Making Spaces: Citizenship and D

C000059885

Also by Tuula Gordon

FEMINIST MOTHERS

SINGLE WOMEN: On the Margins?

UNRESOLVED DILEMMAS: Women, Work and the Family in the United States, Europe and the Former Soviet Union (*co-editor with Kaisa Kauppinen*)

DEMOCRACY IN ONE SCHOOL? Progressive Education and Restructuring

Also by Janet Holland

THE MALE IN THE HEAD (*with Caroline Ramazanoglu, Sue Sharpe and Rachel Thomson*)

* SEX, SENSIBILITY AND THE GENDERED BODY (*co-editor with Lisa Adkins*)

* SEXUAL CULTURES (*co-editor with Jeffrey Weeks*)

DEBATES AND ISSUES IN FEMINIST RESEARCH AND PEDAGOGY (*co-editor with Maud Blair*)

IDENTITY AND DIVERSITY: Gender and the Experience of Education (*co-editor with Maud Blair*)

* *From the same publishers*

Making Spaces: Citizenship and Difference in Schools

Tuula Gordon
Professor of Women's Studies and Social Sciences
Department of Women's Studies
University of Tampere

Janet Holland
Professor of Social Research and
Director of the Social Science Research Centre
Faculty of Humanities and Social Science
South Bank University, London

and

Elina Lahelma
Department of Education
University of Helsinki
and Senior Fellow
Academy of Finland

Consultant Editor: Jo Campling

First published in Great Britain 2000 by
MACMILLAN PRESS LTD
Houndmills, Basingstoke, Hampshire RG21 6XS and London
Companies and representatives throughout the world

A catalogue record for this book is available from the British Library.

ISBN 0–333–66440–X hardcover
ISBN 0–333–66441–8 paperback

First published in the United States of America 2000 by
ST. MARTIN'S PRESS, INC.,
Scholarly and Reference Division,
175 Fifth Avenue, New York, N.Y. 10010

ISBN 0–312–22619–5

Library of Congress Cataloging-in-Publication Data
Making spaces : citizenship and difference in schools /
Tuula Gordon, Janet Holland, and Elina Lahelma.
p.   cm.
Includes bibliographical references (p.) and index.
ISBN 0–312–22619–5 (cloth)
1. High school students—England—London—Social conditions Cross
-cultural studies.   2. High school students—Finland—Helsinki–
–Social conditions Cross-cultural studies.   3. Education, Secondary–
–England—London Cross-cultural studies.   4. Education, Secondary–
–Finland—Helsinki Cross-cultural studies.   5. Sex differences in
education—England—London Cross-cultural studies.   6. Sex
differences in education—Finland—Helsinki Cross-cultural studies.
I. Gordon, Tuula.   II. Holland, Janet.   III. Lahelma, Elina.
LC208.4.M35   1999
306.43—DC21
                                                    99–29160
                                                        CIP

© Tuula Gordon, Janet Holland and Elina Lahelma 2000

All rights reserved. No reproduction, copy or transmission of this publication may be made without written permission.

No paragraph of this publication may be reproduced, copied or transmitted save with written permission or in accordance with the provisions of the Copyright, Designs and Patents Act 1988, or under the terms of any licence permitting limited copying issued by the Copyright Licensing Agency, 90 Tottenham Court Road, London W1P 0LP.

Any person who does any unauthorised act in relation to this publication may be liable to criminal prosecution and civil claims for damages.

The authors have asserted their rights to be identified as the authors of this work in accordance with the Copyright, Designs and Patents Act 1988.

This book is printed on paper suitable for recycling and made from fully managed and sustained forest sources.

10   9   8   7   6   5   4   3   2   1
09   08   07   06   05   04   03   02   01   00

Printed and bound in Great Britain by
Antony Rowe Ltd, Chippenham, Wiltshire

Contents

	Acknowledgements	vi
	Introduction: Do You Wanna Dance?	1
1	Individual Citizens	9
2	Space and Place for Markets: New Right and the Restructuring of Education	23
3	Curricula for Nations	36
4	Invitation to the Dance: Exploring Everyday Life in Schools	52
5	One Two Three, One Two Three: the Official School	65
6	Stepping Here, Stepping There: the Informal School	101
7	'Strictly Ballroom': the Physical School and Space	136
8	'Twist and Shout': Bodies in the Physical School	165
9	Who are the Wallflowers?	192
	Appendix: Methods in Use	204
	Notes	209
	References	214
	Index	227

Acknowledgements

This book is one of the results of a Finnish–English research project entitled 'Citizenship, Difference and Marginality in Schools – with Special Reference to Gender'. We are deeply indebted to the people whose observations and analyses we have used in this book. The Finnish research project consists of Pirkko Hynninen, Tuija Metso, Tarja Palmu, Tarja Tolonen, Tuula Gordon and Elina Lahelma. Pirkko, Tuija, Tarja and Tarja were each specialising in a particular area of the research, but sharing experience and data with us. The keen eyes, sharp observations and innovative interpretations of these women have been irreplaceable for the analysis which we present in this book. Sinikka Aapola and Jukka Lehtonen joined the Finnish research project later; their contribution to the analytic discussions in our meetings has been invaluable. The Finnish team has been helped by a number of people and we especially want to thank Päivi Haavisto-Vuori, Marja Peltovuori, Marita Lampinen, Katariina Hakala and Sirpa Lappalainen.

Janet Holland had two able and committed researchers, each of whom worked with her, undertaking observations and interviews in one of the London schools and some analysis. Kay Parkinson read and commented on the manuscript of this book. Janet's gratitude to Nicole Vitellone and Kay Parkinson is unbounded for their contribution to the work, inspiration and friendship. Janet would also like to thank the Finnish research team, and of course Tuula and Elina for bringing her into the project, and for being such excellent colleagues and collaborators.

We are grateful to numerous people for many reasons, for example for enjoyable and useful discussions on joint interests or for commenting on our papers or parts of this book. We especially want to mention AnneLise Arnesen, Ilse Eriksson-Stjernberg, Mary Kehily, Leena Koski, Melanie Mauthner, Marjatta Saarnivaara, Hannu Simola and Rachel Thomson, and the members of the research network Gender and Education/EDDI in Finland. We also thank Jo Campling for her encouragement and advice.

During the research Tuula, Elina and Janet have worked in the following institutions: the Department of Sociology and Department of Education at the University of Helsinki, the Department of

Women's Studies at the University of Tampere, the Social Science Research Unit at the Institute of Education in London, the Open University, and the School of Education, Politics and Social Science at South Bank University, London. We would like to thank the Academy of Finland for the major funding for this research. We were also funded by the Youth Research 2000 Programme (Finland), the Open University and South Bank University. We are grateful to all these institutions for material support and to our colleagues within them for friendship and discussions.

Most of all, we want to thank the teachers, students and other people at our research schools, City Park and Green Park in Helsinki, and Oak Grove and Woburn Hill in London. This research would not have been possible without their support, friendliness and tolerance for our continuing presence and endless questions.

Last but not least, we want to thank Robert Albury, Dougie Gordon, Mikko Gordon, Janne Gordon, Eero Lahelma, Anna Lahelma and Marja Lahelma for love and support.

TUULA GORDON
JANET HOLLAND
ELINA LAHELMA

Introduction:
Do You Wanna Dance?

When the research team in Finland concluded its main fieldwork period in two schools in Helsinki, we thanked the students and teachers by singing what we called the 'ethnographers' song', with courtesy (and apologies) to Sting and Police (from the album *Synchronicity*, 1983):

Every Breath You Take (by Sting)[1]

> *Every breath you take*
> *every move you make*
> *every bond you break*
> *every step you take*
> *I'll be watching you*
>
> *Every single day*
> *every word you say*
> *every game you play*
> *every* place *you stay*
> *I'll be watching you*
>
> *Oh can't you see*
> *you belong to me*
> *How my poor heart aches*
> *with every step you take*
>
> *Every move you make*
> *every* rule *you break*
> *every smile you fake*
> *every claim you stake*
> *we'll be watching you*

1

Everyday life at school is like a complicated dance with formal and improvised steps in a ballroom consisting of classrooms, halls, stairways and corridors. It is the range of these steps that we gaze at in this book. We examine them in order to explore the part played by the school in the production of difference, and in the construction of citizenship and otherness. In everyday processes and practices students are differentiated along several dimensions, notably gender, social class and ethnicity. In the ethnography we explore practices in schools which seek to normalise school students from diverse social and cultural backgrounds through the notion of the abstract pupil. These processes of abstraction and differentiation have effects on the formation of subjectivities of those in schools.

We are interested in the official and informal processes of the school and the way in which the physical space affects pedagogy and practice; we also want to trace a 'curriculum of the body' (Lesko, 1988). Peter Woods (1990) notes that students entering a new school are intent to find a living space. He uses space metaphorically, but we want to ask specifically how school students make spaces for themselves; space and spatiality are our central concerns. Paraphrasing Philip Wexler (1992), who explores the process of 'becoming somebody', we analyse how school students become some*bodies* some*where*. Whilst our main interest is in how students exercise agency in schools, we also turn our attention to teachers.

By a comparative approach we mean that we compare and contrast processes in Britain and Finland, with illustrative references to the USA.[2] We contextualise our study through a discussion of New Right politics and policies, education systems and the curriculum. By a crosscultural approach we refer to our interest in what constitutes 'a school', and in particular how space and embodiment are implicated there. Focus on space and embodiment have both been neglected in education research; basing our analysis on schooling in two countries and in four schools enables us to extract theoretical and analytical insights which are not completely context-bound.

Historically schools have been expected both to confirm and to challenge social divisions; a continuous strand in educational thinking has emphasised schools as sites of emancipation, and channels for advancing social change (Davies, 1990; Green, 1990; Donald, 1992). Schools then are sites with multiple levels and practices, some of them contradictory, and within them there are spaces for agency, negotiation, avoidance, opposition, and resistance. These spaces are limited, but significant in the context of tensions between emancipation and regulation.

When considering relations of difference we start with gender, and aim to disentangle and challenge binary oppositions: the female/male binary is not taken for granted. Gender places those who are named as females and males in intersecting relations of difference which include social class, 'race' and ethnicity, age, disability and sexual orientation. Gender is dynamic and processual. We *are* and *have* gender; but we can also do gender, avoid gender, ignore gender and challenge gender (Gordon and Lahelma, 1995). Differences *within* the categories 'girl' and 'boy', as well as *between* girls and boys, are also important, as feminists have come to realise from Black feminist and poststructuralist critiques of the category 'woman'.

The within-gender differences are located in the context of inequalities and particular cultural representations which privilege the category 'male' over the category 'female', 'white' over 'black', 'middle-class' over 'working-class', and construct these categorisations as 'natural'. Relations of difference are connected to the marginalisation of some differences. Marginalities are multiple social axes intersecting relations of social and cultural power. In this sense, marginality does not necessarily signify powerlessness but can be seen as an analytical category (Gordon, 1994).

We draw for our theoretical and conceptual position on a range of theoretical perspectives, including social constructionist, cultural, materialist, poststructural and feminist theories, and our work is a contribution to the extensive tradition of ethnography in the sociology of education. The sociological roots of social constructionism are long standing. Recent social constructionist approaches emerge from the desire to theorise individuals as agents with subjectivities in the production of society as well as to consider the constraints and possibilities with which society confronts the individual, and this is important in our approach. There are three central tenets of social constructionism: challenging taken for granted knowledge; historical and cultural specificity; recognition that knowledge is sustained by social processes and that knowledge and social action go together (Burr, 1995). These elements recur in other theoretical perspectives upon which we draw. Poststructuralism is quintessentially social constructionist, emphasising the role of language and discourse in that construction, and seeks far-reaching deconstruction of existing knowledge. Whilst this approach is important for us, our work is not characterised by the heavy textual turn typical of 'post'-research.

Feminism questions taken-for-granted knowledge, and regards knowledge and social action as a pair. Feminist approaches also contain a commitment to analyse the hidden and the marginal. The poststructuralist position is not sufficient for us in this; we therefore retain an element of materialism, in terms of the material base for both social class and other differences upon which human agency is built. Jane Kenway (1995a) characterises materialist feminism as an approach which 'draws on and extends the postmodern conceptualisation of subjectivity'. In this approach the subject is recognised as 'fragmented, dispersed and textualised', but the context of 'globally dispersed and state controlled multinational capitalism and consumer culture' is emphasised (p. 49). We look at processes and practices in everyday life at school in the context of an analysis of the wider social and historical relations in which these are expressed; Angela McRobbie (1996) calls this type of approach 'new ethnography' in contrast to textual anti-essentialist, anti-experience approaches (McRobbie, 1997). Materiality is particularly important in our analysis of spatiality and embodiment. Space is social and mental, and constrained but not determined by the physical. The material body is given meaning through processes of social construction; ideas about the body are social, but they are not entirely separable from bodily constraints and possibilities.

The initial chapters (1–3) contextualise the steps that are taken at school. In Chapter 1 we suggest that the attainment of citizenship is contingent upon giving up special bonds (Jones, 1990); this produces an inherently masculine notion of an individual and a citizen. In Pateman's (1988) view this original conception of citizenship always already included the sexual contract, gender and sexual division. The concept of citizenship is based on the idea of equal individuals entering this contract. However, in practice both 'the citizen' and 'the individual' are positions that are differentially accessible to members of different social and cultural groups.

In Chapter 2 we provide a background for the ethnography through a comparison of the Finnish and British education systems, within the broader context of the New Right politics and policies which have increasingly taken hold in Europe and the USA in the past two decades. Britain and Finland have different educational histories, but in recent years both education systems have been in a state of flux and passed through a period of restructuring. In Britain a process of centralisation of a decentralised education system has been taking place, and in Finland decentralisation of a tightly centralised system. We contextualise our analysis with a comparison of these processes and the education debates which frame them. We examine the impact of neo-conservatism and neo-liberalism on education politics and policies in these two countries, including some comparisons with the USA. We suggest that the relationship between citizens and individuals is redrawn in New Right politics and policies, and that this makes it more difficult to pose questions about social justice and equality in education.

From this broad level of analysis we move in Chapter 3 to an examination of the translation of policy into the schools. In schools students are female or male, and come from different social class and ethnic backgrounds. They are also largely of the nationality of the particular nation state in which the school resides, and this nationality, like gender difference, is a taken-for-granted backdrop in these societies, 'banal nationality' as Billig (1995) has put it. We suggest that one aim of the school is the production of the 'abstract pupil', abstracted from these social differences, en route to become the 'abstract citizen'. In the analysis of policy and curriculum documents in Chapter 3 we examine the way citizenship, individuality, nationality, gender, equality and difference are constructed.

In Chapter 4 we discuss our ethnographic approach, and extend an invitation to you, the reader, to join us and come to the ball. For the ethnography we focused on 13/14-year-old students in two schools in London and two in Helsinki; in each city one school had predominantly middle-class and one predominantly working-class students. Within the school we distinguish between three layers: (1) the official school, (2) the informal school and (3) the physical school. These layers are in practice entwined, but making distinctions between them allows us to analyse aspects of the school which often remain invisible (Gordon, 1993). We use a metaphor of dance to illustrate the layers of the official (correct steps), the informal (improvised steps) and the physical (the ballroom) school. Aspects of spatial praxis in the physical school are of particular concern to us, and we understand praxis as action and practice which can be habitual, but which may also be reflective and creative (Gordon *et al.*, 1997).

Correct steps as well as other rules of traditional dances are prescribed and the master of ceremonies takes care that the rules are followed but can also formulate new steps, often with the dancers. In the official school, traditions direct the pedagogic process, although changes are developed and tried by teachers and innovative students. In Chapter 5 we describe the processes and practices that take place in the official layer of the school. We begin by analysing teachers' work, then focus on students' lives in the official school. We illustrate how 'professional pupils' construct themselves and are constructed in relation to knowledge, individualism and contradictions between control and agency. We show the persistence of traditional ways of teaching but also attempts to make the school and learning more enjoyable. We explore how gender, ethnicity and social background are involved in making the differences through these processes.

In the ballroom, dancers tend to take steps of their own; they step aside, change partners or chat with other dancers. Sometimes their free steps intertwine with the formal ones and are difficult to notice. In Chapter 6 we move from the official to the informal school. We start with the spheres in which the official and the informal school are most intertwined: informalisation of relations between teachers, non-teaching staff and students, and extra-curricular activities. We continue with students' informal relations, and describe how students bind relations of friendship and how differences are constructed, challenged and negotiated in these processes. Ballrooms are arenas for various kinds of feelings; pleasures, desires, anxieties, joys, fears. Schools have sometimes been described as 'the desert of feelings'. We end the chapter by searching for the muted feelings in the desert of the school.

In Chapter 7 we consider the ballroom. The school as a physical space provides a context for the practices and processes of differentiation that 'take place' there. But the physical school is more than a context; it is an aspect in the shaping of these practices and processes which produces differentiation. Decisions about the use of space involve decisions about location and movement of bodies in specific areas of the school. We ask how the dancers make space for themselves and explore how physical spaces become social sites with centres and margins.

Many practices in school work on and through the body; different bodies take up the invitation to the dance in different ways. School rules stipulate permitted and forbidden movement, and discipline in the classroom has a substantial basis in regulated bodily comportment. Moreover, disruption and resistance by students in schools often carry bodily dimensions. Embodiment is implicated in differentiation in schools. Subjectivities assume visible signs; there is a sense in which students 'wear' their specific positioning in school hierarchies. We explore this in Chapter 8 by focusing on curriculum and pedagogy of the body in schools. We ask who wants to dance – and how they dance.

By utilising a comparative, crosscultural approach, discussing two countries, Finland and Britain, and four schools, we hope to be able to discern general processes applicable to the 'school'. We *embody the abstract pupil*, we *spatialise the abstract school* and *problematise the abstract citizen* by exploring the concrete, everyday life of the school.

1
Individual Citizens

Citizenship, individuality and difference

Citizenship sums up the relationship between the individual and the nation state. It is an elusive concept, which has been used as an exclusive and an inclusive social organising principle. In European social thought the concept of citizenship is constructed as universal; but it contains tensions between sameness and difference, us and others, centres and margins. We problematise the universality of citizenship by exploring how it is constructed and reconstructed in schools.

Schooling is a national project and a practice of the state, preparing young people for adulthood. The context of this preparation involves negotiations between difference and diversity amongst young people, and the neutral sameness of 'citizens'. 'Citizenship' frames notions of what it is to be an adult in the political systems in the countries with which we are concerned. A 'citizen' is a member of a nation state and has particular duties and rights. Notions of citizenship are not entirely static. For example in New Right educational politics decreasing significance is attached to equality, equity and social justice, and these are juxtaposed with an increasing emphasis on standards (Chapter 2). Shifting notions of citizenship are implicated in such politics. We want to reclaim the concept of citizenship as a radical, rather than as a conservative, concept.

In European social thought the concept of the 'social contract' is used to explain the formation of the modern nation state. 'Individuals' became citizens through a voluntary contract to maximise their self-interest through organising a higher instance, 'the state of culture' which balances excessive impulses of 'the state of nature'. The development of the modern notion of citizenship was connected to shifts in the way in which the concept of the 'individual' is understood. Raymond Williams (1961) suggests that in medieval times an 'individual' referred to membership of a social group rather than to an abstract unit. With the development of the modern nation state 'individuals' were abstracted from their social location in order to be formally equal carriers of rights and duties, and the concept lost its reference to social relations. Citizenship is contingent upon giving up bonds such as gender, race and social class – Carol Jones suggests that it is by side-stepping particularities that citizenship becomes 'a relationship among equals' (Jones, 1990); it is these abstract individuals who are equal citizens.

T. H. Marshall's (1963) influential theory addressed the problem of formal equality and unequal social relations. He conceptualised citizenship as political, legal and social. In political terms citizens have equal rights particularly in suffrage; legally they are treated the same – but if they are not equal in the market, there needs to be compensation for these inequalities through social citizenship. One impetus for the formation of welfare states was the question of social justice and equality in the political and legal sphere.

Critics suggest that T. H. Marshall's theory has not taken sufficient account of inherent differences in the concept of citizenship, and that relations of difference embedded in the abstract conceptions of citizenship need to be analysed. Carol Pateman (1988) argues that the social contract contains an inherently masculine and ethnocentric conception of citizenship; Carol Jones (1991) proposes that citizenship falsely universalises the particular practices of one group, centring round the rights of men. Nira Yuval-Davis (1997) adds that it is not only gendered but Eurocentric.

The development of the concept of the nation state was concomitant with the separation of the state of culture and the state of nature. A range of binary opposites is connected to this distinction between the state of culture/nature: mind/body, reasons/emotions, rationality/irrationality, abstract/concrete, public/private, independent/dependent, masculine/feminine, male/female, man/woman. Such binary opposites frame the differential access of different groups to universal citizenship. White, able-bodied, propertied men developed the nation state contractually; it was taken for granted that they were able to elevate themselves into the state of culture, to the sphere where abstract individuality was constructed. All women and children and black, working-class men were placed in the state of nature – their emergent individuality remained relative rather than abstract. They were seen to be more guided by their emotions, more embedded in the concrete, more dependent – the second term in the above binaries defined their hierarchical position.

The conceptualisation of these others could be seen as more embodied; they had female bodies, black bodies, worker bodies, bodies with impairments, bodies which were not fully grown. They were seen as more subject to the impulses of their bodies, and their bodies provided more limitations and obstacles in developing objective, rational, abstract thought and the organisation required in the sphere of culture. Citizens should have healthy, regulated bodies; our image of an embodied citizen is not likely to include an aged woman, a woman with a disability.

Over time, formal citizenship rights have been extended from white propertied men to other social groups, and welfare states have attempted to address inequalities through developing social citizenship. But equality in social citizenship is not possible without including cultural, sexual, reproductive and embodied lives. Formal rights are not necessarily easy to realise in practice, and groups for example, with a sexuality which differs from the normative heterosexuality in Western societies, are still in the process of attaining full rights of citizenship (Weeks, 1996). A subject position is required in order to approach the construction of an autonomous individual position. Equal rights policies remain problematic unless sexist representations of women's bodies, or ethnocentric, racist representations of black women's and men's bodies are addressed and iconographies of nationhood are broadened.

Cultural symbols such as the 'English rose' or the blond, blue-eyed 'Finnish maid' embody the gendering and racialising of nationality. James Donald (1996) notes that citizenship refers to a position in formal relations. In that sense, he argues, 'a citizen' denotes an empty place. It is substanceless and tells people what they are, not who they are. Donald compares 'the citizen' to 'I' in linguistic relations – it is 'an empty position which makes my unique utterances possible but which can equally be occupied by anyone' (p. 174). Becoming a citizen is becoming a subject within a symbolic order. Because of this, subjectivity is experienced as a lack. Such an experience leads to identification in fantasy structures – it leads to masks which cover nothing. Donald argues that citizenship and individuality in this sense are performances rather than identities.

We want to put substance on substanceless citizenship. We also want to understand psychic fears and desires in the process of becoming an 'individual citizen' whilst embedded in hierarchical relations of difference. In that sense the empty space of the citizen can become a located place of an embodied unique subject. It can become a space to be talked from. Subjectivity refers to our sense of self, of who we are, and arguing that there is a unique subject is not to imply unitary subjectivity. The subject may have diversity of 'selves', constructed in the multiplicity of discourses within which the individual is positioned and positions himself or herself (Davies and Harré, 1991).

In formal terms children and young people are citizens who in a legal sense enjoy citizenship rights except at those points where such rights are curtailed in their own interests (or in ways that such interests are interpreted by others), or are suspended in terms of inscribed age limits. But generally in national education systems children and young people are addressed as adults-to-be who need to be raised and educated to be 'proper' citizens able to exercise their rights, duties and responsibilities in acceptable ways. They are frequently referred to as dependent, in need of guidance and discipline, but the abstract individual and the modern citizen is independent. So, particularly for children and young people, being an individual and a citizen is a constant process of becoming (Gordon *et al.*, 2000b). We want to explore this process of becoming in schools; how are universality and particularity constructed and reconstructed? We consider official, informal, spatial and embodied processes and practices in the school which contribute to this construction. We also address fears and desires, horrors and pleasures, as well as the mundane and the everyday.

Individual students

The individual, then, is a citizen in formal relations, a symbol rather than a substance. We are trying to construct citizenship which is cultural and embodied and so we need to move beyond theoretical, abstract individuals to consider cultural individualism. Abercrombie *et al.* (1986) define individualism as a political and economic doctrine relating to the rights and obligations of persons. Lukes (1973) states that the concept of individualism has been used to refer to, for example, self-interest, self-assertion, independence, self-fulfilment, natural rights, non-conformity, self-reliance, free enterprise and a minimum of state intervention.

Cultural individualism can both disembody and embody; it can hide difference or expose it. It has been used to reject authority but also to gloss over the relativity of individuals positioned in social relations. Individuality, suggest Abercrombie *et al.* (1986) refers to the incomparability of individuals; it is concerned with subjectivity. Individuality is a process of becoming, which can be displayed performatively, rather like gender in Judith Butler's (1990) analysis; but it can never quite be reached (cf. Gordon, 1994).

To illustrate these abstract arguments we cite ways in which school students talk about being an independent individual. Individuality is an ambivalent goal, particularly for young people since school students are expected to conform to control whilst also developing and exercising agency. Moreover, the agency required in the official school may be different from agency required in the informal and the physical school; the steps to be learned can be complicated indeed. Achievement of learning is a constant process of becoming, an active, personal project. This is illustrated when Noora talks about changes resulting from transfer to secondary school:

> You start taking more responsibility yourself, even though I used to take masses of responsibility in the primary school, more than is normal, sort of. But I actually really felt that I must get a bit more serious and that everything is – I must have a goal.
>
> (FSH)[1]

Noora constructs herself as an active agent in the process of becoming. She refers to this as a decision – hence she operates with a notion of an 'individual'. She also refers to difference when she suggests she has taken more responsibility than normal – in that sense she is talking about individuality, about unique features of human beings, visible only in relation to particular ways of placing others.

That individuality poses considerable demands. For example when Noora talks about teasing and bullying, she says that those who are subjected to mistreatment are also responsible for it themselves. She herself is not teased, because she would not give anyone the opportunity of doing so. Such a quest for individual autonomy can take a heavy toll. Noora struggles between independence, dependence and interdependence. She often comes physically closer than others would wish her to, but she is worried about too much proximity in thoughts, and fears people knowing too much about her. Because of the balancing which is required by being near/far, in exercising agency/maintaining proximity, Noora enjoys moments alone when she does not need to consider others.

The search for autonomy and independence is important to school students, who often talk about school in terms of conflicts between the necessity for 'discipline' and their own need for decision making. These conflicts are greater for some students than others. Noora talks from a position of strength. Although her gender can create obstacles for the exercise of autonomy and the construction of individuality, she has obtained a central position in the social constellation of her own form group in the school. She has dual nationality – this is an epitome of her position as an insider and outsider – it signifies her as different in the sense of being constructed as unique, and provides her with a platform for being bold. As well as bold, she is beautiful.

Other students feel a more acute need for a balancing act. Kati explains:

> I'm sort of quite good, really. In my own way – I have never really been disruptive and I don't know, I think that's good, but some others think that it's bad, so. But I don't sort of loudly spout my opinions, like if something a teacher does irritates me, I don't really say it out loud – you know, some do, like for example Noora speaks really straight, but I don't really dare to, because I worry that if I say something negative it will be reflected in my report card.
>
> (FSH)

In Kati's upper-middle-class family, good school performance is expected and Kati has internalised this expectation as her own. For her the project of becoming an individual has to be secondary to this main goal, where the ideology of individualism is entwined with a process of adaptation to social, cultural and familial values and practices.

Many complex dimensions of difference are raised by students when they talk about themselves and about individuality, independence, rights and responsibilities. Maya, living in London, explains:

> I was born here but I came from India and I'm a Hindu. But I believe myself to be both, 'cause I've been brought up here and I've been brought up to live the ways people live here, but then I've also been brought up to live two different ways. Sometimes I get confused to which way I should be and what I should do and is this right?
>
> (FSL)

When Maya explains to her parents what her friends do, their reply is that she is a different person, and must act in a different way in the context of her own culture. She encounters a blend of social, cultural and familial values and practices like Kati:

> I just get kind of confused but then I kind of disagree with my parents 'cause I think because I live here and because I've been brought up here I should live, I should do the things they do here. But then I also think, no, I should live up to my culture, I should live up to who I really am, to the fact that I'm Indian. So sometimes I get confused as to who I should be.

Although Maya expects herself to work out who she really is, and ways of acting accordingly, she criticises this notion of a unitary self.

> I think that's quite a good thing about me, I mean I don't have this kind of fixed personality, fixed personality that I've got to be a fixed person. I think I can mix with quite a few different people and it will be ok.

Nevertheless she does talk about the process of becoming an independent individual – fixed or not. She explains that both her mother and father like to help her when she has problems. They also offer to help her with her studies:

> but I like to be independent, I like to do things on my own, 'cause in the future I have to. When it comes to later years, I have to do everything on my own, so I like to do everything on my own. Which I do most of the time now.

Noora, Kati and Maya talk about being an individual in terms of solutions as well as problems. The problems they refer to are ones they experience themselves. Santtu, a white middle-class boy, also talks about individuality in relation to multiplicity and diversity, and refers to problems of fragmentation. But he refers to those problems as experienced more by others:

> I reckon I got at least ten selves and you know, they surface in different situations. And then if all those ten were, say, put together, then nobody could bear to listen to it for very long. And sometimes they say in my class, don't show off. And perhaps that

irritates me the most because you can't help it – what mood you happen to be in on a particular day.

(MSH)

For Santtu individuality is something he possesses; it is a source of irritation if it is constructed as a problem by others. His social, cultural and familial relations combine to facilitate his eccentric individuality; an individuality he was able to maintain and foster.

It was more typical among boys to emphasise that they are 'ordinary', 'average' or 'typical'. An 'unmarked position', Bronwyn Davies and Robyn Hunt (1994) note, is a comfortable one. It is also safe – and the safety of it is not open to all students. A male student whom we describe as a 'gender blender' in Chapter 8 suggests that he 'sucks up to teachers', and some have adopted him as their 'pet'. He adds, however, that he is quite an average student; that this is an important project and process of becoming is demonstrated by his repeated use of the word 'average' when talking about himself.

Girls tend to be more ambivalent. Noora, Maya and Kati illustrate the positions of particular types of girls; other strands of individuality can be found in the girls' narratives. Asta talks about her art hobby, which takes up a great deal of her time, and as a result of which she is less able to spend time with her friends. She emphasises that this is her own choice, and as such there is no point in complaining about it. Although she is Finnish-speaking, she adds in English that 'a man's gotta do what a man's gotta do'. A determined, individualistic project has overtones of masculinity. Asta's social and cultural background, as well as her familial context as an only child, feed her project of becoming, though the project is ambivalent for a girl.

For working-class girls the individual project may be less readily available. When Saija was asked how she would describe herself, she said 'I don't know, I don't know what I would say' (FSH). Tiina spent more time thinking about it, but she, too, found the task difficult:

> Well, I don't really – OK, peaceful. Or I don't know if I'm that peaceful. But in school I'm usually peaceful. Outside the school it's a bit different. I can't really say. I don't know really if I can say that I'm peaceful, because I don't know if I'm that peaceful overall. Well, peaceful in school, but a bit wild outside the school.

(FSH)

An even more marked contrast is provided by Siiri; when asked how she would describe herself, she would say 'nothing' (FSH).

Age relations figure a great deal in school students' talk, and the students see themselves in the borderlands between childhood and adulthood. Childhood is constructed in terms of dependence, adulthood as independence. 'Being childish' is an important demarcation, a wedge to be inserted between self and others. It is usually others who are childish – though these 13–14-year-olds may at times describe their sense of themselves as still being small in the face of the world looming large (Aapola, 1997).

The term 'individual' denotes an abstract relation, but for students it is a facet of everyday life in terms of the desire to be unique and interesting, but also to be approved and liked. For some this undertaking is more dangerous than for others – they withdraw into the safety of silence, wanting to blend in rather than to stand out. But again, to blend in can be more difficult for some than for others. Uniqueness and blending in are contradictory as desired states; but being singled out as 'different' can be dangerous and lead to marginalisation.

Marginalisation in schools is most significant as a process, a tendency, but although it is not a particular place to be occupied, the metaphor of place is significant. Marginality is a social relation, but it is a relation which defines borders of the acceptable and normal. Though some students may be gravely marginalised, a more general, widespread feature of everyday life in schools is that particular behaviours, traits and social positions are marginalised. At a particular time in a particular place a student can be in that position – but not necessarily all the time. When marginality is more cumulative it is a serious social problem needing attention and action. But when it is not, it is an effective device of suppressing diversity – the margins are not safe places to inhabit, visit, or be sent to. A great deal of activity in schools involves guarding against marginalisation in the process of 'making space'.

Citizens in space

A citizen is a disembodied body, decontextualised and abstracted from social relations, but at the same time placed in space. The nation state is a place, a bordered territory, the ground of the citizen.

'Space' is a problematic concept which has been taken for granted in the social sciences. In the relatively recent vogue for spatial analysis, space has been understood and defined in a number of ways. The term is often used metaphorically rather than literally or analytically (Smith and Katz, 1993). Terminology tends to run riot, absolute space may mean very different things for example for Harvey (1975) and Lefebvre (1991). Having sifted through a plethora of ways of conceiving and defining space, our focus on space is threefold: we are interested in physical, social and mental space. We approach nations as bordered territories, as organised sets of social relations, and as mental constructs.

Space is physical. Nation states are geographically and politically inscribed; they occupy particular territories with mapped borders. Every society, Lefebvre (1991) notes, 'produces a space, its own space' (p. 31). At this level space is conceptualised as ground, as a three-dimensional grid. By referring to this as physical rather than absolute space, as geographers tend to do, we draw attention to the fluid whilst fixed characterisation of borders which constructs the physical ground for a nation. The fixity of the grid blurs the historical contingency of borders, and can, for example, veil the existence of diasporic nations.

The universality of geography as a subject in the school curriculum suggests that physical space is meaningful in the education for citizenship. In geography nation is presented through maps as a physical space with strict borders. In biology lakes, climate, vegetation and so forth are often presented through maps. The regularity with which maps are presented in history lessons also emphasises the physical space of the nation state – maps of territories that are attacked, invaded and defended. In history the nation state also appears in social relations and as a social space. Maps are sometimes present during Finnish lessons, for example showing how people who use Finno-Ugric languages have moved towards the west. Typically, in foreign-language classrooms, maps of the relevant different countries hang on the walls, demonstrating relationships between languages and geographical territories.

Physical nation space, though typically taken for granted, is created, produced and reproduced (and also contested). Nation state is lived – it is social. The physical, geometric space of a nation cannot exist without practices that assert and reassert it. Lefebvre (1991) notes that 'physical space has no "reality" without the energy that is deployed within it' (p. 13). Processes involved in the social production of space create margins and centres (cf. Soja and Hooper, 1993) through differentiation and domination based on sociocultural and political–economic relations of power. Nation space implies the existence of a market, and armies in readiness to defend the borders of the nation state.

Space is socially constructed, but it is also a dimension through which and over which social relations are constructed (Massey, 1985, 1993; Keith and Pile, 1993). Production of space constitutes and concretises social relationships; people shape and are shaped by spatiality (Soja, 1985, p. 90). Doreen Massey adds that space is 'one of the axes along which we experience and conceptualise the world', (1993, p. 143). Processes of differentiation are part of social space. Complex constellations of centre/margins involve relations of power. Some spaces are more closed than others, and different social groups have differential access to particular spaces.

Nation space is also imaginary and symbolic – it is mental. Its territorial protection is a masculine project connected to evocations of a fatherland (or motherland) to be protected – along with the women and children in it. Social space 'folds into mental space, into representations of spatiality rather than its material social reality' (Soja, 1985, p. 102). The nation state is told and retold in a multiplicity of narratives which constitute what Lefebvre terms 'representational space'. Nation is a mental space which is created and recreated (Karakasidou, 1997). Nations are narratives which have lost their origins in myths of time, but the mythical origins nevertheless provide a context for national iconography (Bhabha, 1990).

Nira Yuval-Davis (1997) notes that since discussions about nation and nationalism often take place in the public sphere, women are less visible in those debates. But gender relations are fundamentally implicated in nationalist thinking, and women are crucial bearers of the nation. The mental space of the nation frames cultural access to particular places in national iconographies and we shall explore this further in relation to practices and processes in schools. We shall also introduce the notion of mental space as a place inhabited in the mind. Such space may provide fantastic and alternative visions – escaping the everyday, perhaps in order to retreat from pain, or to find strength in dreams (cf. Walkerdine, 1984).

National citizens

A range of expectations and assumptions marked the establishing of national education systems. But typically schools were expected to produce citizens in the nation state, familiar with a common culture, common language, common history and a joint sense of future. A compulsory state system of schooling has been important in the construction of Western nation states (cf. Popkewitz, 1991). Newly founded national education systems were often expected not only to inculcate commonalities, but also to produce them. Schooling has played a crucial role in preparation for citizenship, and schools were important in defining what a national citizen would be.

In his analysis of the development of national education systems, Andy Green (1990) refers to Britain as a particular case of nation building through education. Britain had achieved territorial integrity early and its institutions were relatively stable; the nation state could rely on the status and strength provided by the Empire. Nationalism was backward- rather than forward-looking, as in those continental states which constructed national education systems in order to solidify the nation state. The integration of the urban working class was, however, a strong incentive for the 1870 Act to form a national education system. Great worries were expressed about potential revolutionary tendencies among workers, and about the health, fitness and morality of the 'lower orders' (Johnson, 1976). The nature of this project explains the important part played by the liberal market ethos and relatively weak state practices in shaping the education system.

In the United States, education was clearly a national issue, and a concern of the state. Andy Green notes that, whilst a strong connection was forged between education and liberty, a national school system was also expected to maintain order and promote patriotism. It was a key component in developing individualism and liberalism, whilst promoting competition and remaining ethnically uneven.

The geopolitical location of Finland is important in understanding schooling as a powerful national project. Finland's history, with its brutal civil war in 1918 immediately after gaining independence from the Soviet Union, has left a particular legacy (cf. Alapuro, 1988). The aim has been to construct a consensus society with few clashes of interest, and a strong centralist tradition has developed in Finland. Partly because of this specific history, and partly because of the very late development of a national education system (in the 1930s), Finnish education did not clearly segregate girls and boys. In a still very rural society with predominantly small farms, the physical labour of women was necessary both in agriculture and in developing industries (Markkola, 1990). In sparsely populated areas gender segregation was not feasible. Girls and boys went to the same school – though in a few larger cities some of the teaching was gender segregated (Kaarninen, 1995). Homogeneity and consensus were strong aims of

Finnish education, and individualism was far less important in this tradition. In Britain and in the USA the school system clearly differentiated girls and boys in terms both of educational goals and practical separation.

Despite the differences between them, in each of these countries the stated aims of compulsory schooling do not differentiate young people; in schools there is a tendency towards processes of normalisation, framed by conceptions of proper adulthood and the rights and duties of citizens. In this process young people are named as 'pupils' with neutral characteristics and equal opportunities. Schools, then, are characterised by processes of abstraction in the production of universal citizens in a national context. But 'pupils' as actual young people are located in diverse social and cultural contexts. Neutral 'pupils' in the practices of schools become differentiated in the process of 'natural' attitudes shaped by conceptions of the state of culture and the state of nature, and the associated binary oppositions which are fundamental to European social thought. National citizens like Noora, Kati, Maya and Santtu, Tero, Tiina, Saija, Siiri and other students in our study, construct their lives out of the ingredients available in particular historical circumstances (to paraphrase Karl Marx); they deal with tensions between emancipation and regulation, and between agency and control, by constructing themselves as particular kinds of individuals, constantly in the process of becoming.

Citizenship and social justice

Does 'citizenship' as a concept have any potential for encompassing pluralism and diversity? Or does it inherently imply notions of sameness resulting in marginalisation of different others? Does it have potential to enable claims to be made about social justice? Or is citizenship a myth which in its neutrality necessarily hides and maintains inequalities?

Nira Yuval-Davis (1997) sees citizenship as a multi-tier concept which can be applied to people's membership in a variety of collectivities – local, ethnic, national and transnational. Many progressive practices have been based on the concept of citizenship; it has enabled trades unions and the women's movement, for example, to bring claims for rights against the state. This possibility has been extensively utilised by 'state feminists' in the Nordic countries and by 'femocrats' in Australia. Bryan Turner (1993) proposes that in citizenship 'it may be possible to reconcile the claims for pluralism, the need for solidarity and the contingent vagaries of historical change' (p. 11), though his analysis remains gender-blind. Madeleine Arnot suggests that new and more wide-ranging ways are needed to think about what autonomy means for women, and what citizenship can offer (Arnot and Gordon, 1996). Carol Jones (1990) argues that if the multiplicity of women's interests is included in citizenship, this can mark the presence of all those actually or symbolically excluded from it. For her, this 'signals the possibility of shifting the boundaries of citizenship away from nationalism towards multi-cultural community' (p. 812). In Chapter 2, where we discuss New Right policies for educational restructuring, we ask if this is possible and challenge the New Right, particularly neo-liberal, distaste for social citizenship. We return to this question in the conclusions.

2

Space and Place for Markets: New Right and the Restructuring of Education

Introduction

In the United States, Europe, Australia and New Zealand, changes in education have introduced markets into schooling. These changes have taken place in the context of rhetoric and practices constituted by New Right politics and policies. Such developments are significant both at national and supranational levels. We explore shifts in thinking about education as well as the processes of restructuring of school systems which have taken place. Although some seemingly diametrically opposed changes have occurred in England/Wales[1] and Finland, it is of particular interest that the outcome appears to be that the two education systems have become more similar.

Finland has had a strong, Nordic-type welfare state, and compared with Britain and the USA it is a more homogeneous, social democratic society. The Russian tsarist bureaucratic heritage and the modern welfare state have combined to produce an emphasis on public responsibility for the welfare of all citizens, on consensus and the regulation of citizens, and an ideology of equal opportunity. A combination of conservatism and liberalism prevails in the USA and Britain. Free market thinking is strongest in the USA, but Britain has been moving closer to the US model. Finland has also shifted to the right recently.

New ways of thinking about the relationship between economic rationality and educational means and ends began in the USA (Aronowitz and Giroux, 1986; Apple, 1992). Such New Right politics have been connected to the spread of monetarist policies, criticisms of the welfare state, and public expenditure cuts. They contain notions of citizenship that increasingly emphasise individualisation and differentiation rather than equality. Tendencies towards accountability, centralisation, individualism, and closer links between school and industry are what are referred to here as the restructuring of education. Restructuring has taken place in many Western countries in recent decades, and as Knight *et al.* (1993) note, has typically been initiated from the centre, rather than from the local communities of schools.

This major shift has been accompanied by the growth of a considerable body of research and policy literature. As Jane Kenway and Debbie Epstein (1996) note, remarkable in its absence from the earlier literature was a substantial consideration of education research and policy from a feminist perspective. There was often a desultory gesture towards gender issues, or they were ignored.[2]

Schools are sites with multiple levels and practices, some of which are contradictory, as we have noted, and demonstrate in later chapters. In the terrain of these contradictions there are spaces for agency with particular trajectories: for negotiation, avoidance, opposition, resistance, challenge, accommodation, stepping aside, dramatisation, and reinvention. Whilst limited, such spaces for individual agency are important in the context of tensions between emancipation and regulation. Educational policies have addressed these spaces through redrawing the map of possibilities and limitations for individual citizens. Changes have taken place in the context of New Right politics and policies; these include a redefinition of the relationship between nation states and their citizens, the changing significance of the boundaries of nation states, and supra-nationality. The effect of the New Right discourse in each of the countries discussed here has been to move the debate on aspects of the welfare state, including particularly education, to the right, and to embed notions of the market into the system. This setting of the agenda has been so effective that, despite changes of government, many of the policies and practices of the New Right have been incorporated by new governments in these countries.

The New Right politics

The New Right is an amorphous alliance of neo-conservatism and neo-liberalism. It is a confusing, contradictory constellation (cf. Roche, 1992) which would not be of great analytical and intellectual interest, had it not been so influential in the recent development of Western societies, notably in the USA (Reaganism) and Britain (Thatcherism) and more recently in Nordic countries.

The New Right has privileged education as a crucial site for the promotion and realisation of its policies, and for courting populist support (for example through commitment to choice). Education is also an arena where neo-conservative and neo-liberal strands exist side by side, comfortably in some countries (cf. Darmanin, 1993) and more uncomfortably in others. In England/Wales, paradoxically, increasing prioritisation of market forces in areas of policy which had previously been subject to detailed central regulation, coexists with the intro-duction of prescription into an area hitherto characterised by professional autonomy – the curriculum (Whitty, 1989).

In the USA, in the early Reagan administration, concerns about the economy, worries about morality, and fears about the weakening global position of the USA were channelled into education through a neo-conservative revival. Education is, as Cohen (1990) argues, perme-able and becomes fused with issues which arise outside it. There were sweeping efforts to standardise education, which were followed by moves to promote standards and raise accountability (Fuhrman, 1990).

In order to understand widespread international changes in educa-tion we compare the Finnish social-democratic welfare state, and the British model which is based on conservatism and liberalism, but includes social democratic and radical elements. There are also differ-ences in gender relations in the two countries. A majority of British women are engaged in part-time paid work, whereas a majority of Finnish women are in full-time paid work. Public child-care provision is minimal in Britain, and extensive in Finland. Though Finnish women enjoy a great deal more economic independence, the labour market is still gender-segregated, and the pay and prospects of those located in the predominantly male sectors are better than of those located in the predominantly female sectors (cf. Husu and Niemelä, 1993). The USA has the least developed welfare state, and child-care provision is largely in the hands of the individual or family; a gendered division of labour in the home persists. Despite improving life and labour market chances for women since the 1960s, largely due to improvement in their access to education, there is considerable gender segregation in the labour market and a large gender gap in earnings remains (Brenner, 1996). Clearly, as in Britain and Finland, women's situations will vary according to social class, ethnicity and family structure. We are interested here in what possibilities greater formal rights and a more inclusive notion of citizenship give to women, and discuss how education is implicated in these processes.

There is no monolithic New Right (cf. Knight *et al.*, 1993); its manifestations vary. In order to understand the historic specificity of the New Right, the coalitions that maintain it, contradictions in the policies promoted (and in the context of contradictions, the way in which compromises are achieved) and the effectiveness of those policies, one must analyse and compare individual nation states. Roger Dale and Jenny Ozga (1993), while comparing the very different education reforms of New Zealand and England/Wales, argue that 'the blanket use of the term New Right to describe both sets of reforms might conceal as much as it reveals' (p. 66). We start from the concept of the New Right in broad terms, but specify our arguments with more concrete concepts.

Preceding the advent of the New Right, social democratic policies were dominant in education. Belief in education was part of the modernist project in a period of economic expansion and politics which emphasised equity. But social democratic educational policies in both countries were unsuccessful in securing equality of opportunity for school students from different social classes. The social democratic agenda did not address diversity constructed through economic, social and cultural location. Gender and 'race' were marginal in the social democratic agenda (Arnot, 1992). Faith in the ability of the school system to produce social justice slowly crumbled (Hillcole Group, 1991).[3]

In Britain critical teachers and other educationalists had utilised points of autonomy in the expanding education system to promote more radical reforms than were tolerable in the liberal social democratic consensus. There were no real attempts to publicly debate radical education initiatives and to secure community support for them (cf. Gordon, 1986); professionalism and expertise were used as cloaks of safety. The Labour government became concerned with a costly, somewhat unpopular education system which delivered less than it promised. In this situation Conservatives 'knocked on an open door' (Education Group, CCCS, 1981).

The New Right had to kick somewhat harder on the schools' doors in Finland. Factors which facilitated the opening of doors were the need to make public expenditure cuts and dissatisfaction with a traditional, inflexible and authoritarian school system. The main focus of policies had been on the structure of the school system, rather than on the content of schooling. Teaching and learning in schools were criticised as being based on flows of fragmented knowledge, and a more integrated approach was called for. The comprehensive school has also been accused of forgetting the most able students. The education system was an ideal testing ground for combining neo-conservatism and neo-liberalism and centrally led decentralisation and delegation of decision making.

Whilst in both countries there was concern about the failure of equal opportunity politics, there was also concern about their possible *success*. In Britain equality was not a prospect welcomed by all. This was manifested in debates about progressive education and positive discrimination in Britain. Media attacks on practices which aimed to achieve social justice were orchestrated by the emergent New Right. In Finland concern was voiced about the feminisation of education; the increasing success of girls in achieving educational qualifications has led to worries about boys' comparative failure. It can be argued that there has been a crisis in masculinity (Gordon, 1992). Such debates have recently been more prominent in Britain too, particularly in the press, but also amongst educational commentators (cf. Arnot *et al.*, 1996).

There is, on the surface, a fundamental difference between changes in the school system in England/Wales and Finland. The former has moved from a decentralised to a centralised national curriculum and Finland has moved from a centralised to a decentralised curriculum, the curriculum in England/Wales having been one of the most decentralised, and in Finland one of the most centralised. Yet in each, the market has been emphasised, and this has been reflected in cuts in spending in education and the devolution of the management of schools. These shifts are evident in 'market-speech' discernible in education policies and documents: 'accountability', 'choice', 'customers', 'standards', 'assessment'. In both countries individual decisions about the educational path to be pursued have been emphasised, and this individualisation is to be realised through the mechanism of parental choice. Education has been increasingly conceptualised by policy makers as an economic, rather than a social, political, or moral activity.

In the USA, Reaganism in educational policy initiated, for example, the reduction of the federal role, stimulating competition among schools and increasing parental choice (Apple, 1993). There the governance of education has been traditionally characterised by fragmentation, but now states have become more active in regulating the curriculum, assessing student performance and school effectiveness. 'Accountability', 'choice' and 'standards' are also key terms. Emphasis on individuals and their liberties is so ingrained in the USA that there are constant tensions between uniform treatment and acknowledgement of diversity (cf. Fuhrman *et al.* 1990).

Neo-conservatism and neo-liberalism in education

Significant in neo-conservatism is the espousal of cultural identity, authority and standards. In England/Wales, nationalism is strengthened for example by reasserting traditional norms of standard English, religion and narrative national history. Neo-liberalism, and its commitment to the free play of market forces, is apparent in the transfer of responsibility for financial management to individual schools, promotion of competition by giving parents the right to select a school, and the increase of parental (England/Wales and Finland) and employers' (England/Wales) representation on the governing bodies of schools. In England/Wales, schools were also encouraged to 'opt out' of local education authority control. Neo-conservative aspects of policies ensure governmental control of practices in schools. Whilst neo-conservatism emphasises the responsibilities of citizens, neo-liberalism emphasises the rights of individuals. Both contain a shift from collectivism to individualism and from concerns about justice and equality to concerns about competition and efficiency (cf. Gewirtz *et al.*, 1993).

Neo-conservatism is more prevalent in educational policies in England/Wales than in Finland. This can be explained by considering the differing constellations of New Right social groupings. In Britain the New Right gained ascendancy in the 1980s; in Finland it is more fragile – indeed in the present coalition government Social Democrats are the largest party. The New Right in Britain represents powerful, privileged economic and social interests. No groupings capable of wielding such hegemonic power exist in Finland. The more extreme neo-liberals in Britain are libertarians who have forsaken liberal concerns about the general social well-being of citizens; their extremism causes concern among other New Right groupings.

In Finland neo-liberalism is more tied to national concerns, and the geopolitical location of Finland is important in understanding this. Citizenship is a stronger and a more taken-for-granted frame of reference than in Britain, where it has been necessary to promote and to redefine the concept of citizenship, for example by referring to 'active citizenship'.

In Britain the social democratic consensus in education broke down in the 1970s. In Finland the consensus continued till the late 1980s. Finland's history has left a particular legacy. There have been few battles about diversity in recent decades; the aim has been to construct a society with minimal clashes of interest. Devolution in the context of centralised control is, therefore, a more realistic prospect in Finland. Developing national curriculum guidelines has been an effective policy in Finland, with its history of strong centralism; it would have been far less effective in the decentralised education system in England/Wales,[4] where curricular guidelines would have been combed through by critical teachers and educationalists for disjunctures and possibilities for doing otherwise. In Finland the weight of centralist tradition gives more authority to the guidelines (cf. Norris *et al.*, 1996).

In England/Wales consensus politics were challenged from the inside by grassroots curriculum development and anti-sexist and anti-racist initiatives which were added to concerns about social class inequalities. These were attempts to place abstract pupils in their social contexts, and to develop 'relevant' education. The New Right feared liberal/radical local authorities, teacher educators, education researchers, governors, headteachers, teachers and parents. Teachers were also regarded as a problem in the USA; *A Nation at Risk*, the report of the Commission of Excellence in Education, 1988, found teachers guilty of the equivalent of an act of war against the state (Dale and Ozga, 1993). In Finland there was little grassroots action until the latter half of the 1980s and it was soon harnessed by public education cuts and shaped by New Right policies. Consensus politics had operated in the context of an integrated, corporate system and there was little fear of radical groupings obstinately subverting official policies.

In the USA the education system is characterised by such diversity and fragmentation that similar strong shifts in terms of constructing or breaking down consensus are not clearly discernible. It is evident, however, that decentralisation and choice have become panaceas which have been promoted in different levels of educational governance, and promoted by people and groups representing different points of view.

Marketisation of education

Restructuring addresses the relationship between the state and its citizens. We can discern this in debates and policies about 'choice'. The 'consumers' in New Right education policies in countries including Britain, Finland and the USA, are parents (Donald, 1992; Feintuck, 1994). Parental choice centres round celebration of difference (David, 1992). The New Right has its finger on the pulse, unlike social democrats who have not been able to address gaps and silences in social democratic modernising agendas (Arnot, 1991). Education was a central project of modernisation aiming at mastery, rationality, individual and collective social improvement (cf. Dale, 1992). Social democratic policies addressed the surface, but did not tackle inequalities at the root of surface differentiations, and this caused almost inevitable failure. Social democrats were unable to deal with crises of capitalism *and* of gender relations.

New Right politics addresses these issues by emphasising 'the family'. The welfare state, from the perspective of the New Right, is too expensive and too controlling. The wish to strengthen the family is connected to the aim of weakening the welfare state, and shifting some of its public functions to the private sphere. The family is expected to strengthen social stability, and is a crucial site for establishing the sexual division of labour. Through an emphasis on the family there is an attempt to reassert traditional conceptions about the sex–gender system and the position of women in particular (Arnot, 1992; David, 1992). Family rhetoric is stronger and more explicit in public debates and in New Right policies in Britain. But in Finland similar fears are indicated in publicly expressed concerns about women controlling the education of children and about schools as institutions more suitable for girls than boys.

In New Right politics and policies equality of opportunity has become outmoded, and differences have become more acceptable. But in both countries there is concern that the pool of talent for recruitment should not become too shallow. The New Right alliance in education is concerned about control and resistance, and its policies are designed to fragment or co-opt opposition. The alliance is also interested in the efficient operation of the market, and in the ability of the nation state to survive internal criticism and international competition. Most extreme policy suggestions are not successful; there is an effort to ensure a sufficiently wide base for recruitment to skilled and professional positions in the labour market. Thus for example it is likely that middle-class girls will achieve well in school in each country.

Flaws in the operation of 'choice' which complicate the pursuit of individual success may lead to dissatisfaction and criticism (cf. Davies *et al.*, 1992). The difficulties of working-class girls and boys, and of girls and boys of minority ethnic groups will probably increase and lead to frustration and opposition, especially in England/Wales. In practice in more sparsely populated Finland most children will go to their nearest schools, though in larger cities differentiation between schools has increased.

On a more abstract level, there are tensions between 'citizenship' and 'individualism'. The concept of the citizen is dependent on a modern construction of the individual. In New Right thinking the 'citizen' and the 'individual' are becoming more differentiated in the process of the formation of neo-conservative and neo-liberal alliances. Neo-liberals emphasise individual freedom whilst neo-conservatives emphasise duties associated with citizenship; neither are particularly interested in citizenship as a basis for claiming social justice. When trying to understand what is 'new' about the New Right, the coexistence of these two tendencies is important; as are the contradictions caused by one emphasising citizenship and the other emphasising individualism. The New Right has an asocial concept of human beings and an atomistic competitive concept of society (Roche, 1992) – 'equality' is an inappropriate concept and aim in this context. The concept is no longer linked to past group oppression and disadvantage, but is now argued to guarantee individual choice under the conditions of the free market (Apple, 1993).

New Right educational policies are thus vulnerable – but their one remaining strength is the paucity of well-developed alternatives. Educationalists involved in grassroots initiatives in England/Wales have not been able to form alliances in local communities. Critics of recent education policies in Finland have not offered significant alternatives; instead they have glorified the past social democratic consensus without recognising its rigidity and authoritarianism, and without addressing its gaps and silences.

Choice has been promoted as a solution to the perceived problems of US education; Cohen (1990) argues that 'Markets are ... a venerable American solution for political problems.' Choice becomes linked with freedom and individual liberties, and as such remains merely a slogan. Whilst various selection procedures have been established through, for example, gifted and talented programmes and magnet schools, in practice choice does not mean control, though it may mean parental influence. In practice most parents who use the state education system for their children, choose a neighbourhood school. More significant 'choice' is exercised in terms of middle-class (especially white, but also other ethnic groups) flight from urban schools either to private schools or housing outside inner cities.

'Choice' was discussed in everyday life in schools too, and we illustrate it with the words of first a student, then a teacher. A high-achieving male student in Helsinki described 'school' using two different metaphors; one was a prison, a metaphor repeated many times by other students. He also used a unique metaphor which seemed to reflect marketisation in education: a supermarket:

> You can, of course, compare the school to a supermarket for example – where you go to each shelf – and they're like classrooms – you get out when everything's done. So it's almost like the same thing, you go to a supermarket, you go to school. You go from shelf to shelf to see what you buy – you go from classroom to classroom and you stay there for the lesson, and then you get homework and then you go to the next lesson. You go out when you have bought everything you need – in school you go when you've got all the homework and all the lessons are over. Basically it's the same thing, isn't it?
>
> (Tommi, MSH)

Is this the vision of the New Right school of tomorrow? If so, what goods will be loaded on the shelves, what goods will be in short supply, and what goods will be impossible to obtain?

A teacher talks about issues relating to choice of schools.

> I don't really know what's going to happen, because there are sort of schools that are really highly esteemed and then there are schools where you go if you have to. And if this is to be reflected in salaries – what sort of results the schools achieve, and there is the catchment area and you have to take pupils from there – what sort of material do you get. And is it right … that one school gets the top material from its own area and then all the good ones apply there and the other one has to take all the dregs and then the schools will be unequal – I don't know if that's good. Time will tell how it's going to work out.
>
> (Saara, FTH)[5]

This comment reflects teachers' anxieties about parents' right to choose, whilst at the same time polarising student capacities through categorisations of ability utilised as if they were self-evident.

Educational policies emphasising choice have continued in Britain, Finland and the USA, despite the advent of new governments. Criticism of these policies has also continued; choice is juxtaposed with inequality in educational debates. Proponents of choice argue against 'bland sameness for all'; the critics point out that this once meant 'equality of opportunity'. In the course of such debates it is difficult to ask different types of questions about equality that do not ignore the previously hidden diversity and difference. The nature of the debates is somewhat different in the USA, where 'bland sameness' has not been an issue, but equality is juxtaposed with choice. We need analyses that are able to engage with 'the changing nature of social and material diversity and differentiation' (Hey, 1996, p. 356).

De/centralisation

Decentralisation is one of the 'oldest and most treasured political remedies' (Cohen, 1990) in the USA, but it is not a clear-cut process. Reaganism in educational policy initiated, for example, the reduction of the federal role, stimulating competition among schools and increasing parental choice (Apple, 1993). There the governance of education has been traditionally characterised by fragmentation, but decentralisation has led to further centralisation at the state level, as states increasingly attempt to monitor and regulate schooling, school effectiveness, and student achievement. In California local control over curriculum, text selection, and testing has been waning (Witte, 1990). At the school level planning ahead is difficult. One headteacher noted that the direction of education in his school is controlled by 'what you get money for'.

In England/Wales, New Right policies have curtailed the influence of the local educational authorities, some of which have been active in promoting policies of equal opportunities in schools. They have lost resources and some of their responsibilities have been either centralised or delegated to schools. Administrative control has moved substantially to Boards of Governors in individual schools, while policy direction has moved to the centre. In the USA, where power has traditionally been in local school districts, state governments have increased authority and responsibility (Knight *et al.*, 1993). In Finland, planning of the local school system is still the responsibility of local authorities, but management of schools has been delegated to the headteacher and governing body. The Framework Curriculum for the Comprehensive School (NBE, 1994) states that the 'curriculum is an *expression of the local decision-makers' political will* as part of the national education policy' (p. 18; emphasis as in original).

Using Dutch experience, Sleegers and Wessenligh (1993) argue that decentralisation often means only the delegation of executive tasks and workload to lower levels and sub-units of education, and not redistribution of genuine power. They refer to Weiler (1990), who claims that arguments for decentralisation in political agendas are incompatible with the manifest interest of the modern state in maintaining control. The arguments have, nevertheless, important political utility. The rhetoric of decentralisation is linked with an attempt to counterbalance the erosion of the legitimacy of the modern state (see Sleegers and Wessenligh, 1993). The freedom that schools have is more to do with means than with ends; they may have greater autonomy, but there is also increased accountability and more efficient monitoring of results (cf. Singh, 1990, cited in Knight *et al.*, 1993).

In England/Wales, as well as in Finland, delegation of economic decision-making has taken place in the era of economic cuts and the ideology of accountability and choice. While schools have acquired more autonomy in curriculum planning in Finland, the National Board of Education is preparing a new system of national assessment when standard testing in the comprehensive school has not existed before. In England/Wales, despite delegation of decision-making to schools, central control has actually increased (cf. Feintuck, 1994).

Standards versus equality

The status of equality as an educational goal is problematic in this situation. The reforms place little emphasis on the idea that a central task of schooling is to build and protect democracy, and that strong measures designed to promote equal opportunities are important in bringing this about (Middleton, 1992). In Finland and in Britain, promoting equal opportunities is mandatory, in principle. For example, the Sex Discrimination Act in Britain and the Law of Equal Opportunities in Finland place obligations on educational authorities.[6] In the USA the federal Education Act Amendment of 1972 deals with sex discrimination in education. But the concept is defined in different ways, and there are many interpretations of the means to be employed (cf. Arnesen and Ní Chartheígh, 1992).

In Britain an overt attack was made on the policy of equal opportunities in the 1980s. The Secretary of State for Education and Science uttered in a conference in 1988: 'the age of egalitarianism is now over' (referred to by Arnot, 1991, p. 457). In Finland equality is still formally one of the criteria for educational development. In the 1990s, however, the goal has acquired new interpretations. A former director of the National Board of Education argued that equality is still an important goal of education, but not the only one. He explained that when education is developed 'at times equality suffers, at times quality' (Hirvi, 1994). This implies that equality and quality are contradictory. Upgrading concern for the first has downgraded concern for the second. Similar juxtaposition is evident in Britain (Hill, 1990) and in the USA (Kenway, 1990).

In the context of New Right restructuring it is difficult to pose questions about social justice seriously, to criticise the lack of attention given to diversity and to address processes of marginalisation (cf. Kenway *et al.*, 1996). Valerie Hey (1996) suggests that multiple territories of the market need to be held onto, including cultural as well as material practices. New Right politics and policies have addressed weaknesses of social democratic politics and policies in relation to education. Indeed, as we have suggested, the current New Labour government in Britain, and coalition government led by social democrats in Finland, have not sought to alter significantly the educational policies they inherited.[7] In the USA Reaganism has been diluted during the Clinton period, but New Right politics have maintained their hold.

3
Curricula for Nations

'Abstract pupil' and difference in schools

> Some of the pupils are tremendously good and some of them are
> like, a bit worse.
>
> (Erkki, MTH)

Teachers do recognise difference between students in school and act
on it and, as we see in the quotation above, level of ability is a major
distinction for them. Gender, class, ethnicity and nationality do not
come immediately to their minds when asked about differences
between students; ability, personality and behaviour do. Although the
school might aim to produce the 'abstract pupil' in training to become
the 'abstract citizen' of the nation state, students in school do differ
by gender, social and ethnic background and even nationality.
Nationality, for example, is taken-for-granted or 'banal' in Billig's
term (1995), an unremarked part of everyday life in our societies,
where nationalism provides a continuous backdrop. Gender too is a
taken-for-granted backdrop, a self-evident dichotomy so deeply
rooted in our thinking that we cannot see it. And social class too is
hidden in our schools. The 'abstract pupil' is abstracted from social
bonds.[1]

When we discuss gender patterns, it is important to note that
Finnish girls and women have been active participants in education
and, unlike in England/Wales, all schools have been co-educational
since comprehensive reform in the early 1970s. Boys' underachievement in schools, which has emerged in British educational discourse
as a problem only lately (Arnot *et al.*, 1997), has been an issue in
Finland since the 1980s (Gordon *et al.*, 1991). These discussions have

36

a long history in the USA, particularly at elementary school level (Brophy and Good, 1974).

There are also differences in the educational systems in relation to social class. Finland has been a stable welfare state, based on social democratic consensus, and income redistribution has smoothed class differentials in terms of extremes of poverty and wealth, when compared with Britain or the USA. Education is based on a comprehensive system, and the few private schools that exist usually operate with a particular ideology (for example there are some Steiner schools). In Britain and in the USA an essential backdrop for the development of the state school system is the existence of a private sector.

A further important difference between Finland and Britain and the USA is the situation of 'ethnic others' in schools. Finland has been more monocultural than most European states, although the situation has changed recently.[2] It is a novel experience for Finnish teachers to have in their classroom perhaps one or two children who do not understand Finnish, and/or come from a culture which is different from their own. Britain, as a multicultural society, has a long history of children from ethnic minorities in schools, largely concentrated in urban, inner-city areas, and a comparable history of regarding them as a 'problem' in and for education (Gillborn and Gipps, 1996).

One of the underlying ideologies of comprehensive reform in Finland was that of equality of opportunities: the same curriculum and equal resources must be provided for everyone regardless of gender, social background or region (ethnicity was, then, not regarded as an issue). As we have suggested earlier, the principle has never been equally evident in everyday policies as in policy texts. In Britain there is more evidence of equal opportunities policies initiated at a local level. In the 1980s some Local Education Authorities produced equal opportunities (which included gender equality) anti-racist or multicultural policies, and supported schools in developing policies and programmes to deal with these issues and generate good practice (Troyna, 1992). These policies have been challenged by the restructuring and marketisation of schools. We now examine how nationality, gender and social class are emphasised or problematised in Finnish and British national curricula and our research schools.[3] We also refer to the curriculum in the Californian school system.

Citizenship and difference in the national curricula

Education for citizenship

Citizenship education is a high priority in many European countries and is often included in the statutory curriculum (SCAA, 1996). In both Finland and Britain it is a cross-curricular theme and not central in the core curriculum.[4]

Cross-curricular themes in the Finnish *Framework Curriculum* (NBE, 1994) are international education, consumer education, traffic education, family education, health education, information technology skills, communication education, environmental education and entrepreneurship education. Much of the content of teaching and learning about citizenship takes place within the subject history, and specifically within the ninth-grade syllabus of history and social studies. But it is, broadly speaking, a task of the whole school system, and the goals of citizenship education are the general goals of schooling rather than those of any specific school subject. Significant aspects of the curriculum are social skills and the conception of the students as active constructors of their knowledge structure and world view. Growing up to become a member of civil society is regarded as one of the elements of the value base in the curriculum:

> Some of the characteristics of a functioning society of citizens are the citizens' mutual equality and people's willingness to actively participate in attending to common affairs. The members of citizens' society have the right to voice and promote their own opinions. Furthermore, the citizens have a chance to oversee the work of political decision-makers as well as that of the authorities.
>
> (NBE, 1994, p. 17)

The framework does not give many ideas on how these democratic principles can be promoted in school education, nor does it question whether these principles are a reality or an ideal in Finnish society.

In Britain the Educational Reform Act (ERA, 1988) stated that schools have 'statutory responsibility to provide a broad and balanced curriculum' which 'promotes the spiritual, moral and cultural, mental and physical development of pupils at the school and of society; and prepares pupils for the opportunities, responsibilities and experiences of adult life' (ERA, 1988, Section 1). It was recognised that the National Curriculum alone could not provide the necessary breadth and that 'an accepted range of cross-curricular elements' would augment it

(NCC, 1990). 'Education for Citizenship' is one of five cross-curricular themes. The others are health education, careers education, economic and industrial understanding, and environmental education. A 'multi-cultural' cross-curricular theme which was mooted in the early days of curriculum development for the National Curriculum, was rapidly excluded from consideration.

It has been argued that all of these themes contribute strongly to an understanding of responsibilities and rights as a citizen. But they are not high on the agenda of schools, given the demands of the statutory elements of the National Curriculum (Whitty *et al.*, 1993). It is the subject-based curriculum which marginalises these cross-curricular themes, combined with teachers' tendency to 'give priority to within-subject coherence' and 'reluctance to have anything to do with the themes, claiming that they "polluted" other subjects' (Whitty *et al.*, 1993). These authors found that education for citizenship was the least favoured of the cross-curricular themes. It could be argued then that the exhortations to schools to implement these themes could be seen as rhetoric, given the difficulties of taking them up in practice.

Gender (neutrality) in educational documents

The Finnish *Framework Curriculum* explains that clarification and realisation of the set of values upon which education is based is an important starting point, and lists 'basic values in the classical period: goodness, truth and beauty.... Equality among men[!][5] with no respect to sex, race or wealth is likewise one of the starting points for our value deliberation' (NBE, 1994, p. 15). It also states that '[t]he equality of the sexes is an important part of the value basis for the school' (NBE, 1994, p. 17). Equality is interpreted as enabling students to function with equal rights and responsibilities in family life, working life, and society. More concretely, responsibility is given to school counsellors: 'Student counselling also promotes equality between the sexes' (p. 43). Apart from these declarations gender is mentioned three times in the document; documents refer neutrally to 'pupils' instead of boys and girls.

This neutrality is gender-blind, and does not allow for a discussion of gender differences. Nor does it encourage the inclusion and valida-tion of the experiences of girls and women in the content of teaching. A case study of some Finnish textbooks indicated how 'ordinary people' in the curriculum framework were transformed into 'men' in history textbooks (Lahelma, 1992). Another example of gender neutrality which turns into gender specificity is that students can choose either textile or technical handicraft. In an evaluative report the efficiency of the comprehensive school in attaining gender equality is demonstrated in the following way:

> ... in the old primary school, [gender segregation in handicrafts] often symbolized the different approaches in preparing boys and girls for working life. In comprehensive school, such sexist thinking on roles in life has been systematically avoided; instead, the aim is individuality and a study programme allowing for specialization according to personal inclinations.
>
> (Jakku-Sihvonen and Lindström, 1996, p. 12)

Comprehensive school reform has not, however, changed the situation that almost all girls study textiles and almost all boys technical handicrafts. This empirical fact is hidden behind the gender-neutral text. As the guidelines do not address the gendered choice, it is possible for teachers to maintain an essentialist understanding of difference, like one teacher who argued in an interview that 'we must accept this biological difference that girls like different things from boys' (Marjatta, FTH) (cf. Riddell, 1992).

The situation in England/Wales is slightly different. Although there are inconsistencies in references to equal opportunities in the National Curriculum, it is less characterised by stereotypical conceptions than the Finnish texts, and there is some sensitivity to gender issues.[6] However, where references are made to equal opportunities, scant attention is paid to the large body of British research indicating the nature of sexism within educational institutions. Equal opportunities issues and concerns are formally present in the documents, but their stature, significance and definition is ambiguous (Davies *et al.*, 1992; Lahelma, 1993). As Arnot *et al.* (1997) argue, the reforms were not framed or developed with increased gender equality primarily in mind and hence there is relatively little explicit reference to gender in the policy documentation.

Nation, ethnicity and (inter)nationalism

> To foster our national heritage as well as multicultural aspects which have to do with internationalism leads to a new type of clarification of our identity.
>
> (NBE, 1994, p. 10).

In the Finnish *Framework Curriculum* the national heritage appears linked with multiculturalism and internationalism. This way of linking Finnish culture or cultural identity, other cultures and internationalism emerges several times in the documents. One example is in the guidelines for mother tongue; it is stated that literature helps the student to 'understand his[!] mother tongue and phenomena in the Finnish culture, from which he[!] can receive ingredients to understand other languages and cultures, too' (NBE, 1994, pp. 47–8). This 'pairing' of national with multicultural and international values may be a compromise between conservative values which stress nationality, liberal values with a multicultural emphasis and neo-liberalism which stresses internationalism.

Equality and justice are mentioned in the aims of international education:

> The aim of international education is that the student accepts the fact that people are different, knows different cultures, understands that the mutual dependence of people and nations and equality as well as justice are the basis for human dignity. This education, furthermore, aims at arousing the students' interest in international development and events and their reasons and at being ready to have international interaction and cooperation as well as at being ready for a personal contribution and participation.
>
> (NBE, 1994, p. 38)

The changing situation in Finland in relation to immigration is noted: 'More and more students with different linguistic backgrounds are flocking into our schools, making our schools more multicultural than heretofore' (NBE, 1994, p. 16).[7] The rights of immigrants are stated in the same section:

> Children of minority groups have the right to grow up to be active members of both their own cultural community as well as of Finnish society. Tolerance and openness towards different cultural backgrounds, viewpoints, and languages as well as an interest in them pave the way for interaction between students.
>
> (NBE, 1994, p. 16)

Robert Fullinwider (1996, p. 3) argues that the germinal ideal of 'multicultural education' is that the good school must adjust itself 'culturally' to the students, and it must overcome 'cultural' barriers for the students to adjust to it. In the above text the rights of minority groups are in line with this multicultural ideal. But, as Fullinwider suggests, there are many controversies. What is a 'culture' and when is it reasonable to expect a school to adjust, and when a student? The values of the minority groups can be not only different, but contradictory to the values of the society. The format that 'we' have to learn to tolerate the 'others' does not necessarily involve treating others as equals. The potential positive impact of minority children on Finnish school is mentioned in the section on mother tongue:

> Minority children and their parents bring new viewpoints and open avenues to natural international education in a Finnish school. Their expertise in the natural environment, way of life, languages, and cultures of other countries and continents is made use of in the teaching of different subjects.
>
> (NBE, 1994, p. 61)

Although different ethnic groups are acknowledged, an idealistic picture of citizenship and nationality in schools is given. Potential problems are not raised; the word 'racism' does not appear, and there are no references to possible discrepancies between the Finnish and the immigrant child's culture. But these are problems which teachers and students are bound to confront in everyday life at school.

In England/Wales (NCC, 1990) students must be made aware 'that all citizens can and must be equal' and that 'Britain is a multicultural, multiethnic, multifaith and multilingual society'. They must also be made aware of 'the diversity of cultures in other societies, of international and global issues, and of the origins and effects of racial prejudice within British and other societies'. Citizens' rights 'include civil, political, social and human rights and how these may be violated by various forms of injustice, inequality and discrimination, including sexism and racism' (NCC Circular 11, 1991, p. 6). This text promotes a supportive approach to bilingualism in the National Curriculum: 'Linguistic diversity ... provides an opportunity for pupils to gain firsthand experience, knowledge and understanding of other cultures and perspectives. It also helps to prepare pupils for life in a multicultural society by promoting respect for all forms of language' (Runnymede Trust, 1993).

When it comes to the specific National Curriculum subjects in which citizenship might find a particular place – English, history, geography – this focus on diversity is not so apparent. McKiernan

(1993) argues that the National Curriculum was specifically cast in terms of national economic regeneration and identity, and was introduced at a time when concerns about economic survival in a changing global context meant that nationhood and national sovereignty were (as they continue to be) of considerable importance. In practice the balance of subjects in the National Curriculum suggests that questions of national identity and control were pre-eminent, rather than industrial or commercial requirements (Goodson, 1994).

Garside (1995) has commented that, in the revision of the National Curriculum for English in 1995, the range of authors 'represents a narrow view of the English literary heritage, including very few women authors and no black authors or works in translation'. This is despite the general requirement that pupils should be taught to: 'read, analyse and evaluate a wide range of texts, including literature from the English literary heritage and from other cultures and traditions' (English p. 2, NCC, 1990). There is also, in her view, an increased emphasis on Standard English, and an implicit rejection of employing bilingualism positively. In geography, as pupils progress through the stages of education, they are increasingly introduced to 'the wider context' into which places and communities fit, and are required to study, at 11–13 years old for example, two other countries in 'significantly different states of development'. But it is Britain being contextualised into this broader context, from a British perspective.

The subject of history is regarded as quintessentially the place where citizenship can be taught. *Education for Citizenship* (NCC, 1990) gives 32 examples of how to implement citizenship programmes in the curriculum, citing history 13 times. And here the tendency is towards a nationalist approach. Goodson (1994, p. 20) argues that 'the focus on British history in the formative years of schooling indicated a wish to inculcate at an early stage a sense of national identity'.

The History Working Group appointed by the government wanted pluralistic study using a radical 'process' approach to history teaching. This was rejected by the government in favour of an emphasis on British, political, constitutional and war history at the expense of social, local and non-European and new world cultural history; ancient and classical rather than modern history (McKiernan, 1993, p. 50). File (1995, p. 24) points out:

> Post-Dearing history is unbalanced as between local, national and world history. The content is predominantly British national

history. Eighty per cent of curriculum time for the 7–14 age groups is essentially concerned with British or European affairs.

Bracey (1995, p. 9), however, is more positive, and argues that 'the need to consider British rather than English history also shows that there has never been a homogeneous culture within these islands. In this way the long term nature of our multicultural society will be an issue which permeates the History course.' This would of course depend on the way in which teachers take up the possibilities of the curriculum. The perspective of the neo-conservatives in the government at the time of the introduction of the National Curriculum is more accurately captured by the statement of a humanities adviser: 'We don't have a national curriculum for history – we have a nationalist curriculum' (File, 1995, p. 23).

International education and multiculturalism in Finland is more outward-looking and in England/Wales the concern is more inward-looking. This is not very surprising; Finland is a small country that has recently become a member of the EU. By looking outward it tries to clarify its national identity in the broad picture. Britain is, perhaps, in confusion about national identity given its changing and diminished role on the world stage, and concerned about the turmoil within.

Students as 'citizens-to-be'

When she was asked who decided which school she was going to, Pinja (FSH) replied that 'it was totally my own choice', constructing herself as a citizen, capable of making choices. The citizen as 'consumer' and participant, able to make choices are key concepts in the rhetoric of the restructuring of education. But it is parents who are regarded as the consumers of education, not students. The students are not participants of civil society, but learning to be so. In legal terms, children are citizens, but in schools they are often regarded as 'citizens-to-be'.

That students are citizens-to-be is evident in the following extract from the Finnish document: the school 'is to develop attitudes and capabilities in students which will make it possible for them to function as active, critical and responsible members of the society of citizens' (NBE, 1994, p. 17). The concept of a 'citizen' in Finland sometimes refers to a human being in a 'taken-for-granted' way, but in other cases active (as above) and cultural citizenship are highlighted. In guidelines for music, a cultural citizen is one who is able to make assessments in music. Active participation in society is mentioned in environmental and natural studies, and in teachers' guide books, for example:

> The technical development of society makes it necessary for all citizens to exert an influence on the direction of technical development. A citizen needs to understand technology.
>
> (NBE, 1994, p.13)

> ... to support and guide the students' growth into an investigating, active citizen who is interested in nature.
>
> (NBE, 1994, p. 85)

> The task of education is to explain to the students the structure of the society and citizens' possibilities for exerting influence, to encourage them into activity and participation.
>
> (Hirvi, 1994)

The concept 'new Finnish people' emerges in the guidelines for ethics. This implies an interpretation of immigrants as Finnish people, not as 'the other'. Ethics, however, is studied only by the small minority of children who do not participate in religious education. It is possible to regard ethics as a 'niche' for more democratic principles within the educational policies, but what is taught and learned in ethics does not affect the majority of school students.

A new feature of Finnish educational policies is an emphasis on entrepreneurial education. It is a new cross-curricular theme in comprehensive school and is one of the optional courses in the secondary school. Here students are seen as autonomous individuals who should develop 'innate[8] entrepreneurship':

> Through entrepreneurial education, the student's innate entrepreneurship, activity, creativity, and persistence are encouraged. The student should learn to see man's [!] own initiative and the importance of being creative and active as the starting point for entrepreneurship.
>
> (NBE, 1994, p. 42)

In England/Wales, *Education for Citizenship* certainly takes the position that pupils are citizens in the making. It 'embraces both responsibilities and rights in the present and preparation for citizenship in adult life. It helps pupils by supporting them as they develop from dependent children into independent young people.' It does this '(i) by helping pupils to acquire and understand essential information; (ii) by providing them with opportunities and incentives to participate in all aspects of school life' (NCC, 1990, p. 1).

Citizenship can be taught through the subjects in the National Curriculum, through personal and social education and through 'immersion in the corporate life of the school'. The ethos of the school 'can do much to' promote the personal and social development of pupils, offering them opportunities to be involved 'in decisions about features of their life at school, and participation in the planning and organisation of group and extra-curricular activities, schools councils' (NCC, 1990, p. 5). In this conception the corporate life of the school offers a training in the skills, knowledge and capacities which will produce the good citizen.

Most of the current documentation for England/Wales cannot be faulted on using non-sexist, non-racist language, but the SCAA document (1996) does have a tendency to be anti-youth, or at least to express negative perceptions of young people. It is based on a conference called as a result of 'public concern at a perceived degeneration in moral standards, especially among young people' (p. 8) and talks in terms of a 'moral crisis', arguing that 'a significant proportion of young people is now out of control'. This has the ring of an older generation in moral panic, although some delegates felt that young people behaved as they saw others behave and 'previous generations are not blameless: among their legacies are racism, exploitation and environmental pollution' (p. 8).

Individuals and difference in the curriculum of California

'Little is known about the substance of intended curricula around the world – let alone curricula that are implemented in some sense in the classroom' (Meyer and Baker, 1996). To address this we examine curricular documents from California in relation to some of our central issues. The History–Social Science Framework for California Public Schools (1987) emphasises the development of civic and democratic values as an integral element of good citizenship.

> From the earlier grades students should learn the kind of behaviour that is necessary for the functioning of a democratic society. They should learn sportmanship, fair play, sharing and taking turns. They should be given opportunities to lead and to follow. They should learn how to select leaders and how to resolve disputes rationally. They should learn about the value of due process in

dealing with infractions, and they should learn to respect the rights of the minority, even if this minority is only a single dissenting voice.

Students must understand what is required of a citizen in democracy. They need to understand, for example, that a democratic society depends on citizens who will take individual responsibility for their own ethical behaviour, control inclinations to aggression, and attain a certain level of civility by choosing to live by certain higher rules of ethical conduct.

(p. 22)

These principles seem central to sustaining a democracy, and give more concrete guidelines for teachers than the Finnish and British documents. Lawrence A. Q. Blum (1996), however, notes their limitations. He argues, for example, that values of fair play, sharing and taking turns do not go very far in correcting those attitudes that contribute to racial and cultural exclusion, since these values come into play only in the context of an already-defined group. While respecting the rights of a single dissenting voice is highlighted, the framework does not speak of the need sometimes to *be* the single dissenting voice, or even a part of a collective dissenting voice. Blum also notes that the framework does not raise questions about which children are present in a given school in the first place. Because of the wide system of private schools, most schools in California are essentially racially segregated. This is not the case in Finland, nor generally in England/Wales.

Whilst equality is an issue there are tensions between the emphasis on diversity and the ever-present nation, captured in multicultural iconography on school walls, along with national insignia such as flags. Gender is a silent category in relation to race.

Curriculum in schools

We move now from the macro level of national curriculum to the micro level of schools by analysing curriculum processes in the four research schools.

School-based curricula had just been introduced in Finland when we started our ethnography. City Park already had the new curriculum and the teachers in Green Park were working on theirs. In both schools the teachers had found the making of the new curriculum hard; they had a considerable amount of extra work and it was difficult to find time for the necessary meetings. Given the Finnish tradition of a very centralised curriculum, teachers are not used to planning their teaching. But most of them regarded the process as useful or interesting, or at least found something positive in it. Some teachers said that the curriculum process did not give much time to reflect on teaching methods, and that they would have liked to learn to change methods: 'We produce 70 versions of curriculum but the pedagogical process in the classroom does not change.'

Because of the change in education policies, Finnish schools have now considerable space to negotiate their curriculum, to transform their image, and to choose the kinds of educational services they want to provide. But these new freedoms are curtailed by both the centralised control of outcome and the economic cutbacks of the 1990s. One teacher argued: 'when we started to make these curricula, then, it was wow, wonderful, now we really are allowed to do it. But after that came a stop, there was no money, no money for extra lessons … no space, teaching groups got bigger' (Raila, FTH). But she went on to say that despite this there are possibilities for change.

In the process of generating the National Curriculum in England/ Wales, the burden on teachers has been immense:

> But I think on the curriculum on the whole a lot of people are quite for having a national curriculum, except the government just go about it the completely wrong way. There have been major changes at all ends and the problem that comes out of it is the amount of paperwork that is expected…. I don't think people also realise the amount of change and that it takes time to implement things and to work things out. Everything happens too quickly, too much and as soon as people get their head round one thing, bang it is gone.
>
> (Katherine, FTL)

There have been almost continuous changes to the curriculum since its inception in 1988 (Graham, 1993), and the requirements of testing and assessment (at ages 7, 11, 14 and 16), always controversial and often contested, have made additional demands on teachers' time and patience – teaching has become a high-stress profession.

In regard to the requirements of the National Curriculum, some teachers have reacted by ignoring the paper blizzard from the Department for Education[9] where possible. One teacher, when asked how the changes in curriculum had affected him, responded that he took no notice of it and just went on teaching as he always had. Others have responded to the challenge with more and more effort to produce a coherent, meaningful school curriculum.

Unlike teachers in Finland, those in Britain with a history of autonomy in the classroom were used to producing material and planning their own curriculum content. What they were not used to were the constraints and demands placed upon them by a centrally controlled curriculum. Although much of the teaching in each school was undertaken using traditional teacher-centred didactic methods, these were also combined with other, more mixed methods, particularly in some subjects. Collaborative and group work was encouraged in both of the schools, although competition was also a motivating factor in pupils' performance.

Growing up into internationalism and to be a member of the society of citizens is mentioned in the principles and aims of Green Park school in Helsinki. International education is one of the themes, and its aims are acceptance of difference, getting acquainted and tolerance. The curriculum states that students who come from abroad are welcomed and treated in an equitable way.

The curriculum does not include many references to gender or other differences. The word equality is mentioned in home economics, handicrafts[10] and counselling. An exception is in the guidelines for ethics, where equality and the status of women are mentioned as contents to be studied but, as pointed out earlier, ethics is taught only to those few students who do not participate in religious education. Internationalism or the Finnish culture is mentioned in the plans for different subjects, for example the national tradition in arts, national music in music, strengthening Finnish identity and broadening knowledge in culture in mother tongue, learning to understand the differences between cultures and to esteem the cultural heritage of humankind in history. An optional course in cultural history includes the notion: 'We try to learn good, constructive and enriching issues in the multiculturalism in Helsinki.' Racism and difference is mentioned as one of the themes in ethics.

The curriculum of City Park 'aims at producing the endowments that the students need in their duties after the school, in societal life and in interaction with other people'. Students' individuality and difference is, according to the plan, taken into account by offering possibilities for choice. The students will be provided with 'sufficient behavioural skills for interaction in the more international surroundings'. The aims of international education include 'tolerating difference in people', 'participating in the making of the future' and 'meeting other cultures'. In the aims and contents of different subjects international or global questions are mentioned, for example in ethics difference and minorities; in geography understanding foreign countries, nations and cultures; in history understanding differences between cultures; and in handicrafts respect for local, national and international culture. Understanding the importance of equality is mentioned among the aims of home economics. Gender, social class or other differences are not mentioned in the curriculum.

The schools in London do regard themselves as providing a training in citizenship, as laid out in *Education for Citizenship* (NCC, 1990). This is clear from their aims 'to extend their [pupils'] understanding of the world in which they live and to prepare them for adult life, work and citizenship', and 'to help pupils to acquire knowledge, skills and interests relevant to adult life and employment and the ambition to realise their full potential'.

Each of the London schools is resolutely multicultural, and has produced or is producing written policies on a range of issues including equal opportunities in relation to 'race' and gender. Amongst the expressed aims of both schools, reflecting the aims for education in national documents are the intention: to stimulate well-motivated students with lively and enquiring minds into developing responsibility for their own learning; and to assist pupils to develop informed views in the sphere of beliefs and values and to encourage understanding and proper tolerance of the beliefs and values of other people.

The ideas of the national policy documents are more or less apparent in the school documents of all our research schools. The schools do not teach 'citizenship' as such, but the elements are there. Ethnicity and international relations are taken into account. In the documents of the London schools gender is treated with more sensitivity than in the Helsinki documents, which are more gender-neutral or gender-blind, paralleling the difference which we noted in the national documents in each country.

Conclusions

The construction of the citizen in school is a project of the nation state, and we have traced here how this process is presented and construed in the curriculum at the national level. We have seen how, in national-level documents and guidelines, expectations of the school extend beyond curricula into the processes and practices of the school, through which the multiple social contexts of the student are to be distilled into the abstract pupil as 'citizen to be'. The restructuring of education and shifting of the education agenda achieved by the New Right is also apparent in these documents and expectations. Marketisation in both rhetoric and organisation has led to the marginalisation of equal opportunities considerations, and the competitive 'consumption' of education; entrepreneurship has become a requisite for the 'citizen-to-be'; the requirements of national identity and nationhood are laced through the curriculum. And despite New Right rhetoric of curbing the power of the state, the school can clearly be seen as a local site of the state, charged with producing appropriate citizens.

There is a gap between policy and its implementation at the local level which is suffused with interpretation, negotiation, challenge and even transformation. We move now into that space with our ethnography of the everyday conversations, experience and perspectives of people in schools which, as Middleton (1992) suggests, are often rendered invisible by a reliance on the reading of texts. We shall next trace the variety of steps taken by students and teachers in their everyday lives in school.

4
Invitation to the Dance: Exploring Everyday Life in Schools

Introduction

> A small note to say how we've [the class] enjoyed you following us around the school. Your shadow in the background silently observing our actions shall be missed (including your little smiles when someone does something silly!) Only one question, how could anyone bring themselves to note and watch universally dreaded form 9B (is the pay good, or something). Anyway, see you in a next existence ...

A student gave a farewell card with this note to Kay Parkinson on her last day in a London school. The note indicates our place in the classroom where the authors (and colleagues) spent many days; we normally sat in the background silently, an embodiment of an ideal (female) pupil. But we experienced many emotions and evidently revealed our feelings through small gestures.

The ethnographic work was based on previous cooperation among the Helsinki team, and work with the London team was also constructed over a long period of time. The years of sharing were essential background for conducting intensive, collective work in schools. We have crossed borders to work together in developing qualitative, crosscultural, comparative understandings. The pleasures and pains of this type of undertaking are considerable. A notion of 'fun methodology' – making our meetings as pleasurable as possible – sustained us in our demanding undertaking. Our work is grounded in collaboration between a number of people, in two languages, in various spaces and places. We have visited each other's schools, we have talked in London and Helsinki, and also in conferences in

Seville, Amsterdam, Budapest, Edinburgh, in hotel rooms, parks, cafés, restaurants – we have twirled around in rhythms of talk about incidents and observations.

Getting dressed for the ball: planning the ethnography

Our work is based on an analytical distinction between three layers of the school that formed the focus of our interest: the official, informal and physical school. The *official* school is laid out in documents of the school and the state; in our observations in the classroom we focus on lesson content, textbooks, teaching materials and methods, and classroom interaction. We examine the disciplinary apparatus of the school, rules and sanctions, and outline official hierarchies among and between teachers and students.

We chose to use the term *informal*, rather than create a binary opposition between the official and the unofficial, to indicate that the informal school is different from, and not merely a reaction to, the official school; it has a life and a meaning of its own. Here we expand the analysis of classroom interaction to examine interaction between teachers and students beyond the instructional relationship, among students in other areas of the school, among teachers, and between teachers, students and other groups in the school (support staff of various types). School rules are compared with their enactment in practice, informal hierarchies among and between teachers and students are compared with formal hierarchies.

Our focus on the *physical* school, and the possibilities and limitations offered by school buildings and spaces for teaching and learning in the official school, and interactions and hierarchical differentiation in the informal school, was innovative at its inception. In this connection we draw on Giddens' (1985) discussion of time–space paths in Chapter 7. Here we contrast rules about movement, talk, noise and the use of spaces in the school with the informally sanctioned and forbidden practices of students. As we have suggested earlier, the school as a physical space provides a context for the practices and processes that take place within it, but it is more than context, it shapes these practices and processes, and in this way can produce differentiation between students.

We have developed a metaphor to capture the relationship between the official, informal and physical layers of the school; that of the dance.[1] Dance, Maureen Molloy (1995) suggests, is 'structural and processual, involving set moves and individual improvisation, group patterns and individual performance' (p. 108) and, usually, both women and men. Here the *physical* is the dance hall, or dance floor, the space in which the dance takes place and in which bodies move, as well as the dress and other embodiment of the dancers; the *official* is the rules of the dance, the formal steps, movements and dress codes prescribed for the specific dance (for example the minuet);[2] and the *informal* is all the exchanges that take place around and between these two elements (verbal, physical and other contacts).

Ethnographic steps

Once we had made the decision to pursue our interests by studying everyday life at school, and to use ethnographic methods, many more decisions followed: how we should prepare for the study, what methods to use, what places and spaces to occupy, how to record our observations and experiences, analyse our data, and write them up. These are important decisions; ethnographic research is diverse and multi-faceted, and no simple solutions are available. All the researchers are committed to collective, feminist research, and we wanted to ensure that we undertook collaborative and collective work in which the difficulties of such an undertaking were turned into strengths. Without this kind of effort an ethnographic study of four schools in two countries would have been impossible. The multiplicity and variety we have witnessed has facilitated an approach where very little is taken for granted.

Sara Delamont and Paul Atkinson (1995) have criticised the work of educational ethnographers as 'all too familiar', and argue that there should be a commitment to making the familiar strange, to reflexivity in data collection, analysis, theorising and writing, and that ethnographers should take an eclectic and pragmatic approach to research and not see methods, disciplines and schools of thought as 'sectarian doctrines with iron barriers between them'. They advise the approach of 'promiscuous bricoleurs, selecting whatever techniques, theories, or insights can be best deployed in any particular project' (p. vi).

They propose several ways in which the familiar can be made strange so that ethnographers can see beyond what everyone sees in the processes of schooling, and we have adopted three of them in this study. The first is a focus on gender, which will throw light more generally on the processes constructing difference in the school setting. They suggest that much of the excellent feminist material is lost to mainstream ethnography, sociology, and sociology of education in a feminist or women's studies ghetto, and draw attention to a range of work which has rendered the familiar new by attending to aspects of gender in the school. The second is the basis of the current research, crosscultural comparison. A different perspective can be gained on the familiar by comparing and contrasting what happens in schools in different cultural contexts. The third is to draw on the ethnomethodological approach, which has at its heart treating every-day life as problematic. The important principles here are recognising that every researcher uses his or her 'member's knowledge' (p. 10) when studying schools and classrooms, and that this itself should be posed as problematic.

We have all spent time in school as a school student. As part of our collective work on this project we did memory work together on our school experiences. In memory work the participants produce narra-tives about particular themes from their own experience which are then explored in group discussions. It has been used successfully to explore aspects of sexuality and emotions (Haug, 1987; Crawford *et al.*, 1993). In memory work shared cultural codes can be tapped, and in this instance we had the added advantage of being able to compare similarities and differences across cultures. We examined these indi-vidual memories of experience at school in the light of more general categories of sociological analysis, such as class, nationality, gender and difference, and in relation to our feelings, behaviour and responses during the ethnography in the schools. The Finnish researchers also included memories and dreams in their research diaries.

An ethnographer entering the field is preparing to gaze, record, interpret and analyse, but what does this gaze mean. Foucault (1980) has argued that the surveying and controlling gaze is a technique of modern power. Starting in disciplinary institutions, it is based on architectural and organisational innovations through which adminis-trators managed their populations through exploiting visibility. The gaze was then incorporated into the detailed observation of the habits and histories of individuals required by the modern disciplines and practices of medicine, science, and the science of man. Each then became linked with surveillance. And as Foucault (1977) points out, the interiorisation of this surveillance leads to the production of 'docile and useful bodies'; a requirement in his view of the modern nation state. In the school the surveying and controlling gaze is one of the techniques for producing the requirements of the 'abstract pupil', and ultimately the citizen. We have also linked both the gaze and the interiorisation of surveillance to the production of gender hierarchy.

There are continuities and discontinuities between the surveying gaze and the gaze of the ethnographer. When researchers backed by the authority of the academy enter a school, they gaze with some power. But the situation is complex, and researchers can be seen and experience themselves as balanced between power and vulnerability, as we see from descriptions of our own experiences. Qualitative researchers in the social sciences today confront a double crisis, of representation and legitimation which is associated with the interpretive, linguistic and rhetorical turns in social theory (Denzin and Lincoln, 1994).

David Morley (1997) suggests that the poststructural moment, particularly in cultural studies – itself moving towards the ethnographic method – may have tipped the balance too far into the textual, and quotes Elspeth Probyn's comment on ethnography, 'just as practitioners in other disciplines seem to be drawn to ethnography because of its promise to delve into the concrete (in the hope of finding real people living "real" lives), ethnography is becoming increasingly textual' (Probyn, 1993, p. 61).

Morley's and Probyn's argument is with the influential work of Clifford and Marcus (1986) which set the groundwork for a predominantly textual approach in postmodern ethnography, and their desire is to know what is the relationship between the textual and the real. Morley wants to avoid the disabling of empirical research by what he sees as a muddled relativism which eschews the notion of truth. Marshalling support from Massey (1991), Tomkins (1986) and Fish (1989) he argues against the deconstructionist, postmodern epistemological position in cultural studies (and ethnography) that maintains that since facts can only be known from a particular perspective and are situated within interpretative frameworks, they cannot be known as facts *per se*. In contrast, the argument is that if you accept the idea that any fact or set of facts can *only* be known from a perspective, or world view, this assertion is no longer sufficient to invalidate any particular fact.

Judith Stacey (1990), in discussing her experiences of doing feminist ethnographic work, notes the difficulties and complexities in the interaction between the researcher and the researched. In her book *Brave New Families* one of her research subjects comments on what has been written about her by saying that she can never be 'pinned down', alerting us to the fact that as social researchers we do not just realise the meanings of the researched, but make meanings, create knowledge of the social world from our own perspective(s). Stacey calls for rigorously self-aware feminist cultural accounts, humble about the partiality of our vision (Stacey, 1988). Whatever the shifting epistemological sands upon which the ethnographer stands, and the status of the 'facts' which s/he presents, a reflexive practice which recognises both the constraints and the possibilities of the perspective from which the study has been undertaken, and the multiple positioning of both researcher and researched can provide a basis for producing knowledge of the social world.

Leslie Roman notes that feminists have tried to develop research approaches that go beyond both objectivism and subjectivism, neither neutrality nor relativity is a sufficient guise for the researcher. She calls for the consideration of 'underlying structures, material conditions, and conflicting historically specific power relations and inequalities' (Roman, 1993, p. 282). Like Angela McRobbie (1996, 1997) she calls for ethnographic accounts which do not dematerialise the social and the cultural. Thus feminist approaches can no longer assume themselves to be inherently egalitarian, nor other approaches to be essentially reifying or masculinist. Leslie Roman criticises both voyeurism and intellectual tourism in ethnographic approaches, including short cultural immersion and involvement in the lives of the subjects under study.

The way in which we have attempted to conduct ethnographic research also affects how we write it. Studying schools provides rich material to surprise and to startle; accounts can be rendered in a gripping style of semi-warfare. We have tried to focus on stories of cooperation as well as on stories of conflict. We do not see teachers as agents of the state, with a sole interest in control, and every limitation is for us, as for Giddens (1985), an opportunity for enactment. We frame the events in our schools in the context of politics and policies. We try to materialise the cultural order we have observed, and the patterns of interaction which constitute that order. Our main focus is on gender, but we have tried to take difference seriously; we are constantly talking about students as gendered and belonging to particular groups, and then disentangling these constructions to think about them from a different perspective.

The schools

The pseudonyms of our two Finnish schools are City Park and Green Park. City Park is in the central area of Helsinki and the local catchment area is middle class. The school also has a number of classes with extra emphasis on the performing arts, and students with an interest

in these come from a wider geographical area. Overall a large proportion of students come from middle-class families. A majority of the
students are also white and Finnish. Green Park is located outside the
centre of Helsinki in an expanding urban district. It is in a traditional
working-class area which has become more heterogeneous as a result
of this expansion, but average income and educational levels are lower
than in the City Park catchment area. The majority of students are
also Finnish and white although there is a larger proportion (still
small) of students from different ethnic groups than in City Park.

The two British schools are Oak Grove and Woburn Hill. Oak Grove
is a state mixed comprehensive, in a predominantly working-class
catchment area in London, with a very ethnically and culturally
mixed student body. The school has many characteristics of an urban
inner-city school although it is located outside the centre of London.
It caters for a range of special needs. Woburn Hill is a mixed grant
maintained school which also has an ethnically and culturally mixed
student body, and is located in a largely middle-class, but still socially
and ethnically mixed, area outside the centre of London. The school
is in high demand and has a selective intake, in terms of ability and
other characteristics that the school regards as desirable, and students
come from a wide geographical area. There is a special interest in the
performing arts.

All the schools are secondary co-educational schools, but the
Finnish schools cover three age grades, from 13 to 15 years, whereas
the London schools cover the secondary age range 11–16 in five age
grades, and each has a sixth form up to the age of 18 or 19. Secondary
schools in Finland then, are in general smaller than those in
England/Wales, and the largest school in our research had about 1000,
and the smallest less than 400 students.

Access to schools was no easy matter (cf. Troman, 1996). Schools
were under pressure to perform, teachers suspected surveillance,
school management sometimes expected surveillance. The process of
negotiation to gain access was lengthy and often unsuccessful, particularly in London, where schools had been subjected to some years of
pressure and overload through the introduction of the National
Curriculum, were subject to demanding inspection by OFSTED (the
Office for Standards in Education), and were thrown into competition
for students who could perform well in exams through the quasi-
market which was the mechanism for funding. This meant that the
image and performance of the school was crucial and schools were
wary of anything which might lead to criticism.

The Finnish ethnography involved all six researchers in two schools concurrently for differing lengths of time over a period of a year. In London the research took place in the two schools in the study sequentially, Janet and one other researcher in each school for one or two days a week over two terms.

Finding your feet: methods in practice[3]

Gazing with intent

In our ethnographic practice the mode of our observation appeared to reflect that of the ideal student; quiet, industrious, observant, diligent, writing copious notes. We also questioned whether this mode of behaviour represented that of the ideal student, or of the ideal *female* student. And what exactly is going on here? Is this a playing-out of our own experiences of school, memories having been invoked by the memory work we had undertaken, and by the sheer fact of being in a school. One observer remarked almost with astonishment on the powerful feelings of being back in her schooldays evoked by being in one of the schools, a school which was in fact very different from her own school. So can we see this response and mode of behaviour as linked to the personal? Or is it more self-consciously the ethnographer, the voyeur, donning the (gendered) mantle of the insider to divert awareness of outsider status? These layers of meaning have implications for our observations and for the interpretation which we make of them. Sensitivity and methodological, positional self-awareness is required by an ethnographer who occupies an ambivalent, contradictory and vulnerable position in the school.

One of the most concrete points of vulnerability can be seen as embedded in embodiment. When women in their thirties, forties and fifties position themselves in classrooms full of 13–14-year-olds to observe and to participate, there is no ready-made position available for them. Finding their own space, physically and metaphorically, can be a daunting process. As we were also interested to talk to teachers, we were ambivalent borderliners in a space where institutional practices constitute 'teachers' and 'pupils' in different locations. If we veered too far in one direction, our movement in the other direction became more difficult.

Participation in some activities – physical education, exams, advising on and tasting their cooking – could bring us closer to the students. Drawing, instead of writing notes, in an art lesson brought students to the researcher, eager to discuss her picture. It was useful experientially too, giving us insights into the feelings and emotions which swirled around the classroom. When two of the researchers participated in a mathematics examination, and handed in their papers to be marked, they were surprised by the anxiety caused by this: 'will I get an embarrassingly poor grade'; 'will the other researcher get a much better grade than me?' When a researcher was practising long jump in physical education, she noticed how her efforts heightened when the jumps were measured after the initial practice period. The elation she felt when scoring her first goal in football was tremendous. She felt happy about her achievement, but also experienced great relief in 'having passed' as a competent participant, when incompetence, particularly during the early period in the school, was a common occurrence (cf. Hey, 1996).

Emotions were part of what we observed, and of what we experienced. An observer's notes recall the range of feelings that we recorded during our stint in the classroom:

> ... anger, boredom, disappointment, sometimes even fear, loneliness, ambivalence, uncertainty, joy, excitement, tenderness, disgust, hurt, intolerance, sense of injustice. Not to mention headaches, sore wrists, stiff necks, aching backs, oxygen deprived brains ...

The roller coaster of feelings we encountered reflected partly our own ambivalent positioning, but were also more general instances of what Jenny Shaw (1996) calls the 'anxiety-ridden' and 'anxiety-driven' experiences of education. But we must emphasise that we also experienced many feelings of happiness, as the above quote demonstrates. When we were away from schools we missed the people there, and when we finally left the schools our sadness and sense of loss was considerable. For example, as the Finnish team has been in the process of reading our research diaries and diaries of our own meetings, we have been filled with a mournful yearning.[4]

As a result of the ambiguities of our positioning, throughout the whole time we spent in school, we were constantly negotiating entry: can I come to this occasion; can I join in this special activity; will I be able to participate in this conversation; can I sit here? Our experiences as qualitative researchers, our preparation for and participation in our fieldwork whilst at the same time members of our disciplines and institutions, constructed a complex and shifting positionality for us.

We sometimes felt that we had not spent enough time observing some aspects of the school: for example, observing the students at break time, or observing the activities and interactions of support staff, when instead we had spent the time in the staff room, with other researchers, or frantically making arrangements for whatever was to follow. But with such an enormous amount of time spent in the schools, these gaps, although annoying, were not too onerous. They could often be filled from the experience of another member of the team. Ethnographic research, even when carefully planned in advance, as ours was, is full of surprising and unexpected situations. The Finnish team has discussed this in terms of 'suction' of the field, where an irresistible pull draws you in unanticipated directions. Part of this suction is a result of human relationships which, in the context of research relations, operate in many similar ways to any social and cultural interaction (Hey, 1996).

Asking questions

Our aim was to interview all of the students in 'our' classes, and with minor, and one major, exception, we were successful in this. In Helsinki a few quiet boys did not want to be interviewed. There was some feeling that if we had tried a little harder they could have been persuaded, but our position was that this was a voluntary activity for the students, so no pressure was applied.

As well as in interviews, we asked questions in many other ways. For example, in a questionnaire we asked the teachers and students to produce a metaphor for the school, 'School is like …'.[5] The metaphor was used to uncover the types of response to the school which would not be discernible in observation, and would not necessarily emerge in interviews. 'Metaphors translate, invent and betray … [they] both conceal and reveal … clarify and confuse' (Gordon and Lahelma, 1996, p. 303). For this purpose we also used an association list, in which interviewees were asked to give the first thing that came into their head on a series of prompts. The associations were particularly useful in relation to notions and understandings of gender difference and nationality.

We have struggled to maintain a hold on material, social, cultural and psychological dimensions in our analysis of everyday processes and practices in schools. We have constructed intensely collective working methods among the researchers – but the collaboration with our research subjects, teachers and students, in the course of the analysis has been slight. Day-to-day concerns in the business of schools makes it difficult to develop cooperation, particularly when our focus is on both students and teachers. We have been aware of this, and have tried to avoid voyeurism – we have not encouraged students or teachers to tell us more than they want to; we have not made efforts to intervene in situations which appear very intimate; and, importantly, we do not portray and illustrate all of our data. The collaboration among researchers provides some balancing for potential problems caused by this reticence – in the context of joint discussions a range of situations and utterances can be considered in order to gain insight without injury.

Leslie Roman (1993) argues that researchers interact with and therefore also alter the social relations they are studying. Doing work in schools lessens this impact, as the processes of habituation and routinisation – though interlaced with the surprising and the unexpected – are so strong that alteration of these is difficult even when it is the specific aim of educators. We hope that we have had some impact in the lives of students and teachers we met and came to know – as they have had a tremendous impact on us. We do not want to remove our own subjectivity, nor do we want to objectify the subjectivities of others – as ethnographic narratives sometimes do, and as Leslie Roman also notes. More work is to be done in order to integrate a contextualised, materialist, cultural approach to schooling which is also intensely collaborative and respectful of its subjects. Material issues relating to the process of conducting research are also important, though often underplayed in final texts. We, however, wish to present an account of our everyday work.

Ethics and anonymity: who are the dancers?

There are critical issues of ethics and anonymity in this, as in all ethnographies. Being allowed to venture deep into the experience of a particular group, having access to information which these groups cannot withhold, since the gaze of the ethnographer, whatever her interpretation, is upon them, places a burden on the researchers to protect the participants and preserve their anonymity. But the issue of informed consent is complex. Is there a once-and-for-all decision about taking part in the research, or is it open to negotiation during the course of the research.

We had guaranteed anonymity for participants, but confidentiality, again, is very difficult in an ethnography. Ethnographers choose names for their schools to disguise their identity, and speak, for example, of the school being located 'in a large urban conurbation'.

We have made it clear that the schools in our study are in London and Helsinki, and have sought to guarantee their anonymity by general descriptions, which match a number of schools. Here the tension is between giving enough information to give contextual life to the data, and too much which may identify the school. Although we identified the year groups with which we worked, a slight vagueness about the exact dates that we were in the schools would make it more difficult to identify the students if the identity of the schools were discovered.

For reasons of anonymity we have often not mentioned from which school an example is taken, and we marked the extracts from field-notes as ObsH and ObsL. As mentioned earlier, we have identified quotes from individuals by a pseudonym, plus gender (M/F), whether a student, a teacher or a member of support staff (S/T/SS), and whether in Helsinki or London (H/L). Sometimes we have blurred even these categories.

Our place in the ball

When we came to their classrooms most of the students had a very vague image of a 'researcher'. For some the image may not have changed; their associations for the word 'researcher' included: 'physician', 'works at the laboratory', 'professor'. Many of the associations did relate to us, either to tasks they saw us doing: 'interviews', 'asks questions', 'wants to know', 'curious'; or more personally 'you', 'a woman with glasses'. Many of them reflected a positive relation to us; some associations included 'nice'. The card to Kay quoted at the beginning of this chapter indicates that our participation in the classroom might sometimes have been enjoyable for the students.

While the ideal of the observer in the classroom may be to melt into the furniture, to observe and to scribble without stirring the air, an incident in one school demonstrated just how sharply observers are themselves observed. In a mathematics lesson students were taking turns to act as 'the teachers' and asking questions using the overhead projector, and during one of these lessons two boys took the opportunity of writing and displaying the following lesson notes of the classroom observations of one of them on the overhead projector:

Jere threw a piece of paper at Ismo.
Jukka received our visitor in an unpleasant way.
Pete helped the teacher to write on the blackboard because her cat
    had mauled her middle finger.

Heikki is bawling (as usual).
The girls are sitting quietly as in St Paul's Church.

These lesson notes neatly encapsulate the concerns of the researchers. They cover the official, informal and physical layers of the lesson; visible and audible action as well as stillness and silence is recorded; and they contain an apt comment on gender difference. They also place the researcher in relation to the class, with a note on her unusual (unacceptable?) behaviour (slipping out of the role of the ideal, industrious, female student) in being late arriving at the class. The reaction to the lurking presence can range widely, from 'To tell the truth, sometimes I didn't even notice you were there' (the happy fly on the wall) to 'And where were you last week!?' after an unavoidable absence in regular attendance on the part of the researcher, from a student with whom she had never exchanged a word. It is clear, however, that the observer is observed, placed, and responded to, albeit not always with her knowledge. Overall, the warmth of interaction and the pleasure of observing were such that, though being in schools was hard work, we have missed these schooldays. We joined the intricate dance of the school to understand the complex and multilayered steps everyday life there involves.

5
One Two Three, One Two Three: the Official School

Introduction

The rules of traditional dances change over time, and more flexibility is allowed today, but the basic rhythms of steps and pauses prevail. Masters of ceremonies apply the rules in different kinds of situations. They know how to direct the dance if the group of dancers is particularly large, if the ballroom is in some way unusual, or if some of the dancers are in wheelchairs or are reluctant to participate. The master has to ensure that the orchestra is in tune; the dancers are supposed to learn what is important for the dance, to act and dress properly, and to obey instructions.

We start our story about life in City Park, Green Park, Oak Grove and Woburn Hill by analysing the official school. To understand traditional dance you must know the formal steps of the dance; to understand what we call the official school you must examine the written curriculum, formal hierarchies, pedagogic relations and the disciplinary apparatus. The dance itself, like the contents of learning, follows the rules more or less accurately. Dancers are supposed to concentrate on the steps; they should not step aside to hug their friends or reveal feelings of delight or disgust. But for dancers, the steps are not always the most obvious nor the most important things that happen during the dance, although the movement itself might be enjoyable.

In the school context we use the word 'curriculum' when we refer to the content of knowledge and the planning of teaching and learning, 'pedagogy' when we refer to relations in teaching and learning, and methods and contents of teaching. 'Pedagogy is about the interactions between teachers, students and the learning environment and learning tasks' (Murphy, 1996, p. 17). The pedagogic relation organises social relations and interaction in schools, and positions teachers and students in an institutionally defined instructional relationship. This is, Philip Wexler (1992) argues, a quintessential relationship, a proto- type of many situations where a more experienced, usually older and socially superior person advises and guides a more inexperienced, usually younger and socially inferior person, who carries out instruc- tions in an orderly, dutiful manner. In schools the pedagogic relation is a dichotomous category: the teacher is the one who knows and teaches, and the student is supposed to learn; the teacher is a citizen, and the student is learning to become one; the teacher is professional and mature, the student is neither of these things. Martin Mills (1997) argues that 'discourses of "professionalism" and "maturity" legitimate existing institutional relations of power founded upon a separation between the categories of "teacher" and "student"' (p. 37). The peda- gogic relation is based on difference and authority.

This dualism, that is often taken for granted in pedagogic discourses, hides negotiations and challenges. In saying this we are not denying the power relation, since pedagogy is always related to power. Below we argue that we can find professionalism and maturity in student positions as well as teachers, if we look for them. The dancers know the rules of the dance, they can predict the wishes of the master of ceremonies and the orchestra's next tune, they can devote themselves to the whirls of the dance or use the situation for their own instrumental needs, they can act innovatively by producing new steps in cooperation, or they can deliberately step aside and resist the rules.

Teachers at work

'It's like a picture of life itself, everything is there' (Elna, FTH) is how one teacher described the school. Secondary school is a workplace for teachers and support staff. Teachers are alone with the students in the classrooms but together in the staff rooms. The staff room is a place, but also a spatial metaphor for teachers working in a school, and in staff rooms hierarchical relations as well as cooperation are acted out.

In Finnish schools only the headteachers have officially different status from the rest of the teachers. With recent legislative changes the increased autonomy invested in schools has led to increased power for headteachers, both in relation to economic decisions and to the curriculum. Although some made critical remarks, most of the teachers were satisfied with the organisation of their school and co-operation with colleagues: 'This staff room is good, organised, it helps that we know about everything and discuss decisions' (Inkeri, FTH).

Apart from the official power structures, teachers sometimes argued that age, gender and teaching subjects did lead to different positions in the hierarchy. One teacher said: 'Because I am the last one who came here and I'm the youngest, people don't respect me, I don't have a permanent job' (Aila, FTH). Physical location in the staff room can reflect hierarchical differences too: 'For example, this table of mathematics teachers, people respect them, both because they are all on this same table, and because they are teachers who have been here for years' (Raila, FTH).

The new educational thinking with its emphasis on school-based curriculum planning in Finland cannot succeed without teachers' cooperation. The tradition of the Finnish schools, however, is strongly based on working individually, and the organisation of the school day makes it very difficult for teachers to cooperate unless they are willing to use much of their spare time at school for this purpose.

In schools in England/Wales the hierarchy is formally more extended. The headteacher holds a position of considerable power, and with local management of schools, the potential for power and control (within the framework of responsibility to governors) is great. But headteachers exhibit different management styles, ranging from autocratic and controlling through to democratic and employing considerable delegation of power. There are several grades of teachers, each with salary and responsibility implications, but the major hierarchy in schools would be headed by the senior management team. There were some suggestions in these schools of rifts and lack of communication between senior managers and teachers further down the hierarchy, as there might be in any complex organisation. A member of the management team in one school, discussing relations between senior management and teachers, pointed out:

> It's difficult to tell. It's always very difficult when you actually are in management ... one is never privy in the way that one is as an ordinary classroom teacher to the general feelings and thoughts of the staff room. And I think that's right and proper.... On the other hand, we like, we do try to keep good relations with them, I think by and large we do. I don't think there's any great animosity towards senior management. I'm quite sure there are people who

would like senior management to do different things and operate in different ways, but that's the same in every school.

(Robyn, MTL)

And at least one teacher agreed that this particular manager was 'doing a good job, not closed, if someone has another idea or disagrees will listen to them and act on it, might disagree with it and say no I don't agree with it, but will still listen, so is doing a good job' (John, MTL).

But contrary views of management figures were also held:

I just think once you get into senior management you are out. You are in a different ball game, you are not in the front line any more and I think people like [headteacher] forget that completely, or they have never actually been in the front line for too long.

(Katherine, FTL)

The hierarchy and expectation of career progression could cause discontent or resentment in London schools, if people thought for example that younger teachers were coming into the school and progressing more rapidly than was thought appropriate, or passing over others who had served longer. Some teachers in the schools we studied showed great loyalty, and could spend their entire teaching career in one school:

There are people that have been here for thirty-odd years ... it's like a womb for that I think, and I think also because people are afraid to leave it. One of the reasons I've decided to leave is because I need to get out of this womb and go and experience the real world.

(Thomas, MTL)

Many teachers in all of our schools were rather satisfied with their profession and their own school. It was not difficult for them to find good aspects of being a teacher: freedom and variation in daily work was mentioned regularly as well as working with other people, and, particularly with young people.

JANET: Have you enjoyed it here?
ALISON: Loved it, yeah. Excellent, brilliant. Nice school actually.
JANET: What do you think of the school in general?
ALISON: I like it. I mean there's things that you get, you know, that

you get upset about and – you do have to work hard here.

(Alison, FTL)

A wonderful, lively occupation. It's hard sometimes, but never monotonous. Always new young people in front of you. A very good occupation … you can laugh more than usual here. When students are in a good mood, they kind of spoil you. (Katri, FTH)

In spite of general satisfaction with their work, teachers often talked about problems. While working with young people was among the good aspects of the work, it was also among the bad. Teachers felt they had to use their whole personality all the time in their work: 'If you are feeling bad, it's easily reflected in your work. Then it's rather hard, because you don't necessarily want to show it' (Raila, FTH).

Busyness was mentioned as a negative aspect of the profession. The pressure on time pervades a teacher's work. It is related to work on the curriculum, but also to the organisational structure – breaks (very short in Finland) are filled with responsibilities such as keeping watch in the playground or running a club. Older teachers say that schools had a slower rhythm before recent changes. There is not enough time to talk with other teachers, the work load has grown, papers follow teachers home and it is difficult to get the school out of your thoughts in leisure time: 'The bad side is [being in a hurry]. 18 different groups a week run in front of your eyes. How can you dive under everyone's skin?' (Risto, MTH).

There are also more general reasons for some teachers' dissatisfaction. They argue that the teaching profession has lost its public respect. In England/Wales, teachers have worked under increased pressure resulting from fast and onerous changes in policy and practice since 1988, and New Right campaigns of vilification in the media. Some of the London teachers did refer to these problems, and to specific issues within their own schools.

In Helsinki, teachers did not raise the issue of educational policies. Most did not have strong opinions on marketisation, and discussed it only when asked: 'I wonder what I can say on such a big question' was one response. Many of them were hesitant about choice for parents and students. Fear of growing differences between schools was mentioned by a few teachers in Helsinki: 'Are we going to have a system of good schools and bad schools – seems frightening' (Inkeri, FTH). Some of them thought that the comprehensive school should remain comprehensive. Tero (FTM), for example, was not happy about growing differentiation between schools: 'We only have good [talented] pupils, for whom the criteria are drawn somewhere in heaven. And you might ask me if this makes any sense, this is a comprehensive school, isn't it?' Some teachers were worried about the relative popularity of their own subject when students have more opportunities for choice, and teachers may be left without lessons.

But other teachers valued the advent of parental choice; one argued that it has a positive effect on their relation to school. Neither of the Helsinki schools was afraid of losing students, which must have affected their views. Teachers and educational commentators in England/Wales have been worried about falling rolls in the light of league tables based on exam results, which affect parents' desire to send their children to particular schools that are not doing well, with fears that unpopular schools will enter a spiral of failure and decline. These were not problems for the schools in the study. One of them was in very high demand, and operated a system of selection for its intake, and the other had a specialist niche which meant that its position was not at risk.

During the time of our research in Finland economic cutbacks had not had a very great effect on schools.[1] A deputy head said that, of course, there is never enough money, but cuts have not been great enough to hinder the school's work; she said that it is possible to find many ways of saving money. Some teachers did complain about the large size of teaching groups and lack of other resources, for example for remedial teaching. Some feared that student choice might leave them with too few lessons, and competition amongst teachers for students might affect the atmosphere in the staff room.

London teachers have longer experience of the effects of markets. The following teacher was concerned about many aspects of the new politics. While appreciating that education should be accountable, she felt that schools opting out of local government control led to a waste or misallocation of resources which could provide services across a local education authority, and that school provision should be planned as a system, not left to the decisions of individual schools:

> Taking it a bit too far really isn't it? I mean schools are becoming increasingly like businesses, anyhow, especially at this place being grant maintained and things. But then you know, if you're, the government's only going to give education a certain amount of money isn't it? And if one school's better off because they've opted

out, then another school's worse off. Because you know, that shouldn't happen. I suppose I am concerned.

(Alison, FTL)

There are, thus, in both countries, tensions between cooperation and autonomy, as well as between cooperation and hierarchy in teachers' thinking about their work. Cooperation is a prerequisite in the new educational policies; at the same time the new policies foster individual competition and hierarchical divisions.

Professional pupils

What is a 'pupil'? In the Finnish language the word 'pupil' is *'oppilas'*, which is normally used to refer to young students. 'Student' is *'opiskelija'*, which in Finnish refers to upper secondary or older students. The former can be translated as one who learns, the second as one who studies. The English words 'pupil' and 'student' do not have the same connotations, and are used more flexibly. In this book we use the word 'pupil' as analogous to the abstract 'citizen' – both are abstracted from social relations of gender, class, 'race' and ethnicity. In the everyday life of the schools 'pupils' are particular children and young people, who tend to be perceived through natural attitudes as, for example, girls or boys. To signify the role of the 'pupil' we use it as a formal term. When we want to refer to young people in our study, we talk about school students.

In both countries, when students were asked what they associated with the word 'pupil/oppilas', many of them referred to the informal rather than the official school: 'friend/mate', themselves or some of their friends, and others referred to their youth – 'child', 'young'. Students' feelings of lack of agency and autonomy are reflected in many of the Finnish associations; a pupil is 'the one who is taught', 'a person who obeys', 'one who listens during the lessons', 'under control' or one who 'tries to manage through this institution'. In relation to the official school, the London students tended to refer to a 'learner', 'learns', 'working', or 'supposed to work'. This type of response occurred in Helsinki particularly in some girls' associations where a more active participation was suggested: a person who 'studies', 'a student', and, for one high-achieving girl, 'eager to learn'. Both official and physical school are present in 'a person sitting behind the desk and studying very hard'.

The ideology of democratic education is reflected in the thinking of many of the Helsinki teachers and they tend not to emphasise the hierarchical relation in their associations to the 'pupil'. Associations were related to working together; a pupil was 'colleague' or 'collaborator' to some teachers. 'Child' or 'puberty' occurred a few times, as well as teacher's responsibility to supervise and teach: 'one whom we try to direct' or 'one who should get some learning here'. New educational policy was reflected in the thoughts of some teachers: 'customer' and 'employer' were mentioned. We had fewer associations from teachers in London, and they tended to emphasise both youth, and large numbers, for example 'hordes'.

Neither students themselves nor teachers referred to competence in their associations for 'pupil', although students do have competence as 'pupils'. Whilst starting to visit schools when preparing for our research we were struck by the variety of skills that moving through the school day required from school students. The Finnish team developed the term *'professional pupil'* to refer to those skills. To become 'professional pupils', secondary-school students need first to learn appropriate behaviour in and outside the classroom. They have to learn the basic features of the pedagogic process, the hierarchical relations within the school, and the possibilities and spaces for, as well as limits of, student agency.[2]

Much of pupil professionalism is strongly interwoven with tradition in education. Halpin *et al.* (1997) argue that the 'integrity' of tradition derives not so much from the simple fact of persistence over time, but from the continuous 'work' of interpretation. That work is carried out to identify the strands which bind present to past. One of the traditions of schools is written school rules that are made available to all students. They provide regulations on what pupils are supposed to do, and what they are not allowed to do at school. We have noted (Gordon *et al.*, 2000d) that rules are mostly related to the physical school (Chapter 7).

When asked about the rules in the interview many students claimed that they could not remember them. But they often revealed detailed knowledge of how they are supposed to behave at school:

> I don't know any rules, actually. I don't know them, but I suppose I can guess what they're like. Everyone knows what you are supposed to do at school and what you're not supposed to.
>
> (Lasse, MSH)

> I don't know many of them [the rules] really, but they're quite strict

some of them, but I don't know, I haven't got a copy of them or anything so, and I haven't actually read any of them, so um, I probably break a lot.

(Melissa, FSL)

Professional students must know good manners, and during our year in schools young people's lack of good manners became an issue of public debate in Finland. A school in our study devoted a week to this topic:

In display cabinets outside the hall were different kinds of eating equipment, and students had a competition about whether a particular fork was for oysters etc. And who is supposed to be introduced first, the older to the younger person, or a man to a woman, or does it matter.

(ObsH)

Teaching middle-class habits seemed to be central in 'good manners'. But they also emphasise gender difference, as we have shown elsewhere (Lahelma and Gordon, 1997). Teachers, when asked about their educational aims, often mentioned good manners in one way or another. But they gave a wider meaning to the notion; they referred for example to the need for an absence of teasing and sexist language, for tolerance, taking care of others and for equal opportunities, as in the extracts below:

If we decide that we don't have teasing in this school, and if the staff is committed to it, then teasing will decline. And it's the same with good manners.

(Mikko, MTH)

The Code of Conduct and the rules which are new this year will have been given to them and discussed with them, the bullying one, equal opps one, probably I think that's it, that's probably all that's relevant.

(Alison, FTL)

Teachers referred to good manners in lessons. For example, when students were joking whilst completing questionnaires, the teacher said 'There should be nothing that is contrary to good manners. If there is, I'll contact parents' (ObsH). This threat in relation to parents might indicate an underlying idea that it is parents who should pay attention to their children's good manners.

We saw situations when teachers did not always behave well themselves. Some of the students were sensitive to this. Noora said of a teacher: 'And he [teacher] shouted there [in the dining room], and I was kind of ashamed for him. I got up and told him that he should never come and shout at the lunch table' (FSH). She also tries to find legitimate reasons for the imbalance of behavioural demands for teachers and students, here recognising the ritual purpose they may have:

> In primary school I was angry because we had to stand up when the teacher came in. I regarded it as really humiliating, because the teacher never stood up when a student came in. Then I went and asked a teacher and she told me that when the teacher comes in, the lesson starts and everybody is quiet and stands up, and I understood that it's quite all right.

Professional pupils know the importance of peace and quiet in work. Teachers regularly remind students that they should respect others' need to work in peace and quiet, and students often wish this too. Students' instrumental relation to schooling is reflected in their hopes to be able to concentrate on learning, and girls, especially, often argue that teachers should not let the boys fool around.

There are many examples of lessons when there is absolutely no peace and there were constant reminders of rules and manners attempting to ensure quiet and disciplined work, intertwined with teaching. In the groups we followed it was predominantly boys (but not all boys) who were disruptive, and in many lessons teacher's time and energy was concentrated on some boys who had their own agenda:

> Teacher calms the students down, 'sshh', claps her hands, 'Matti!' 'Erik!', turns her gaze towards the knocking and speech, asks Sami quietly to move, reprimands Santtu, Sami, glances at Matti, wrinkles her forehead, reprimands Matti on the cap, to Matti: 'Matti, stop now!' Her voice gets a bit higher, 'Kalevi', to Matti 'Would you please move one desk further, Matti.'
>
> (ObsH)

Boys' disruptive behaviour is often particularly visible and audible during the lessons when the teacher is not in control. The following researcher's comments were from a lesson of that kind:

> Some difference between girls and boys in this class, though both talk, make a lot of noise, move around, the girls are more likely also to be engaging with the task (although some boys do too). Boys' activity is often more boisterous.
>
> (ObsL)

What is less obvious is that teachers also disturb students when they are working. Often students, especially girls, did not want to stop their work when the lesson ended or between a double period, but teachers normally wanted them to leave the room. One teacher, however, did begin by saying 'Sorry to interrupt' when he gave instructions. Such a simple sign of respect for students is rare.

Professional pupils also have to learn to work in a group – although often alone in a group (Jackson, 1968) – and to take account of other people, as teachers repeatedly reminded them. Saku often commented on other students' and teacher's talk; teachers sometimes became annoyed, and he was reminded: 'You are in a group, you must not live a life of your own' (ObsH). Students need to accomplish balance between the requirements of the collective and the ideal of individuality. Learning to take account of other people, sociality, empathy and tolerance were regarded as important goals for many of the teachers. When teachers tried to teach students not to shout out answers, but to raise their hands, they often emphasised that everyone must be given an opportunity to participate. Students basically agreed, although in practice they often forgot or ignored the hand-raising rule.

A professional pupil, then, must follow many formal rules and act according to 'good' manners, and consideration for others. This was not as evident in the daily life at school as were the many ritualistic reprimands about formal behavioural rules. Drawing on our observations in California, consideration for others was clearly expressed in a meeting organised for new students in one school. The most important principles of student professionalism were summarised by the deputy head:

> Everyone is to respect another person. You are to call a person by his or her name. Everyone has a right to personal space. [Illustrates that space with hands] We want everyone here to be a respected

person. We respect people's personal property. If you do those three basic things we will have a great and wonderful school.

(ObsC)

These principles represent the ideal, and aim to ensure the autonomy and agency of individual students in groups. The students are informed that in order to be professional they must not infringe on other people's rights; whilst individualism is often competitive, it can also be mutually cooperative. It is clear here that professional students are not merely to behave in ritualistic accordance with the rules, but in a way that gives space to others – and to themselves.

Making knowing citizens

School knowledge is divided into subjects following the classical division of academic disciplines (cf. Goodson, 1994). For example, history and geography are at the centre of various curricula – as they were in the period of nation building – while modern social sciences are at the margins. The weight of tradition has persistently challenged curriculum changes; Bronwyn Davies and Robyn Hunt (1994) refer to this as 'teaching-as-usual'. Classroom practices are amazingly enduring; when we started visiting schools we were struck by a sense of familiarity, based on our own schooldays. There is more audiovisual equipment, teacher–student relations are less formal, but despite changes there are persistent practices which have developed over a very long period, and which constitute popular understandings about what a 'school' is like.

The new concept of learning is defined in the Finnish *Framework Curriculum* (NBE, 1994) as learning by various means to gather information, using data processing skills and independent study. This concept, and the new role of the teacher as a facilitator rather than as a dispenser of information, are well known by teachers.

> I think that learning and learning to live are much more than knowledge about facts. And secondary school, which is the institute for general education, should give more things that you need in your life rather than separate pieces of knowledge.
>
> (Aila, FTH)

But there are still lessons where 'knowledge' is distributed from teachers to students, and some teachers feel that this is what they should do. One teacher felt bad because 'we are always in a hurry to cover the syllabus and to get on'. She regrets that, even when there are interesting themes to discuss, there is not enough time. Teachers often admit that their methods are traditional; some of them arguing that students are conservative and want to work that way, others suggesting that time pressures do not enable them to work differently. A teacher in London reports that she has moved from progressive to traditional methods because she feels that is what the students can handle:

> I have become more and more traditional recently. I was much more small group etc. perhaps ten, twenty years ago, but ten, twenty years ago children had the self discipline to cope with it. A lot of the children I now teach don't have those disciplines, I don't know if it is the fault of the schools that we haven't instilled it earlier on, or it's the fault of the family. But I find that a sad loss, so I am becoming more traditional and using more old fashioned methods, that is a bit sad for me, disillusioned is the word.
>
> (Beatrice, FTL)

In one instance students complained that they had not covered the curriculum fully, as evidenced by the fact that they could not answer some of the questions in a test a teacher had set them. The teacher disagreed, pointing out that they were obliged to think to answer the questions, which would not be exactly in the format that they had learned the topic concerned (ObsL).

It is not surprising that students often regard learning as a package they have to get into their heads, and find difficult to keep it there:

> Take a biology lesson, there it's good that you're supposed to be quiet and listen to the teacher – it's good, because then you get these things in your head and you don't need to read for exams.
>
> (Sinikka, FSH)

Mathematics does not fit in your head ... I don't like to learn really, because I'm afraid that it suddenly vanishes from there [knowledge from the head]. And you have to remember so much all the time. And there's the compulsion that you should know it well, and such difficult tests. And then, some teachers think that their subject is the most important ... I reckon I'm the only one who has these thoughts – the others just study. But I get tired, so much knowledge

I must put in my head each day. And I am afraid that I will forget it, it's so frustrating.

(Auli, FSH)

When we asked teachers about their methods, they mentioned a range which did not include 'copying'. We have observed many episodes with the teacher standing by the overhead or blackboard, talking and asking detailed questions, and students answering and copying the contents into their exercise books:

Teacher shows the overhead line by line, asking questions, asking for small details: 'What is the positive and what negative impact of ...?' 'Is it bigger or smaller ...?'.

(ObsH)

Sometimes the text is difficult to read. Below is an extreme example of an absurd ritual of copying:

Teacher uses the overhead and remarks that somebody has broken the glass. Somebody says that we cannot see, the letters are too small, and the glass is broken. Teacher puts the front light off. A boy suggests that the teacher gives them a copy of the overhead. Teacher: 'At school one writes and learns'. Some students complain again that they can't see. Teacher: 'Okay, let's get it a bit bigger'. Students ask what the words are. Two girls walk to the overhead in order to see.

(ObsH)

Many students complained in interviews that there is too much writing, or that continuous copying prevents learning: 'it's so hard to be there, when she puts some words of a song on the overhead and it's such small text that you can't see' (Milla, FSH).

The central position of textbooks in Finnish schools was noted by external evaluators (Norris *et al.*, 1996). Although, in our research schools, teachers also used other materials, the authority of the text was not often problematised. One teacher sighed to the researcher: 'The contents of the book doesn't stay in their heads.' The following extract illustrates respect for the 'knowledge' in textbooks:

The examination shows how well you have studied, and how you can understand. Many of you tell their own stories that are not in the book or in the exercise book. You should trust the book and the exercise book. Your own opinion is not always right.

(ObsH)

Students usually hope for more varied teaching methods and to be able to decide themselves how to work. Some of them want to go on more visits, some want to conduct wider project works, either individually or in groups, 'something different from the normal teaching'. Taru (FSH) describes her ideal teacher as follows:

Hmm, I think one who listens to the students, asks their opinions on how to work, that it is OK if we do it this way, and that we do as much as possible different kinds of group work and projects and so on.

William (MSL) describes what he gets and what he prefers:

WILLIAM: Some do quite a lot of dictation and others do worksheets and work from books probably because it's less work, and others write things on the board and you just have to copy it down, and our [subject] teacher talks for about half an hour and you've got to do loads of work in five minutes at the end of the lesson, so there's all different ways.

KAY: And which do you think is best out of those?

WILLIAM: A mixture, from some lessons do work from books, others just explain things and just keep a balance of all different, all the different ways of teaching.

And Norma (FSL) describes the advantages and disadvantages of different methods:

I prefer group work – 'cause you have your different opinions, you can put it together and sometimes it's individual work I like, because if you get a grade and like some people do more work in a group and some people do less, and they all get the same grade, it's not really fair, so sometimes it depends on what sort of work it is.

(Norma, FSL)

Many students prefer group work; they can talk to friends and get help when they need it, appreciate the possibility of changing the use of the space in the classroom when desks are moved around to facilitate group work. Others dislike being forced to work with people they do not like.

> Group work is better because you can, you know, gather opinions from other people. You can socialise with other people. You can work as a whole and make a, produce something better, because you're taking all the good skills from other people and using them, putting, contributing your best skill into it.
>
> (Tony, MSL)

> You might end up with somebody you totally hate or dislike and you'd rather be with your friends on this.
>
> (Hadi, MSL)

Teaching and learning is more traditional in Helsinki schools. Although our London schools are also teacher-centred, and a great deal of the work is routinely conducted, more student-centred methods are used. The long tradition of decentralisation in England/Wales has facilitated school-based development of curriculum and pedagogy, whereas in Finland the previously strictly centralised system did not give teachers much scope to develop their work. Although routine teaching and learning is the usual practice in Finland, there are also many examples of teachers challenging students to try harder and integrating themes from different disciplines. They sometimes indicate that it is not so bad to give incorrect answers, that it is important to try out your ideas:

> Teacher emphasises independent working, tries to get them to find out for themselves and to propose answers. 'Good, Joona, who will continue Joona's idea?' 'Erik is on the right track. Why?'
>
> (ObsH)

The following notes from two lessons in London are examples of different teaching methods. In the first one, the teacher used a variety of methods, and control was less apparent:

> This is a history lesson about the Black Death, Plague. The students are involved, there is quite a lot of noise, and movement, but they are engaged, typified by April and Kathy, who, although they talk a lot amongst themselves, are mostly on task, and always very eager to answer questions. Methods: the teacher talks to the students, but

invites answers, and they offer, by calling out and putting up hands, he calls on those with hands up. He reads, then gets them to volunteer to read, which they do. They put up hands to attract his attention when they are working and he walks around checking the work. He uses maps, brings coloured pencils/pens (for the boys I note) uses an overhead (the girls want to close the blinds when he puts it on), has backup (extension tasks) for when they have finished, and quite a few of them do. When one boy claims to be good at maps, the teacher provided a more complicated map than he has given the rest. He does not give the impression of being controlling, provides lots of stimulation for the students, is very well prepared and supplied with materials, and engages the students.

(ObsL)

The lesson is lively, but well organised. This contrasts with a lesson in which the teacher is not in control:

Lot of movement, noise and activity. A group of girls who are essentially working on the task, also talk, and sing intermittently throughout the lesson. There are some squabbles over equipment, some boisterous body play by girls but mainly boys. One girl wanders about, squeals at something someone on the other side of the class says to her, and returns to her seat. Two boys spend a lot of time sliding about on their chairs and bumping into each other, with a lot of noise. Two others beat a drum tattoo on the desk.

(ObsL)

A common fear for teachers is that a lesson will disintegrate into chaos. Traditional methods are tried and tested, teachers have developed skills in using them, they seem safe, they seem to enable the teacher to deal with those students (often boys) who are boisterous, whilst the silent students (often but not always girls) contribute to the success of the lesson by carrying out the allocated tasks. A whole range of elements contribute to 'teaching-as-usual' and help to maintain a classroom order the rudiments of which were laid down some 300 years ago in Prussia (Green, 1990).

Making individual citizens

> I think we are, we are trying to create citizens, but we are trying to create thinking citizens, or citizens who, erm it's not autocratic I think that's what I am trying to say.
>
> (John, MTL)

In schools, students are on the path towards adult citizenship, defined in terms of individuality (Chapter 1). An ambivalence on the part of teachers lies in the paradox of individuality and collectivity in students. Bronwyn Davies and Robyn Hunt (1994) suggest that, for learning to take place, students have to work collectively, although learning, in the context of 'teaching-as-usual', is thought of as an individual activity, and individual performance is what is assessed. Students also value collective, cooperative work, as suggested above.

We asked students to describe themselves as 'pupils'. Their responses contained notions of individuality, achievement, behaviour and competence and illustrated ways in which students are implicated in the process of making differentiations in the official school. A competent pupil achieves well and behaves well, and this is the yardstick with which students compared themselves.

'Ordinary' or 'average' occurred often in students' descriptions of themselves: 'Well, I'm kind of average, not very good, not very poor, so that you're attentive in all lessons and don't skive and do homework whenever you can and at least you try' (Teijo, MSH); ' I'm not brilliant at school work but I'm not terrible at it either. Um ... average' (William, MSL). Students usually saw themselves as not very good, not very poor, but in the middle; fairly quiet, fairly well behaved, often regardless of how they achieved or behaved. For example, although Marianne (FSH) is a high achiever, she starts her answer modestly. 'Well, [I'm] kind of average achiever, I suppose. I don't know. I've done rather well, kind of, done fairly well in tests and ...'. And Justin struggles with claiming his competence

> Erm, well, I don't want to be too big headed but [*laugh*] everyone says that I'm quite good at most things, I mean obviously I am not brilliant at everything but I'm, I don't, I think I don't, I could work harder, but my results are usually quite, I am happy with them and I've got quite high standards, ... I think I could work definitely work harder, but on – I think I am like kind of quite good on average.
>
> (Justin, MSL)

Struggles towards competence were evident in students' self-evaluations to a greater extent than struggles towards individuality. 'Average' can be seen as a norm which students construct and with which they then compare themselves. When students started with positive or negative statements, they often neutralised them in the following sentence. For example Sami, a working-class boy who is low-achieving and who is, his form teacher suggests, in danger of becoming marginalised, explains that though he does not 'achieve very well in school', his achievement is 'good enough' (MSH). Anni is among the highest achieving students, but she does not emphasise it: 'good enough, OK in school and all that, I don't fool around all the time like some people, I don't know – like moderately good' (FSH).

Most students emphasise that they are ordinary, normal, average, not specific, and, despite the value attached to individuality, they do not describe themselves in particularly individualistic ways. High achievement is not always positive in students' own hierarchies and carries a risk of teasing, as does low achievement. One teased boy was described as follows:

> Well, he's a bit professor-like ... his hair is always neatly done and he wears glasses and – it's certainly also envy and others not getting on as well as him.
>
> (Anu, FSH)

And a high-achieving girl who was teased reports:

> Everyone calls me a bod,[3] but I don't mind. I used to in the first year, but I don't any more. They don't call me all those jokes about – because they know I'm not a bod. I don't work twenty-four hours a day.
>
> (Shardia, FSL)

Normality is not only defined in relation to achievement, but also in relation to behaviour. Auli (FSH) thinks that it is not 'normal just to study' but 'sometimes one has to loosen up'. Elisa (FSH), who evaluates her achievement highly, not only refers to her competence as a learner, but also as a professional pupil who has adjusted to school rules.

> Well, I think I'm rather good, because I've received excellent marks from almost all tests. And I listen rather carefully and I don't do any

terrorism during the lessons. I don't mess up the desks and I do what I'm told to, I think. I've not been in detention once this term. I've done just what I've been told to, I've done, like, everything that I've been told to. And I don't shout to others during lessons, so that I think that teachers don't have to comment on me.

(Elisa, FSH)

Sami, on the other hand, regarded himself 'kind of bit wild', as did many boys who suggested that they were a bit boisterous but not excessively so. Some girls saw themselves as having difficulty conforming to appropriate behaviour: ' No, I think I'm quite loud. I think I'm, I'm not a very good, I wouldn't call myself a good student, with a halo over the top' (Sara, FSL) and her friend Fiona describes the difficulties she encounters in trying to change her reputation with teachers from bad to good:

In the first and second year I was a bit of a bad girl.... You've got to learn, if you don't want to get in trouble, you've got to be good, which is all right.... [I'm] Sometimes bad, sometimes good, but at the moment you know, I'm trying to be good, but I ain't in the habit of just ... [in one lesson] I think oh no, I'm going to be good this lesson because I've been really out of order shouting at the ... but then she'll, I'll just be sitting there and she'll say: whose talking? Fiona! Sara! and so I'll just get fed up with it and think, why should I be nice to her, if she's not going to be nice to me.

(Fiona, FSL)

The 'ordinary pupil' is gender-neutral. In line with current trends, girls in our groups are high achievers in schools more often than boys. And, in relation to the schools' criteria for good behaviour, boys disrupt far more often than girls. Students' self-evaluations do not follow these patterns so clearly. When girls evaluate themselves, they seem to compare themselves with other girls, and boys with other boys. Justus (MSH) explains this clearly when he describes himself as 'quite an ordinary male pupil'.

It has often been argued that girls are regarded as more conscientious than boys at school, and that teachers, parents and the students themselves do not look for excellence in them (e.g. Walkerdine and Lucey, 1989; Sunnari, 1997). Auli does not trust her own competence and illustrates the pressure students feel to cram the knowledge into their heads:

I kind of get worried, because I don't understand, and I wish that someone would help. And there's no time, because all the time the teacher gives more information, and more, more. And there's no time for the earlier knowledge and the one before that. And it's so terrible that you feel like throwing the book on the floor and going to sleep. But you can't concentrate on sleeping, when you feel bad all the time because you should be listening to what she's saying. And you don't understand anything, because you haven't understood what went on before.

(Auli, FSH)

Boys often claim both competence and a position as an individual. Matti is constantly constructing himself as an individual. He says that he does not want to answer very simple questions. He often makes an issue of his knowledge. 'I'm wise, more intelligent than others', he claims in one lesson (ObsH). Although his claims are often ridiculed by other students, there are nevertheless several occasions where some boys are constructed, and construct themselves, as competent students.

Teachers might have problems with students who do have a high level of competence; they can appear as a threat to the authority and control of the teacher. One teacher did not see students as empty vessels waiting to be filled with knowledge:

And it's, they're not easy kids, it's not like they're all sitting there desperate you know, empty just waiting to be filled or anything, they're, there are some hard kids, nasty kids in the school, and the fact they are intelligent probably makes it harder to deal with, 'cause psychologically they can take you to pieces, and I think we, we haven't supported our staff very well in the past, I think that's somewhere I'd like to, and if staff feel confident, if staff feel encouraged then it will go through to the pupils.

(Thomas, MTL)

Girls construct their competence in different ways. The following extract is from a mathematics lesson of the group of boisterous boys and quiet girls, some of whom are the highest achievers in mathematics. In this group boys often protest when one of the girls answers questions. Here the teacher tries to encourage the boys who do not see the point in the task they are working with, for example by wondering: 'you never know what kinds of scholars [male] you are going to be'. Ismo notes the girls' competence and makes the difference with 'us boys' and 'them':

PETE: What use is this?

Teacher walks towards him. Says something about the diagrams.

MANU: The reason why this diagram has been invented is so that teachers can fail students. All this group is going to fail.

ISMO: Not Sonja and those [girls] ...

Teacher gives the class a task. Some boys ask for help.

ISMO: Now you have to come and be my private teacher.

Girls sit quietly all the time. Some of them look ahead, some around them.

(ObsH)

We observed many episodes when students start to say 'I don't understand'. It is often girls who do so, often girls who are high achievers and willing to achieve. When boys start to say 'I don't understand', teachers sometimes take them more seriously. This way of talking can be an attempt by the girls to get the teacher's attention while s/he is engaged with talkative boys.[4]

Teacher shows. Anni keeps on murmuring: 'I can't, I can't'. Anni tries, looks desperate, sighs: 'I don't understand this, I don't understand these'.

(ObsH)

In these situations girls often help each other. 'When you need help, then you can ask your friend', Tiina (FSH) says. In one lesson when the teacher interacts mainly with boys, joking with them, giving them commands, appealing to them, notes on girls include following observations:

Taru asks Milla something, about the exercise, I assume. Hille asks for Milla's advice. Milla says she has calculated it in her head. 'You won't be able to do it anyway.'

Milla seems to be ready. She looks toward the window. She fingers her nose. She looks at her exercise book. She rubs something out. Taru turns to her and asks something.

Nelli asks Milla if she is done. Nelli asks how she got the answer. Milla explains.

(ObsH)

These observations reveal aspects of the internal dynamics of girls' relationships. Everybody turns to Milla. She is helpful, and girls seem to get more individual help from her than from the teacher. But she will not help Hille, and responds in a belittling way to her request. Girls can be friendly and helpful towards each other, but not necessarily and not always (cf. Hey, 1997; Gordon *et al.*, 2000a).

Valerie Walkerdine has described middle-class girls as being under considerable pressure to achieve (Walkerdine, 1997). Kati explains why she has to achieve:

> I have to be good at school, because my sister is good at school, that means that I have to, [my cousins], they are also very good at school, yes, they all have excellent grades, so I also have to, or I would be too different.
>
> (Kati, FSH)

More general personal qualities seldom occurred in students' evaluations of themselves as pupils. As a pupil you are not an individual person, but related to the obligations of schools. Henna, however, refers to her personal characteristics and to relations with friends.

> Well, I get mad rather easily and I'm quite talkative. And sometimes, when I'm in a bad mood, I start to shout. And I'm very quick-tempered and my mouth is always wagging. And sometimes I'm rather peaceful. And I'm always on the go and I always need to have something to do. And normally, I go with my friends and things like that.
>
> (Henna, FSH)

Henna describes herself both as quick-tempered and as peaceful; inclusion of several seemingly contradictory strands is typical of students' perceptions more generally. Individuality is not a coherent identity for the students. This is not surprising, as individuality is desired, but at the same time a potentially dangerous position to occupy. There is a fine line between being an 'individual' and being too different from others. Age relations are structured in such a way that children and young people are in a subordinate position; if being an 'individual' is a process of becoming for adults, something to aim for rather than something that is already achieved (Gordon, 1994), then this process is doubly difficult for students in schools.

Between control and agency

Education has a dual task of regulation and emancipation (Chapter 1), and this dual task is visible in everyday life in schools. As Bronwyn Davies (1990, p. 344) argues, the belief that children must be 'socialised' into known and accepted ways of being, and the belief that fundamental to those known and accepted ways of being is a conception of an 'individual' who does and should stand outside of and above those forms, creates a paradox. This leads to a constant tension between control and agency in schools.

One of the self-evident features of the school is that teachers have the right and responsibility of controlling students. Teachers do not like this aspect of their work, but it is something they regard as their duty: 'what I like least in the job is the control – whether it's evaluating examinations or shouting in the corridors, I regard it as the same control' (Elna, FTH). Control is most visible in the classrooms. The following teachers use judicious combinations of voice, silence and gaze as methods of control:

> Methods of control involve picking out the noisy ones and naming; use of a reprimanding look and a click of the fingers – no words are necessary. The teacher does a mime act to silence the student, and the student complies, the message is understood.
>
> (ObsL)

> This teacher can indicate what he wants by casting his eye in the direction of the person he wants to respond. He also uses more dramatic techniques, banging a board cleaner on the desk with a loud noise (or a ruler, whatever is to hand) to call the class to a halt and silence.
>
> (ObsL)

When students describe their teachers, they often use the word 'discipline'; they like a teacher who has 'good discipline'. But this is followed by words such as 'relaxed', 'sense of humour' or 'freedom'/'liberty'. Students want to have organised lessons where 'the teacher allows freedom, but not too much, should be kind of strict' (Kari, MSH). Many students admire one teacher: 'Vilkko is good of course, she kind of gives more freedom, but she also keeps discipline, doesn't let people do whatever they want, but there's a relaxed feeling, and some discussion with friends is allowed' (Tommi, MSH).

When students were asked what their ideal teacher would be like, they (often giving examples from their own teachers) favoured someone who could control them, but was not too strict, who let them talk, but not too much, who could have a joke and a bit of fun with them, but who made sure that they did the work: 'Somebody who can get on with their pupils but still be able to hold authority over them, you know, still get their respect ... and be able to control them when they're having a hyper day' (Sylvia, FSL).

Order in the classroom is essential for students who understand the instrumental value of schools. They have to learn, and they cannot concentrate on learning if others mess around in the lesson – and if they themselves mess around. 'Good discipline' was desired not only by high-achieving students but often by those who, from our observations and their own admission, themselves challenge it. As Manu (MSH) said: 'I like history, because we have good discipline, then we can concentrate, and learn better.'

Teachers often emphasise that good discipline is 'for your own good'. Sometimes it is a last effort to get control in a situation they can no longer handle:

TEACHER: Did anyone hear?... it's because you squeal all the time ... let's agree that you raise your hands, it's the practice in this school ...
Timo, Auli and Marianne raise their hands and answer.
TEACHER: Shut up, Eino!
Teacher asks Matti [who does not raise his hand].
Perttu falls from the chair. Janne answers. Perttu asks something. Eino asks something.
TEACHER [*looks angry and says*]:   What is this with erasers? Erasers fly around all the time in the classroom ... no one listens.... I have to repeat everything three times.... Stupid mess!
Teacher shouts. Students become quiet.
TEACHER: You should work in this kind of silence all the time.... It's not for me, but for your own good.

(ObsH)

Teachers have many opportunities to demonstrate the hierarchical relation between themselves and students. They can punish through grades and detentions. They can threaten that they will not let students do enjoyable things in the lesson unless they behave. A music teacher might say that they will only study 'theory' if students continue to be noisy; a science teacher can threaten note-taking instead of a practical session. Teachers might forbid working in pairs if students are not quiet, or they may threaten to get in touch with parents if students do not behave as they should. These are everyday micro-politics of power in schools, and teachers can use these techniques of control collectively with the whole class or with individual students.

Students are often aware of a teacher's use of control, but even when they dislike it, they may not be willing to challenge it too openly. Noora and Salli are high-achieving girls who know how to get along with teachers.

> I think that it's stupid that teachers can use their power by giving detention or low marks, you don't dare to say anything to them.
>
> (Noora, FSH)

> If I disagree with the teacher, then I give my opinion, but not too strongly, not so that the teacher regards it as annoying. You should respect teachers because they are the ones who give you marks.
>
> (Salli, FSH)

Salli assumes that teachers might not like her comments, and is careful in how she presents her opinions. She is in a class of performing arts, where many girls are high-achieving, talkative and sometimes critical. Some of them have learned that teachers do not like outspoken girls (see Chapter 8). While teachers regularly told us that they do like this group of intelligent and active girls, Ida, from the same group, argues: 'teachers regard us as a problem group. We're noisy and more critical than others' (Ida, FSH).

Teachers' position of power is also vulnerable. The construction and negotiation of the 'order-that-is-to-be' (Davies, 1983) in the classroom takes place during the initial encounters with the teacher (see also Lahelma and Gordon, 1997). This construction is not conducted by the school and the teachers alone; students are active participants in the negotiation of that order. Bronwyn Davies also emphasises the collaborative nature of this venture. When students are not willing to collaborate, the teacher is in a very difficult situation. The position of a teacher may also be vulnerable when students are united and determined. One teacher had a severe conflict with a group that was positive that the teacher had treated a girl unfairly. The situation was finally resolved, although both the teacher and some of the students remembered and reflected on it much later. When a solution to the conflict was found, the teacher asked for understanding from the students; she realised that she had lost the 'position of a teacher' and wanted the students to grant it to her once again.

The ebb and flow of routinisation/control and enactment/agency raises questions of power and resistance. Research in sociology of education contains a strong strand of studies analysing schools in terms of power being exerted over school students. For example Bowles and Gintis (1976) see the education system as a powerful mechanism of reproduction of relations of domination. Power is represented by teachers and invested in them by the school organisation defined through educational politics and policies which reflect dominant interests. Pinja (FSH) talks of two teachers whom she does not like using the terminology of power and hierarchical relations:

> They both are like 'I'm a teacher and you are students', they use it, because they have power and they can behave as they want to, because we are on a lower level.
>
> (Pinja, FSH)

And Julie (FSL) similarly criticises several aspects of this hierarchy:

> Well they think just because they've got a good position in the school, or they're a teacher and you're lower than them, that they can treat you however they want. I find that a bit upsetting really because, just because they're older and – they feel that they have control over us, that they can do what they want with us ... and we're just here to learn and not to be bullied or anything by them.
>
> (Julie, FSL)

Challenging unpopular teachers sometimes seems to be a method of breaking the dull routine of school days, a bit of fun. One teacher in a poorly managed lesson came into open conflict with a group of students. At one point the teacher left the classroom on the grounds that some of the male students were misbehaving. Boys commented after her departure that 'this is no fun anymore, when there's no teacher to shout at' (Heikki, MSH) or 'I don't want to wear my cap any more, because it's not forbidden' (Manu, MSH). Before the conflict erupted, students tried, on several occasions, to negotiate with the teacher, but the teacher did not recognise these attempts.

Complex relations are involved in the process of making individual citizens. We concur with Davies and Hunt (1994) that power and powerlessness are also transitory; students are positioned, and position themselves, in different ways. In some situations they are defined, and define themselves, as individuals who can exercise agency, and in others as pupils whose competence requires the acceptance of control. Most students, like teachers, dislike descent into ever-looming chaos, and consider the need to relinquish their agency as necessary, even though many of them may at the same time resent it.

Making the difference[5]

Making gendered citizens

School and teachers can influence gender construction in many ways. Teachers can unwittingly contribute to gender differentiation in direct ways, for example by treating girls and boys differently. Contents of teaching and the habits and structures of institutional life in school can communicate traditional images of masculinity and femininity. There are also situations when intervention by the teacher might reduce bias and disadvantage in that instance (cf. Acker, 1988; Ruddock, 1994). Students themselves also engage in processes of making the difference, actively reinforcing the gendering of social processes in school.

Gendered processes were different in the various groups that we followed. Apart from the predominantly female class of performing arts it was generally more often boys than girls who were at the centre of teachers' gaze and observation.[6] In classroom discussions teachers interact more with boys, as previous research also has demonstrated. Many teachers, however, make a conscious effort in classroom interaction not to treat girls and boys differently. We see this effort in observations, and in interviews many of the pupils assert that this is the case: one student remarked that 'There's no sexism here', and many insist that boys and girls are not treated differently, 'They treat us basically all the same.' But others report, and we can see running throughout our discussion of the ethnography in this book, that teachers' expectations of different behaviour from girls and boys do affect the ways in which they teach, respond and behave towards students.

In the content of schooling, gender and equality were not often explicitly on the agenda. There were, however, moments when discussions of this kind occurred. One example from a Helsinki school was a lesson of religious education. The teacher was explaining that Jesus Christ spoke of equality and justice for the poor, for sick people, for women, for children, for those who were despised and for sinners. Discussion on gender equality arose in this group where girls were in the majority. Some of the students talked about the poor position of women in some countries that they had visited and in Islamic countries. The teacher said 'You should be satisfied, girls, that you are women, here in Finland where we do have gender equality. Do you remember how it was in Israel?' Here gender and nationality were intertwined in a way that 'other' countries were described as different, as unequal.

There were instances when teachers attempted to engage the interest of both boys and girls, or to raise gender issues. In a home economics lesson the teacher argued that there are not specific jobs for men or women. Different synonyms for the words 'girl' and 'boy' were discussed in a Finnish lesson, and sexualised ways of addressing girls were taken up as an issue by the teacher. But most of the time gender is taken for granted; often a 'human being' turns out to be male in this taken-for-granted discourse.

Teachers sometimes set girls and boys in competition to spur responses from the other: 'Why are only boys raising their hands?', or argue that 'girls write good answers'. In these situations it is clearly not all of the boys who raise their hands, nor all of the girls who write good answers. There are examples when students themselves question this categorisation:

> *Teacher asks who has a microscope at home. Markku, Lasse, Jyri and Pasi raise hands.*
> TEACHER: Boys have it, that's typical.
> SAKU: I don't have one!
> TEACHER: You don't have to say you haven't got one!
> SAKU: But you said that boys have it!

(ObsH)

Although there is a taken-for-granted understanding of gender difference which was acted upon in school processes by all participants, there is a difference between London and Helsinki here. In London schools there is an awareness of gender and ethnic difference which is incorporated into school policies and often apparent in teachers' practice and student responses. This was not apparent in Helsinki schools where, for example, students are often categorised and addressed 'girls' and 'boys'. For teachers this categorisation is self-evident and so unproblematised. The existence of a school policy on equal opportunities, as in the London schools, might have its effect on everyday processes by raising teachers' awareness of the issue.

Nation/ality

Teachers grapple with issues of nationalism/internationalism and ethnocentrism/racism in their everyday work. Their thinking and ways of dealing with these issues are diverse, and are dependent on the ethos of their particular school, their own political outlook, their pedagogical preferences and, in secondary schools, their particular subject. For example language or geography teachers find it easier to ponder these matters – teachers of technical drawing or of mathematics find it more difficult to respond to questions dealing with these issues.

> I think internationalism comes up in geography all the ... time, particularly the increasing integration of the globe. Yes, I try to emphasise in geography, above all, that we are sort of responsible for each other, in biology as well we are, of course, and not simply within the borders of Finland, but that we should think in a more comprehensive way, and understand that responsibility extends to the whole globe. It's not so much that we think internationally, but that we think globally.
>
> (Maija, FTH)

Finnish teachers talk about becoming more European, and about the importance of extending notions of being Finnish, and of developing more inclusive ways of thinking. In subjects that deal with Finland, being Finnish and Finnishness, teachers emphasise that students need to understand their own cultural heritage in order to be able to embrace more international perspectives. Particularly teachers of Finnish stress the need to develop one's own identity in the context of a national language and heritage.

Most teachers consider the Finnish heritage as a positive resource that can be built on in developing global understanding, internationalism and inclusive attitudes. But a few also consider the focus on national heritage as a potential burden, and some discuss the dangers. For example in music teaching the emphasis on Finnish music, and in particular the practice of singing national songs, has been a millstone which alienated too many people from music as a subject in schools. Emphasising the geopolitical situation of Finland in history can, as teachers acknowledge, lead to exclusive patriotism and xenophobia.

Teachers talk in terms found in the Framework Curriculum. They emphasise the importance of internationalism, and tend to refer to it as a taken-for-granted pair with nationalism. But when they discuss their own practices and talk about how they actually try to tackle internationalism and confront ethnocentric Finnish attitudes, the issues are less clear cut. Many teachers seem to expect and assume that the issues will come up in lessons, for example in the context of discussing population growth in geography, or in disentangling nationalist stereotypes in languages. Teachers explain that, when these questions emerge, they do discuss them, and that stereotyped, ethnocentric or racist comments by some students are usually confronted by other students – and if they are not, then the teacher will pause to initiate discussion.

This type of approach is potentially haphazard and counteractive. If teachers rely on opportunities for reflective discussion to develop on the basis of negative comments by students, then nationalism/internationalism and ethnocentrism/racism are discussed in the context of the problems raised. Such problems typically focus on 'others', and the mirror is turned on them by 'us'. In this situation there is less chance of discussions developing, where the mirror is turned on 'us'; 'we' and our 'ethnocentrism' is not the starting point. The 'others' are posited as 'different', albeit ones to be understood and tolerated by 'us'.

Both London schools had an ethnically mixed student body and in one the school ethos valued diversity and difference. The differences were built upon, and drawn upon in lessons, where appropriate, for example comparing experiences of different religious practices, or cultural celebrations. There were also representations of different cultures in material placed on the walls in classrooms and hallways, as well as items produced in art lessons on the basis of different cultural backgrounds (masks, for example). As a result there was no assertive image of British culture, but it was the invisible backdrop against which otherness was portrayed. When asked in interviews, some of the young people identified themselves as British, often with difficulty in making the identification, but found it extremely hard to describe what they meant. Two teachers took opposing views on whether they thought of themselves as British or English, exemplifying the confusion and ambivalence inherent in the concept of Britishness as nationality.

I prefer British rather than English. We should not be segregated as a nation, rather say British. Although the Scots, Welsh and Irish would probably not agree! For me 'English' has negative connotations, some say it has – it's because it's very patriotic – to do with patriotism. Which is not always a good thing in this country, can be associated with hooliganism. [She had linked the notion of 'British' with 'sport' earlier.] For me English is negative and British positive, although I wouldn't argue the toss if someone said I was English.

(Alison, FTL)

And the other:

Anyone who was born in the British Isles no matter what their nationality is, and whose family are in the British Isles. I think it does conjure up issues of colonialism if you like but at the end of the day everybody has to have some sort of identity. I know some people who call themselves Black British or Asian British which maybe is a better way of putting it. But as regards the National Curriculum, there is a nice little phrase in the Dance Curriculum about British National Dance, and that immediately conjures up primary teachers prancing around a maypole. So I think the Government and the National Curriculum need to be clear about what they mean by the word 'British' because I think immediately when somebody says that I think it immediately sounds racist to me and very colonial, I shudder.

(Katherine, FTL)

In Woburn Hill, difference was not explicitly celebrated, in fact it was subsumed into the overall requirement of the 'good' achieving pupil, the hegemonic norm. This was explicitly recognised by some of the pupils. It might even create some confusion of identity, where they were being 'educated to be English', although from a different cultural background, as in the case of Maya in the introduction, and Rita:

I feel more British than Indian, well more English than Indian. I know that at home I would say that I was English – er Indian, sorry. But when I come to school I feel English, and when I go outside – because last year we went on holiday to India and I saw relatives and stuff, they didn't treat me totally as an Indian person. They treated me more English. So it's hard to say.

(Rita, FSL)

In some instances students from different ethnic groups made a very clear separation between the school and its culture, and their own culture. For example, some were taking language lessons to examination level in their own language at Saturday school. When asked if they would prefer to take the lessons in school, even though this would mean a reduction in their work load, they preferred not to do so.

Making sexual citizens

Schools play a major part in the construction of sexual identity, of masculinity and femininity, and as with all major institutions of society this takes place within a heterosexual matrix, a 'grid of cultural intelligibility through which bodies, genders and desires are naturalised' (Butler, 1990, p. 151). Some argue that school is the major site for the production of hegemonic masculinity, constructed in opposition to the 'other' of femininity and homosexuality, since it offers a condensed range of experiences in a sustained and mandatory fashion (Connell, 1989). Sexuality permeates every level of the school, but it is hidden, suppressed or disciplined. Epstein and Johnson (1998) suggest that (in Britain) the social framing of sexuality in the media and political discourse tends towards the further closeting of sexuality in the school, reinforcing a 'split between the treatment of sexuality within student culture, with a focus on fun, excitement and identity as well as anxiety, and the dull regulation of the official sexual (desexualized) regime of truth produced in schools – the regulation of clothing and make-up; the denial of the libidinous in teaching and learning; the caution of the sex education lesson; the policing of masculinities via homophobic abuse; enforced invisibility of sexist harassment' (p. 128). Sex education lessons are the space allowed in school for discussion of the sexual, but as Epstein and Johnson suggest, the overall control and suppression of sexuality, and the legal and public discourse constraints within which these lessons are taught, lead to caution, and often inadequacy in meeting young people's needs for information.

Sex education in Britain has been a site of considerable struggle in recent years, reflecting both the grip of the New Right on education policies and practice, and the conservative and liberal threads within it. Rachel Thomson (1996) discusses some of the politics of sex education in Britain and struggles over its place in the curriculum, as do Epstein and Johnson (1998). In general conservative voices would deny or limit sex education, arguing that it encourages sexual activity;

progressive voices urge that young people should be given information so that they can make their own choices and exercise individual
agency. The quality of sex education in Britain has typically and
historically been very variable, but in general reproduction and its
avoidance has been a major focus, particularly for girls (Thomson and
Scott, 1991; Haywood and Mac an Ghaill, 1995; Kehily, 1996; Holland
et al., 1998). What is lacking is the 'discourse of desire' (Fine, 1988), a
discourse that would enable the young people, particularly girls, to be
the subjects of their own sexuality.

In Finland, teaching about sexuality takes place in the context of PE
(health education), HE (family education) and biology. Although sex
education has not been attacked by the New Right, health and family
education are less emphasised in the 1990s. School nurses give
information about sexuality, and sometimes people from health
organisations, for example, come to the schools and give lessons.
Some teachers say that they take up the issue when a suitable situation
occurs, for example when students use sexist language. We have
observed examples of sex education integrated into different subjects
in this way, but emphasis has often been in biological facts. Sex education materials widely used in schools in Finland emphasise
heterosexual relations, intercourse, reproduction, and the dangers of
unprotected sex (e.g., Aapola, 1997; Nummelin, 1997).

Addressing difference

We have noted that the abstract 'pupil' is abstracted from social bonds
– gender, ethnicity and social class are not often made explicit in the
official agenda in schools. This was true especially in Finland. The
schools in London do have explicit policies for equal opportunities,
and these policies made the issues of 'race' and gender, at least, somewhat more open. These divisions are much more pronounced in
Britain. If you try to hide or ignore differences, they tend to appear in
school processes and the content of education as self-evident, banal
categories.

In the San Francisco Bay Area schools that we visited issues of difference were openly addressed. Teachers regularly discussed with us how
to challenge inequalities caused by ethnic, social and gender differences, though gender was more mute than other differences. Various
cultures to be found in California were present in lesson contexts, in
pictures, aphorisms and poems on classroom walls and murals. One
example of living multiculturalism was given in booklets of poems
and pictures prepared by students. The booklets presented a powerful

picture of the sorrows, pleasures and anxieties of young people from various cultures and with diverse experiences of life: for example, the experiences of being black in America, of arriving as a refugee from Vietnam, of being pregnant, of falling in love, of being harassed.

We are not arguing that educational policies or practices in schools in California (or in the USA generally) are more egalitarian than in Britain or Finland. We are aware of the huge differences in resources between public and private education, of 'savage inequalities' (Kozol, 1992) in American schools. However, in some schools there we saw examples of inclusive pedagogies that helped us to see behind the 'banal' inevitabilities in the schools that are more familiar to us (cf. Delamont and Atkinson, 1995).

From pupils to citizens

Training for citizenship is not explicit in the schools in our study, and specific citizenship education is not a significant feature, despite its existence as a crosscurricular theme in England/Wales. The training takes place more implicitly, through the construction of a 'professional' pupil and a 'good' pupil. Professional pupils learn the expectations embedded in the school organisation, the ethos of the school and the different customs and interpretations of teachers. Students are expected to have or to learn 'good manners', they are expected to be polite and courteous and to have consideration for others. These are moral values with which few of us would disagree. However, the particular manifestations of such moral values, and their outward signs, may be culturally specific. Training to be a 'good pupil' involves processes through which diversity can become hierarchical difference. If national norms are based on the universalisation of specific middle-class cultural practice, students are differently placed in relation to the 'good manners' which symbolise a 'good pupil'. The goal of a 'good pupil' is more attainable for some individuals or groups than for others. The ease with which students can become 'professional' and 'good' is differentiated in the everyday life of the school.

'Professional pupils' or 'good pupils' have various kinds of wishes and dreams. Philip Wexler (1992) reminds us that young people in schools are engaged with each other in the interactional work of making meaning. Here we have followed the rules and the official steps of our dance. We have noted some stubborn traditionalism and empty rituals that emphasise differences between the dancers, but also noted innovative elements. We have listened to the plans of the master of ceremonies and to the dancers' wishes to widen the choreo-graphies, but in a way that maintains the elegance and dignity of the dance. In Chapter 6 we move on to sidestepping the dance, and come closer to the spheres in which the young people strive to 'become somebody'.

6
Stepping Here, Stepping There: the Informal School[1]

Introduction

Lurking in the interstices of the official school is the informal school, with its possibilities, alternatives, tensions and pressures. The official steps and movements become diversified. Various exchanges take place in order to negotiate where and how to step – though the alterations also follow from silent interaction, implicit understandings, where small signals are sent, received and interpreted – and joint action results. Perhaps some loner or soloist has not joined in, or has not been encouraged to or allowed to, and hence observes the movements of the others from a marginal position. Such a retreat may also have more to do with stepping aside with thoughts on different tunes, different movements and different partners – even a different dance floor. Among those who are dancing, a range of verbal, physical and other contacts are taking place. They are making contact – moving in unison, stepping in tune with others, all searching for similar rhythms. They may be developing their own steps, making a difference, constructing a display, making a mockery of the expected steps, or moving round lazily, not wanting to make the effort to learn the proper steps, or moving around clumsily, finding the correct steps difficult or impossible. Whether they are dancing according to the rules, using official, formal, or informal, altered steps, they may at any given moment be feeling energetic or tired, happy or sad, excited or frustrated, in tune with others or lonely and in discord.

In this chapter we develop a picture of the school further to include multiple dimensions and a range of alternative universes. We explore classroom interaction that is not part of the formal teaching–learning agenda, not inscribed into conceptions of the pedagogic relationship.

We describe informal activities of school students and we explore the hierarchies they construct, deconstruct and reconstruct. We consider interaction between different groups in schools, including support staff, as well as teachers. By doing this we aim to deepen our picture of making differences.

While we have chosen the term 'informal' to avoid a binary opposition between 'official' and 'unofficial' school, and draw attention to the separate lived meanings inherent in the informal school, it should be noted that the informal school exists in relation to the official. The parameters of the informal are set by the official sphere. In the informal school students dismantle the mantle of authority (Gordon *et al.*, 2000d). We ask what the informal school does in, with, to and against the official school. School students make spaces in the official school, but use the informal school to make spaces too. We consider how, and to what extent, the informal school is integrated with the official school, and begin our discussion by focusing on the informalisation of student/teacher interaction. We also focus briefly on the informal school of the teachers. Other staff in schools move, often invisibly, in the interstices between the official and the informal school. We examine how students make connections – how they develop joint interaction and friendships, but also ways in which they construct hierarchies and differences through teasing, bullying, naming, cussing and sexual harassment. We look at anxieties and pleasures they experience in these activities. We explore informal relations of gender, ethnicity and class and see these interactions as fluid, dynamic and processual. We look at students exercising agency. We also search for ways in which they challenge gendering and 'racing' of others. We look for stories of cooperation as well as for stories of conflict.

Informalising the official school

The forgotten people at school

Teachers and students are easily regarded as the important people in the school, and the rest of the staff – nurses, caretakers, cleaners, kitchen staff, welfare officers[2] or administrators and school secretaries – remains forgotten.

Neither teachers nor students said that they knew members of the support staff very well. Teachers were aware of the marginal positions of support staff in the school: 'cleaners, for example, probably feel their work rather isolated, we don't even remember to inform them about everything' (Elna, FTH).

Support staff had problems in becoming integrated into the school. In both countries school nurses are employed by the health office. In Finland also caretakers, cleaners, kitchen staff and secretaries have a different employer. This means that organisationally they do not belong to the school institution. A nurse reflected her role at the school: 'What am I? I'm not a worker in the staff room, but neither am I a worker at the health centre' (Mirja, FSSH).

Members of the support staff suggested that their special role as adults but not teachers is very helpful for some students. Boys who seem to have few friends come to talk with a male caretaker, and a nurse noticed that girls come to her office when they have problems that they do not wish to discuss with the teachers:

> It's kind of the tip of iceberg that they came to ask for aspirin or something else, my role is bigger than only taking care of their health, like physically – the mental side is even more important. It is only that, I don't know why it's easiest to come to complain about headache rather than to complain about feeling bad.
>
> (Tellervo, FSSH)

This support role was also mentioned by the welfare assistant in one of the London schools; she also dealt with health and safety issues, since the school nurse was provided by the Local Education Authority and shared between a number of schools, and so was in the school rarely.

> I do first aid and accidents, but they realise that not all upsets are physical. The children who come to me might be upset by something which is going on at home, or their work.
>
> (Estelle, FSSL)

When asked what types of problems they might bring to her she responds:

> Everything really, might have a row with their boyfriends, not getting on with school friends, worried about exams. They might be feeling stressed if they have not done well in a test. Parents have high expectations of them.

The relationship between the official and informal school can be illustrated by the way that, in the official school, the importance of members of non-teaching staff is often ignored. A caretaker comments about the lack of respect that teachers often showed him:

> The teachers are a mixed bag. Some are OK. Some don't even say hullo to me, would not pass the time of day unless they want something. It is difficult sometimes. They do not always understand that I have a multitude of things to do every day. They want what they want done then and there.... Eric Moore treats me with respect for the position of the job. He sits down and discusses staging, seating, [for concerts, performances] does not take me and my work for granted. Others will go ahead and arrange something without thinking that they need to consult me, that it will have an effect on my work. ... Robyn Watkins makes decisions without discussion or consultation, which gets my back up. He does not have the basic courtesy of telling me what is going on.
>
> (Andrew, MSSL)

These members of staff are not regarded as taking part in the pedagogic process, although they often do in many different ways, for example by filling the gaps during times of economic cuts, as described by Valerie Hey (1996). Their impact in practical citizenship education is obvious in our schools. For example, nurses give sex education; welfare officers help solve the problems, for example, of immigrant children and of bullying; kitchen staff, caretakers and cleaners steer students' behaviour in their everyday life. Apart from welfare officers, others conduct these tasks without special training, using their tacit knowledge (cf. Hey, 1996).

Technicians and assistants of various types can provide support for teachers in the teaching task, but they can also impede that task. Science and other practical lessons are disrupted and delayed through the absence of expected equipment/materials, or their failure to function. In one instance no gas was flowing to bunsen burners in a science lesson, and the wrong video was provided for a lesson. This called for considerable mental agility from the teacher who had introduced the video she expected.

Kitchen staff, cleaners and caretakers are representatives of working-class people in schools and, with the exception of some of the caretakers, they represent female working-class. The invisibility and marginalisation of these people reflect for the students the hierarchical structure of the society. In London a caretaker described how he mediated between the working-class children who hung around the (largely middle-class) school causing trouble, and those within. He explains to the rowdy boys that the students in his school are not all 'nobs', that there are a range of children from rich to poor in any school. He suggests if they are envious of the students in the school, that they probably would not like it, it does not suit everyone and they would be unhappy if they came to that school.

Teachers' informal school

'We work a lot here, but then we also know how to enjoy ourselves', one teacher described the atmosphere among the staff in her school. In one of the schools, especially, teachers' good informal relations with each other seem obvious; friendly chatting and bursts of laughter are heard in the staff room along with professional discussions. Many teachers feel that they would like to spend more time in the staff room with colleagues, but during short breaks there is little time for relaxation. Teachers often have supervision responsibilities, they have to prepare for the following lesson, students might come to them with problems, they might have telephone calls from parents, they may need to plan or discuss problems of students together. When students want to continue the work during a break teachers might remark that they must go, because 'I have to get my cup of coffee' (ObsH).

Sometimes the easy and relaxed relations between teachers carry over into their official relations as well, as in the following long staff meeting:

> The staff meeting went on and on. It seemed to me, however, that teachers did not get that tired, because the atmosphere was pleasant. I looked at Pekka Kalela, who was like a wild boy in the classroom. He teased 'girls', threw paper, said 'quiet, I want to listen' when the 'girls' whispered, Mikko Nieminen joined every now and then. Touko Kettunen played with a Rubic cube. I admired the head teacher's way of chairing the meeting. I had the feeling that she had it all in her hand, but listened to the others and gave time. But it really does need time.
>
> (ObsH)

This extract also demonstrates gendered patterns in teachers' informal relations and the analogy of gendered patterns among students is evident. Staffroom culture mediates the official school and can produce a lens for viewing events in school through commonsense discourses – stereotypes, rumour, gossip. In Helsinki schools there were fewer male than female teachers, while in our research schools in London, as more generally in secondary schools, the gender distribution was more even. Many female as well as male teachers in Helsinki argued in the interviews that it would be better to have more male teachers, often referring to informal, rather than pedagogic reasons.[3] The reasons put forward in one case illustrate how the staff room is an arena where dominant ideas can be reproduced and applied in the school setting. One teacher mentioned that students, especially children of lone mothers, need male teachers, and continued that she misses the staff room of the old pre-comprehensive school, where they had more male teachers, as men discuss 'general issues' whereas female teachers, she argued, discuss homes, families and private issues. She also argued that men have a better sense of humour. The image of male teachers as more relaxed and bringing interesting issues to staff room discussion was shared by some male teachers. However, we saw female teachers engaged in friendly, lighthearted conversations as well as serious discussions on pedagogic or broader societal issues – and male teachers talking about families. 'Normal' equal gender balance is desired in staff rooms as well as classrooms.

Informalisation of teacher/student relations

Teachers often try to maintain distance from the students. Elna (FTH) said that she does not tell the students much about herself:

> it's kind of my own space, so that they could sometimes use it as a weapon, it is kind of protecting oneself. And I think that students have the same right, that they don't have to answer if I asked about their leisure, they don't have to answer me if they don't want to.

This suggests a sense of vulnerability and also tact towards students' privacy. Teachers' informal relations with each other are also more or less hidden from the students. Students know that teachers 'sit and drink coffee' in the staff room, and some say that it is unfair, because they themselves have to go outside. But teachers do not often talk to the students about their informal relations. One teacher reported that when some female students were visiting the staff room (which does not happen often) and saw a leaflet about the teachers' forthcoming party, they were astonished, they could not imagine that teachers go out and drink together.

Gender is an important issue in the informalisation of student/ teacher relations. The few male teachers in Helsinki schools often taught boys only groups (PE for boys and technical handicraft). During these lessons male discourses of harsh humour, physical power and violence could be observed – at least by a female researcher who might feel herself to be an outsider. Male teachers' physical strength was often emphasised and admired by boys, as in the extract below:

> Teacher notices that Matti is trying to wind some handle open but cannot manage it, teacher comes to help, says: 'Many people think that you need power in this ... [*winds the handle open*] ... and so it is.'
>
> (ObsH)

Masculinity enacted by male teachers was not uniform. Both in boys-only groups and in mixed groups, male teachers also revealed caring and sensitive behaviour (cf. Mac an Ghaill, 1994). For some boys their positive relation with some of their male teachers is entwined with their liking of the subject they teach. Eetu respects his male PE teacher's sense of humour and past work in a job he admires:

> Sports, it is nice, because it's also my hobby outside, and I like to play football and ice hockey, and we have a nice teacher, not kind of serious. He can tell jokes every now and then, and he is friendly, and he has been a sports trainer and is quite nice.
>
> (Eetu, MSH)

Girls' relations to their (mostly) female teachers are sometimes emotionally laden. When the relation with a female teacher is not good, a girl might feel very sad about it:

> ... I don't like the teacher so much. In the beginning she was quite terrible with us, but we were terrible to her, and then she would explain things to others and kind of discriminated against me, ignored me if I asked for help. But this relation between us, it was like a kind of wave, there were periods when we hated each other and periods when we liked each other ... sometimes this teacher is just irritating, but then sometimes she is really nice. She's like that.
>
> (Mari, FSH)

Sexuality in student/teacher relationships is one of the hidden back-drops that is not often discussed. A male teacher said that the most difficult incident in his career was when a female student fell in love with him. Sexuality can also be used by female students to challenge the authority of male teachers, or as a strategy of resistance towards the sexism of male teachers (Anyon, 1983; Skeggs, 1991; Kehily and Nayak, 1996). Students in the Finnish interviews did not mention their teachers in sexualised terms, with one exception. Some of the girls complained about the sexist jokes made by one male teacher.[4]

Teachers are also vulnerable to sexual harassment by students. For the (female) teachers, insults directed at their bodies and sexuality are difficult to handle. This is true even for experienced teachers who are used to calming down disturbing and aggressive students. Sexuality is one of the spheres through which male power over women is constructed and enacted – and sometimes perhaps challenged. It is also a sphere for the construction of hegemonic masculinity (Carrigan *et al.*, 1985). Referring to the sexuality of female teachers and suggesting homosexuality for male teachers provided ways of challenging teachers' authority for students (Lahelma, 1996). Our interviews with teachers revealed that some of them have experienced humiliating sexualised comments from students, and we saw some instances during lessons (Hynninen, 1998). Some of the teachers preferred to dress in a neutral way to deflect attention from their sex or sexuality. In the London schools students noticed and commented on relationships, or potential relationships, between teachers, a way of breaking down officially prescribed teacher/student relations and a form of social learning of the adult sexual world. When filing into a young male teacher's classroom a student murmured 'Miss X sends her love'.

Official informalisation – extra-curricular activities

The routine of day-to-day life in schools is interrupted by special days and celebrations. In Helsinki schools, for example, Independence Day, Christmas and Spring feasts are celebrated in traditional ways; religion (hymns) and nationality (the flag of Finland) are often part of the event. Feasts are planned and rehearsed, and they also consist of students' musical and other artistic presentations. In a school of perfoming arts these presentations are part of the official curriculum of arts teaching, in others they include more students' out-of-school activities. The London schools each presented a school play during the fieldwork, and each took considerable effort and energy in planning, preparation and performance, on the part of both teachers and students. The performances took place in the evening. One was a glossy spectacular, a musical with the school orchestra providing the music, and older students putting on a polished and professional performance to a packed audience. The other was also a musical, but a more low-key event, with fewer participants and a smaller audience.

Official celebrations are situations when students and teachers, sometimes also parents, gather together in the main hall (Palmu, 1998). These events provide an opportunity to emphasise good manners (Lahelma and Gordon, 1997). Students are under severe control because order in the overcrowded main hall is more vulnerable than in the classrooms. Loud singing of hymns during Christmas celebrations in one school led teachers to suspect that students were ridiculing the event. On this occasion a group of girls performed their own parody of a traditional Christmas play. Their performance contained sexual innuendo and political comment and was regarded as provocative by some teachers, and an official reprimand took place the following day.

Schools also have days with special focus. During 'Tender Day' in Green Park emphasis was on 'taking care of each other'; on 'Boys' Days' in City Park male teachers organised different kinds of activities while female teachers had a training day. In one of the London schools, on the final day of school in year 11, before moving up to the sixth form, the students could come in without uniforms, and the day had an air of carnival about it for them. Sports days took place in all schools and, in London schools, students are taken on trips where they undertake rugged, outdoor activities. Schools are involved in competitive sporting activities with other schools, and (in London) with junior sports leagues. In London schools many events are organised on a house basis, through which pupils are encouraged to both collaborate and compete, and to experience the relationship between a smaller community within a larger whole. Focus is often on cross curricular issues during extra days, and students enjoy these days. For teachers, organising such events was extra work, and indicates their commitment.

At official celebrations gender is displayed more openly than in other situations. It is often girls who sing, play or dance. It is often boys who take care of lights, loudspeakers and other technology. In musicals in London schools both girls and boys took part in the performances, whilst more technical aspects were often in the hands of the teachers and other staff. When students and teachers dress for festive occasions, their dress is less neutral, and female clothes are often more feminine than during normal school days.

Besides extra-curricular events, official informalisation is a more integral part of school processes in London. During the longer lunch break students are engaged in a range of activities, playing football, tennis, talking to each other and so on. In Helsinki schools students are involved in official school processes for a larger proportion of their school day. This is reflected in school metaphors discussed in Chapter 7 – students in London make more references to the informal school than students in Helsinki.

Making connections: friendships

Social interaction in the school is extremely important to students, as their associations for the words 'school' and 'pupil' reflected. A 'school' is a place for studying, for work, and can be boring. But 'school' is also for meeting other 'pupils', with whom experiences in the official school are shared. A 'pupil' was associated with the pedagogic relation (Chapter 5) but, more importantly, 'a pupil' was a friend, 'nice people in our class', 'cool', 'me' and 'we'. Other students in form groups or teaching groups are potential mates with whom laughter and jokes can be shared, and small victories in the everyday life of the school achieved. They may also provide distraction and temptation, as Noora illustrates; she describes the embodied meeting ground of the official and the informal – this space is located in her head.

> Pinja sits next to me, and if I decide that I'm going to listen during this lesson and then Pinja is there next to me, and she's fidgeting so, and then I don't have the energy all the time to listen to Pinja with one ear and to the teacher with the other, so I'll rather sort of join in with Pinja.
>
> (Noora, FSH)

Relatively peaceful, routinely constructed lessons without any special incidents or dramatic events contain a range of possible alternative experiences for students. The possibilities and limitations are not only an external field, not just the formal steps and the current tune – whilst it is played, students may find themselves tempted to hum another.

Starting school is characterised by buzz and nervous excitement. Students are milling around, trying to hang on to those they know, make the acquaintance of those they do not, but whose clothing, style and bodily comportment signified potential for sharing, and avoid those whose bodily insignia indicated likely indifference or possible threat (Gordon *et al.*, 2000d). For students having or finding a friend reduces the chaos of the school (Shaw, 1996). There are also students who shy away from the crowds, looking for quiet corners where they can observe the setting and work out safe ways of entering it.

In Green Park and Oak Grove, the schools with a more local catchment area, the process of settling in was on the one hand easier, because students were likely to know one another already, but on the other hand it was potentially more difficult, as local social differentiations, hierarchies and past disputes were brought into the space of the new school. Some students were keen to make a 'fresh start', but others familiar with their past could make this new beginning more complicated to achieve.

The making of friendships was for many a fast process. A school as a place feels unsafe for those who are alone; in the words of one student: 'in the beginning it was a bit like everyone sitting in their own place and looking around wondering: dare I walk past that one?' (FSH). For students, having one friend, a circle of friends, groups to talk to, or groups in the margins of which they can place themselves, made life more manageable. Friendship groups formed rapidly in the first year, and then adjustment and realignment took place over time. Students' perceptions of loners as people who were unsafe in the school were usually accurate. Hierarchies and differentiations often solidified at the expense of those who were marked as not belonging. Joining in the teasing of others was a way of ensuring one's own safety. Conflicts and discord will be discussed below – here the focus is on strong incentives for making connections in order not to fall under the feet of other dancers when the tempo speeds up.

Friendship groups are most often single-sex and patterns of friendship are infused with dominant notions of gender and gender-appropriate behaviour. Frequently the appropriate gender behaviour for the official school can be reproduced in the informal. But there are a few gender-blending soloists who move between different constellations, and socialise with both sexes. They often do not have a particular group and they tend to enter into shifting constellations and alliances. The social skills of such students are often considerable. Mixed groups are more likely to form around particular activities and spaces. For example in one of our schools there was a mixed-sex group that consisted of smokers who spent their breaks together, and who also met outside school. The girls and boys were friends, but would also form shifting heterosexual relationships. These could be of quite short duration and, where a mixed friendship group existed, it was often important to reinstate the friendship between the pair, to maintain the cohesion of the larger grouping, when the couple 'split up'.

> Sometimes they cause problems 'cause like when people split up with each other they ... I find the ones that have split up, they totally hate each other and don't talk to each other after that. That's kind of, I don't know why but that's the bad thing about the relationships.
>
> (Maya, FSL)

Girls, and sometimes boys, outlined the shifting friendship patterns, and characterised some of the groupings: 'There's our group, that's quite loud, and then there's the other group that, they tend to be quiet' (Fiona, FSL). Another confirms 'Like in the girls there's two groups, and I'm friends with all of the girls in our class but I'm not like good friends with all of them' (Rita, FSL). And another 'there's kind of the popular group of girls and boys and the not-so-popular group of girls and boys, and I'm in the not-so-popular, but you find watching the popular group of girls and boys, they do tease each other a lot, about appearance mainly, things like that, but not, nothing too bad you know' (Sylvia, FSL).

This type of teasing is often interpreted as an expression of interest in the opposite sex – such interpretations were often given by teachers – but some of the descriptions given by girls in interviews suggested that such banter could border on sexual harassment. Girls had to take care and know where to draw the line – as the group was forming, the girls were required to make constant interpretations of what they considered acceptable and what was unacceptable. One boy was reported for 'pinging bra straps'. His punishment was to write an essay about the history of the brassiere. The girl who reported this incident in an interview thought the punishment matched the crime, and they also found the essay informative. Quite often, the girls considered the boys in their form or of their age to be 'immature' – this was a frequent association to the word 'boy'. Girls, in contrast, were 'mature', although some clearly did not think they wanted to be involved in heterosexual relationships at all at this point, 'I just haven't really thought about that kind of thing much. I'm just happy with my life as it is' (Maya, FSL).

Friendship groups in schools consist typically of students who are of the same age. Secondary schools have clear age demarcations, and most students are not likely to cross these boundaries. Age relations are hierarchical, and older students were active in maintaining the difference between themselves and younger students, and in that way they were better able to ensure some privileges which were not available for the younger ones.

> I think a lot of the older children sort of take advantage of them being older, and well I know when we were in the first and second years we got a lot of sort of pushed out of the way, and 'oh, you little first year' and stuff like that. But we don't as much now, I suppose because there's people that are younger, smaller than us.
>
> (Sadie, FSL)

Barrie Thorne (1993) notes that children who do not play with older or younger people at school are more likely to do so outside school in their spare time spent in their local area. Schools, then, can be powerful in instituting and maintaining particular boundaries (cf. Aapola, 1997) – and hence could be influential in dismantling them.

In our Helsinki schools there are no clear ethnic groupings besides the Finnish ones; students from other ethnic groups were few, and were also differentiated by gender and age. These students then had to find places in ethnically mixed groups. Students from ethnic minorities recounted experiences of racism and the need to develop a hard shell, and some withdrew from the fray. If students spoke Finnish, they were more likely to find a location in the social constellations. If they did not, they were likely to be very lonely, and might for example pair up with some other lonely student. Each of the schools in London had a wide range of different ethnic groups within it and very clearly stated anti-racist (as well as anti-sexist) policies. In the classes followed, friendship groups, from observation, could cut across ethnic lines, although in some instances best friends might be from the same ethnic group. Many of the students in interviews said that they valued the diversity and the opportunity of meeting and finding out about people from different cultures, and some find support in the diversity, perhaps in contrast to racism experienced in the broader society. One young woman who was having some difficulty reconciling her home culture with English culture said:

> But then there are lots of people in our class who are from other

cultures. You know if I find it difficult to talk about my culture or something or behave the way I have to be, it's ok, 'cause they're there and stuff, and we're proud. A lot of us are proud to say what we do in our different cultures, how we speak and stuff, you know, because in our class you don't get racist people, who make racist comments about your religion, so that's ok.

(Maya, FSL)

Friendship groups did not tend to cut across social class demarcations (although in London there were some examples of cross-class friend-ships), and school achievement and personal styles and temperament were also important. Students were very skilled in reading small iconographic insignia in dress, hair and make-up when choosing whom to try to acquaint themselves with. Schooling is, indeed, an 'experience of interminable definition', as Valerie Hey (1997, p. 31) argues; this applies to the informal as well as the official school.

Balancing acts: girls and boys

The prototype of dancing is groups of female–male couples. In (co-educational) schools in teaching groups a gender balance is seen as ideal: there should be roughly the same number of girls and boys in each class. In London schools most classes were evenly balanced, although one had a slight preponderance of boys, and this was largely viewed as a negative characteristic. The classes we have followed in Helsinki had differing gender balances. One class consists of mainly girls, with a small minority of boys, one class consists of boys, and rest of them have roughly equal proportions of girls and boys. Students who were allocated into 'uneven' classes often expressed surprise, regret and disappointment. Strongest feelings were expressed by boys in an all-male class (Metso, 1999). 'It's a bit weird class ... it hasn't got a very good atmosphere' (Pertti, MSH). The boys described their class as wild, and students in other classes used similar descriptions when referring to this form. Girls were supposed to counteract this wildness, and continue with the business of the official school even when boys around them were messing about. The drama of boys becomes more disruptive when there are no girls to maintain a 'bedrock of busyness' (Sharp and Green, 1975). This does not offer very enviable positions for the girls.

The girls in the predominantly female class also tended to long for a balance. Some of the girls expressed pleasure and relief that their group was not all-female; there were at least some boys in the class.

Several girls thought that, when boys are a minority, the situation is against them. They are not quite like boys any more.

Single-sex groups are out of the ordinary in the Finnish comprehensive system. They do not replicate the notion of gender balance and therefore they seem inappropriate. Notions of complementarity are built into conceptions of gender. In single-sex groups such complementarity does not operate, and 'boisterous boys' become more boisterous. 'Quiet girls' do not seem to become even quieter in single-sex groups, but when the backbone of the hierarchical order of the class does not include more visible and audible interrelationships among boys, the relationships between girls become more focused and complex.

Though girls and boys describe themselves or others in a range of ways in other contexts, in discussions about the constitution of their classes, gender was demarcated. The student arguments construct a desire for balanced gender which is hierarchical in the proper direction: boys are in the majority, and they are clearly seen and heard to be so – as they most often are in mixed classes. Boys in a minority do not seem quite masculine enough – it is difficult for them to be 'proper' boys who assert their centrality. Not all boys want to adopt such positions. Leo, after his initial surprise and worry, liked his class despite the female majority. His memories of fierce battles among boys for a leading position in his class in the primary school were still fresh in his mind. Moreover, he had a central position in the class, acquired through being a reasonable, reliable, decent male in the official school.

The idea that the presence of girls is needed to tone down excesses of boisterous boys, and the presence of boys is needed to tone down the excesses of bickering girls, does not give a very happy picture of the relations between genders – or of relations amongst them. Girls are positioned precisely *as* girls, and boys are positioned precisely *as* boys. Their behaviours partly replicate, partly alter and repudiate these notions. But despite alterations and repudiations, it is the replication that is most often visible to them and to teachers, because of the strong social and cultural notions of gender balance. This balance rhetoric is powerful despite the fact that there are a great many social contexts where single-sex groups dominate – for example in many sectors of the labour market. Depressing in these discussions were ways in which girls described themselves using negative cultural constructs, like one of them who laughed when she thought about a female-only class: 'that would be a real flock of awful cackling hens'.

Girls together

Despite culturally constructed, materially scaffolded and psychologic-ally internalised yearning for a gender balance, girls mostly interact with each other, and boys mostly interact with each other in school. Nevertheless it seems that boys form the framework for many of the things that girls do, and girls form an audience for the boys.

There were tensions between our observations and what girls said in interviews (Gordon *et al.*, forthcoming 2000a). To an extent these tensions are visible in feminist research as well: on the one hand girls seem very supportive of each other, and on the other they seem capable of hurting each other a great deal. Our observations in schools indicated that the interaction among girls was important and helped them in the process of making spaces. Girls were usually (though not always) less salient in the classroom than boys; past experiences of controlling actions by teachers and restrictive behaviour by boys have contributed towards a more quiet demeanour among them.

Valerie Hey, in her study of girls' friendships, was interested in notes that girls wrote to each other. When she asked girls why they do that, they explained that 'if we say things out loud people will hear that we are having arguments and start picking on us' (Hey, 1997, p. 56). Girls may have had such harsh experiences that some of them fear boys; one girl explained that she and her friend burst out crying when they saw their new class with such boisterous boys.

> Anni is [my best friend in the class]. I cling onto her, because she has been with me since the first grade. And she's the only one from our class who has come [to this school]. So because of that I cling onto her, and she sometimes clings onto me.
>
> (Auli, FSH)

If girls have patterns of interaction amongst each other it is easier for them to find a place in the classroom which grants an acting position. Nelli's time at school is spent in two different teaching groups. In one of them the boys are boisterous and noisy, and the girls are quiet 'as in Saint Paul's church', to quote a description given by a boy earlier (Chapter 4). In the other one, Nelli explains, many students talk, and girls join in too. In the first one, as she does not know anyone well, she remains relatively quiet. In the other group, however

> as you talk with others ... then you shout out the answers to the

teacher as well at the same time ... if you know someone ... but if you are alone in the class then you end up saying nothing and you don't raise your hand.

(FSH)

Nelli refers to 'shouting out' answers. Our observations suggest that Nelli is not in the habit of 'shouting out'; she tends to put her hand up and wait to be given her turn to speak, although she will shout out occasionally if she needs help and the teacher does not notice her. But her choice of the phrase 'shouting out' indicates that Nelli has a sense of having a voice through supportive interaction among girls.

Sonja, who is in the same two teaching groups as Nelli, also gets frustrated by the boys. Sonja is a self-confessed 'bod' and hopes for more space for concentration. She argues that girls' quietness is partly a consequence of the control exerted by boys; if a girl says something out of turn, she is likely to be confronted with 'pointing fingers' (FSH). Nelli does challenge boys; though she talks about being quiet during the lessons, she is also assertive and 'answers back'. She concurs with this in the interview, but adds that, when you do talk back, you must harden yourself to hearing comments for about a fortnight afterwards.

In another teaching group where there are both noisy and quiet girls and boys, Henna acts a bit like boy soloists, but this position is not as easily available for her as for boys. Our observations indicate that teachers control her; when several students may be giggling and shouting out 'silly' answers, teachers may reprimand only Henna. Henna's voice is loud and 'girlish', and she sometimes gets on teachers' nerves. She challenges boys when they mess around, telling them to stop talking or throwing things around, and appealing to the teacher. Valerie Hey (1997) suggests that one assertive position open to a girl in the classroom is provided by the female teacher. Henna almost 'shadows' teachers when talking to boys. But direct challenge may be difficult; mostly her noisy complaints are supported by notions of professional pupilhood and school rules. In the interview Henna describes her class by referring to divisions between girls and boys. The interviewer asks her to say more:

HENNA: Manu and Pete and them, they always interfere with other people's business – you get lots of comments. It's as if you weren't allowed to say anything at all. You should just be quiet and not be yourself.

ELINA: Do you think it's particularly you who gets comments?

HENNA: That's it – not the others so much. You know, every time I open my mouth, I always get comments. As soon as I say something, I can hear 'jäkä, mäkä, mäkä' behind me. It's always like that: quiet!

ELINA: How do you feel about that?

HENNA: Sometimes it's really frustrating. I get really irritated when they always say something when I talk. You always get commented, you know, she's wearing childish clothes, she's a bit childish and so on.

(FSH)

The tense moments here reveal the vulnerability experienced by girls; they have learned to watch out for the boys who are successful in the informal school. Some girls have obtained a reputation of being 'hard'; they have crossed the threshold of 'ordinary girlhood', and have more space and leeway than 'ordinary' girls, for whom surveillance is not suspended to the same extent. But there are many ways in which gender relations are played out. Other enactments by girls, in relation to boys, are withdrawal, conformity and self-discipline, or challenge, resistance and physical self-defence, and include joining as audience or sometimes as participants.

Girls need each other's support – and often also get it. Although girls refer to boys who control them or at the very least cramp them by being so boisterous, interaction among girls can redress the balance. Girls are important for each other; if they are marginalised in the informal school, they can crawl from the margins through mutual support. We observed girls interacting in a supportive way. They move their desks together, hold hands, comb each other's hair, lean on each other, hug, write notes to each other, quietly make funny faces egging each other on, wave fingers, clap hands, hum tunes, whisper, giggle, talk, etc. Their interaction at times is very embodied: 'Pinja leans on Heini, with her head on her shoulder. Ida leans on Noora. And Jatta leans her elbow on Ida's shoulder' (ObsH).

Yet in the interviews, though girls do talk about their own friends, often divisions and conflicts among girls are emphasised, and it was striking to hear girls describing conflicts between groups of girls. Valerie Hey has found girls' friendships to be weighted with difficulties. Her argument is persuasive, but is not entirely applicable to our data (Gordon *et al.*, 2000a). She studied girls' friendships more broadly – we do so in the school context, where their support seems important at least in the arena of the classroom. Valerie Hey suggests that interrelationships among girls can cause them even more harm than control exerted on them by boys. Her focus was on the informal school, and her involvement with the girls with whom she interacted extended beyond the school. When we place the informal school in its entwined relation to the official school, girls' joint support seems crucial in helping them to make spaces. We are thus focusing on a whole range of interactional patterns among girls. Valerie Hey has also wished to redress the balance of research on girls and schooling; girls' interpersonal relations and ways in which they are positioned and position themselves in schools do not create a girl-friendly nirvana, nor oppositional heroines (1997, p. 126), and we concur with that. The marginal positionings that girls inhabit or the 'borderlands' which they visit and revisit, become more habitable places from which they can also escape when girls interact to develop mutual strength. But such positionings are also fraught and ambivalent; whilst making connection, they also talk about splits and divisions which are located in relations of difference among girls. Considerable emotion and desire is embedded in girls' interaction amongst each other (Hey, 1997; Kenway *et al.*, 1998).

Boys in crowds

We saw more collaboration among girls than among boys; but a common phrase among boys is that they are all friends:

> Well in my class I could say that – I won't say best mate, because best mate, or sort of best mates could be classified, but I don't want to use such an expression, but let's say some good types are, say (*he lists most of the boys in the class*) well I'll say that all the boys are OK but these were the nicest ones.
>
> (Santtu, MSH)

and that they collaborate:

> Yeah, we usually sit next to our friends and discuss with them and the people behind us and in front of us. If we get stuck they'll always help out – quite, it's nice that way, as a form.'
>
> (Tony, MSL)

Though boys tend to emphasise that they are all mates and move in crowds, in observations there are a lot of examples of boys controlling each other.

Boys can be amusing situation comics who interpret the mood of the students and communicate it to the teacher. They can cement teaching groups together, in opposition to the teacher; but also in connection with the teacher, including them in the humour. The jokers and the soloists can make everyday life at school more interesting; although also more exhausting. We got frustrated and tired with the noise made by (some) boys; or fumes caused by illicit experiments in chemistry lessons. Boys are constantly reformulating their hierarchies, partly through a display of physical prowess (cf. Kehily and Nayak, 1997).

Yet there are also many instances of joint masculinity, around hobbies for example – sport, music, computers, cars and motorbikes. Boys enlighten and inform each other about these issues. Some of the slapping, pushing and shoving is not so much a display of aggression, but a legitimate way for boys to make contact with each other and to touch each other. The need to be 'masculine' leads to inner censoring of legitimate ways of making contact. Boys who try to touch others without slapping them on the shoulder or tapping their heads face the risk of having their sexuality questioned.[5]

Sampsa describes complex patterns and shifts in the interaction among boys; his description captures several strands that were commonly used by boys in our interviews:

> Sometimes it's like, you know someone's irritated, someone's in a bad mood, and someone else on the other hand is in a good mood, and then some small thing comes up – something bad is said, then the other one says something bad. And then someone has to go in between, so that they won't start fighting. Then they make up, and tomorrow they'll be in a good mood. But if both of them are in a good mood, then it's sort of messing around. And if both of them are in a bad mood, it can be sort of peaceful.... Well, I don't know. Sort of on average I could say that it's fairly peaceful, me and my own mates.
>
> (MSH)

This description demonstrates the existence of a rather lively homosociality where, instead of crowds, the prototype for male interaction consists of two boys experiencing conflicting or corresponding moods.

Máirtín Mac an Ghaill (1994) suggests that dominant definitions of masculinity 'are affirmed within schools, where ideologies, discourses, representations and material practices systematically privilege boys and men' (p. 4), and a range of masculinities are contesting in this quest for dominance. R. W. Connell (1989) notes that social power is accessible to those boys who are academically successful. Such a boy may, like Peter Redman, find a solution in 'muscular intellectualness'; a way of taking and making space by 'pushing people around intellectually' rather than physically (Redman and Mac an Ghaill, 1997). Tarja Tolonen (1998b) argues that it is difficult for boys to step aside from the social order of violence, though they can develop different stances in relation to it. Those male students who are less successful in gaining recognised spaces in the official school do so by claiming other sources of power resorting to aggression, sports and (hetero)sexism (Connell, 1989).

Anoop Nayak and Mary Kehily (1997) suggest that the range of homophobic displays utilised by boys in schools are part of the process of negotiating coherent masculinity. They are also bound up with attempts to negotiate particular positions in the hierarchical order among boys. Sexual cultures are implicated in the shaping of relations of schooling. The intensity of the homophobic displays results, Nayak and Kehily suggest, from the fraught nature of gender and sexual relations within school, as well as from the uncertainties and vulnerabilities of boys.

Manu is a low achiever. His attendance record is reasonable; he does not get into conflict in lessons. He has sufficient social skills to occupy the place of a joker in his class. Other students either participate, gaze as a willing or reluctant audience, but are unwilling to risk intervening. Manu is joined by Pete who occupies a similar position. The interactive drama created by these two is a customary ingredient of most lessons they attend. Manu's and Pete's comments may dramatise the official school in a manner which positions them against the grain; but their comments may also produce a sense of shared hilarity among students and teachers; at times their humour rescues situations in which most are uncomfortable but no-one can find a way out.

But humour controls and orders others and constructs hierarchies of the informal school in ways which few dare to challenge. Manu's control of girls starts by ridiculing them in the official school. At times he participates in the teaching–learning dialogue by using a voice which is at the same time coy, shrill and timid, his sarcasm demonstrating the professional pupil as conformist, simplistic and female. The interviewer was surprised when an extremely well-behaved, quiet and conscientious girl with very high school achievement described classroom interaction and the position of Manu and Pete in it:

> They form sort of – if being funny is plus, and being quiet is minus,
> it would be plus–plus–plus ... when there's the combination of
> Manu, Pete and Jere. Fun is always assured.
>
> (Milla, FSH)

Tommi, a lively, boisterous boy who is also conscientious and keen
to achieve well, criticises Manu's and Pete's 'hardness'. Tommi's
masculinity is softer; his hair is long, he wants to be considerate, he
does not like processes in school where students control and 'oppress'
each other. Tommi is steering a course in the official and the informal
school, trying to be successful in both; in the interview his desire to
achieve well at school is emphasised more than his interest in proving
himself in the informal school. Tommi was likely to be searching for
'muscular intellectualism' referred to above. He had already partly
achieved this position through his responsibilities for the use of information technology in the school. Heikki is critical of control asserted
by boys for whom 'having a go at each other is almost a way of life'
(MSH). He addresses the gendered and sexual nature of that control.
'Some boys like Jere have a go at girls on the basis of what they look
like – and he's no model himself, so I don't know why he criticises the
way girls look. I don't know. Perhaps he wants to show that "I'm
hard", "I'm having a go at a girl".'

Henna challenged Manu and Pete, and criticised them; she felt they
in particular administered the kind of control with which she was
frustrated; she felt that she had too little space to assert herself. We
have already discussed ways in which Henna challenges the control. A
further dimension of this control is its gendered and heterosexual
nature. Pirkko Hynninen (1998) uses an example where Henna is
repeatedly silenced in a way that sexualises her as an object of male
gaze and assessment.

When wild, boisterous boys draw the attention of the teacher (and
often of the researcher too – Chapter 8), girls remain marginalised. But
because of the assumption of balance, there is nevertheless clear
awareness that there are girls in the classroom. It may escape both
teachers and observers that there are also quiet boys in the class, and
these boys are marginalised too. References to 'all' the boys doing this,
or 'all' the boys behaving like that render the quiet boys entirely invisible, which suits some of them. A few of the quiet boys in our study
achieved rather well in school. They were interested in computers,
and seemed to inhabit a world of their own, and a couple of them used
chains of computing codes when they answered questionnaires

administered by researchers. They seemed to be making margins their centre, whilst assuming credibility in the official school through their achievement, not through a visibly, audibly active participation in classroom interaction. They protected their own space, and a quiet group of boys in one class did not want to be interviewed, and usually avoided contact with the researchers.

These quiet boys are not homogeneous, and some of them have a range of social and cultural resources to draw upon. They may be stepping aside from particular forms of masculinity, but utilising or inventing others; so their marginalisation in the audible and visible interaction of the classroom does not render them powerless. But some quiet boys are teased, bullied and victimised; their marginal places can be extremely lonely and painful.

There have been extensive debates about a crisis of masculinity in education and about problems of boys in schools, and these debates need to be critically addressed. Jane Kenway (1995c) suggests that, though generally men are in a superior structural relationship to women, 'there is also no doubt that for certain men this is not the way it feels' (p. 77). A problem with the crisis debate is that too often the culprits are supposed to be women teachers or female students (cf. Gordon, 1992). However, problems are also caused by battles within hierarchical masculinities where some boys can draw on the resources offered by the official school (to the detriment of their status in the informal school), some can draw on the resources offered by the informal school (often to the detriment of their status in the official school) and (a small group of) boys can construct their position in the physical school through control of space and embodiment. The last group of boys may be steering their own course, using violence or the threat of it, but their position is usually weak in the official and in the informal school; other students may not challenge them, but nor do they respect or socialise with them enthusiastically, except when expedient (cf. Tolonen, 1998a). When boys experience insecurity in their masculinity, they are likely to 'lash back' (Kenway and Fitzclarence, 1997).

We have focused on 'girls together' and 'boys in crowds'; though we have disentangled the idea of homogeneous gender groups, differentiating between them nevertheless reproduces complementary heterosexuality. In this context gays and lesbians remain invisible in schools, whilst homophobia is visibly performed and portrayed, as Anoop Nayak and Mary Kehily (1997) have observed. Debbie Epstein (1997) suggests that the 'dual Others to normative heterosexual masculinities in schools are girls/women and non-macho boys/men' (p. 113). Questioning the heterosexuality of boys in particular is a daily occurrence in schools; this questioning is done by girls as well as boys (Lehtonen, 1998). We return to it below when we address teasing, bullying and name-calling.

Anxiety and pleasure

Jane Kenway and Lindsay Fitzclarence (1997) suggest that 'emotional neutrality' and 'hyper-rationality' are core values structuring schooling. Schools are often described as boring places that do not touch the concerns of young people; teachers stress the importance of industriousness, and application in the official business of teaching and learning is to be learned through perseverance and determination. Learning experiences in other places and situations are thought to be increasingly important, and particularly in secondary education routine processes are thought to pass students by (Aittola *et al.*, 1995). Time spent in school generates a range of complex, diverse social situations for students (and teachers) to deal with in which powerful, varied emotions are triggered. When the steps have been learned – or when they are so difficult that they seem impossible to learn – boredom can set in; a boredom which at times seems to know no bounds in the strength of feeling it generates. When the steps do not work out, or when others seem to be taking up all the space and only tight corners are available, and collisions are a constant threat, then incredibly strong anxiety, pain and fear are experienced by some. On the other hand, when the tempo and steps have been learned, the dancing is smooth and the rest of the body takes over increasingly from the head, the enjoyment can be considerable. When in unison with one or more others new, imaginative steps are generated, the pleasure can be immense. If students experience heterosexually constructed desire, the excitement of contact can be thrilling. If that desire is same-sex instead, the necessity of hiding one's feelings can be devastating.

Jenny Shaw (1996) suggests that anxiety-making situations are an integral part of the social technology of teaching. Marking, testing, examinations and grading all produce fears, nervousness and disappointments – as well as pleasure and a sense of accomplishment for students who have good results. We have argued that the dual tasks of education are maintenance and regulation, as well as social change and emancipation – these are constitutive of praxis in schools, and discernible in tensions between control and agency. Unconscious processes, psychological configurations and emotions are involved in the exercise of agency; these are manifest in different ways of exercising agency and in the fear and anxiety, as well as pleasure and enjoyment, of being agentic.

Students used references to emotional states or language evoking emotions extensively. They talked about torture, nervousness, fear, horror, loathing, disgust, bitterness, uncertainty, spite, anger, panic, shock, sadness, being scared, shame, envy, self-pity; many negative emotions were used to refer to school, teaching, teachers and other students. Fewer emotional words were used to describe positive experiences and sensations. Students do talk about wonderful teachers, wonderful subjects, wonderful friends, excitement, pleasure, but less so. A sense of very strong affiliations and of dislikes and uncertainties emerges. Students in our study are at an age where they are still children, not quite children any more, and not yet young adults. They are to be responsible, well behaved, capable of using initiative, but also obedient, flexible and patient. In the course of their daily lives at school students experience contradictions as professional pupils. Auli's (FSH) experience is that pleasure is something that you pay for: 'Well I have this principle that I enjoy myself now and then I'll suffer. Although I know that the suffering will be really appropriate.' She explains further: 'Sometimes it may be that I'll be a bit boisterous and the teacher really gets mad. And then it's really dramatic. Or I'll give a wrong answer and then it starts, everybody's giggling and the teacher stares and everybody waits. It's awful if you don't know.'

The possibility of not knowing, and exposing yourself, is something that particularly girls say they fear. It is likely that this fear is shared by some boys, but they did not express it in the same way. There are girls who enjoy attention, who enjoy performing, and who thrive in such situations. But many girls expressed a very strong sense of anxiety about having to be the focus of attention in the classroom. 'You can really see when I'm nervous, because my hands shake, my knees shake and my face gets red and my ears get red, and I feel as if I'm boiling' (Lotta, FSH).

Generally their talk contained fewer references to emotions. Transfer to the secondary school made some of them nervous; in this context fear of 'initial harassment' of newcomers was expressed, and name-calling, teasing and bullying continued to upset some boys. Otherwise they expressed irritation, disappointments, reluctance; there were occasions when some teachers were awful, scary, argumentative, etc.

Boredom was often part of the vocabulary when talking about the official school. Arguments were often mentioned when interaction among students, and particularly among boys, was discussed.

Many of the fears and anxieties experienced by students are initiated outside school, at home, by friends, by strangers who abuse and harass in the streets, by concerns about pollution, war and injustice. Generally it seems that students have to get used to the possibility of ridicule; whilst this causes sadness, the best strategy, as we were told repeatedly, was to learn to laugh at ridicule.

Paul Corrigan (1987) suggests that schools do not just teach subjects, they make subjectivities. Pain, fear, anxiety, laughter and pleasure are involved in these processes. Mary Kehily and Anoop Nayak (1997) argue that pedagogic practice must be sensitive to students' cultures and to the power in social relations; these are played out between groups, within groups and in individual psyches. Any attempts to change pedagogic practice will interfere with psychological patterns, although this often remains unacknowledged; there are exceptions, such as Jane Kenway's and colleagues' (1998) work on the effects of feminist practices in schools on girls. It is necessary, they suggest, to acknowledge the heterogeneity of girls. They have differing social and cultural stakes in education, and also differing investments in it – and differing access to subject positions.

Pleasure and enjoyment

Books on education rarely discuss pleasure. Pleasure is a complex notion involving the possibility of pain; it is always potentially transformative, and therefore unsafe. Pleasure is often connected to sexuality. What you feel and what you desire are as important as what you know.[6] Desire can be defined in many ways, and an important strand in definitions refers to yearning that eludes fulfilment. If one desires pleasure, this yearning is risky, as the goal seems unattainable. Girls often have high expectations of education, because they want to construct autonomous adult lives, and their observations of women around them might suggest that such an undertaking is not easy. Education is one avenue which potentially opens a path towards satisfying adulthood. Girls desire education, as well as desiring *in* education. In this situation playing safe is a sensible, though potentially a fraught, position to adopt.

It is easier for girls to adopt a quiet demeanour, and have fun when there is a protective group of girls around them. We often observed girls huddled together during lessons, talking quietly, whispering, perhaps letting out an occasional guarded shriek or a peal of laughter. Often they are getting on with their work and make sure they follow teaching sufficiently to be able to perform in the official school. They might do so even though they are bored, and they can adopt humour as an aid to deal with this boredom. Subtle irony used by quiet girls sometimes surprised us in the interviews; Auli was asked what she does not like in school:

> When we write about fish. I hate that above everything else. We had fish stuff in biology last autumn. We had to identify perch, pike – everything, and even what they eat, sort of. That's really – hmm – clammy! And now we have that again in biology. [Interviewer: You mean fish?] Yes. I got salmon for my enjoyment now.
>
> (FSH)

The wry turn of phrase suggests participation and detachment at the same time. Auli does not wish to get into trouble. She gets her fun playing safe. When she talks about what she likes in school, she refers to 'teasing' teachers who do not teach her; hence they do not know her, and she is fairly safe from disciplinary action as she is careful not to overstep the mark. Fun is achieved by girls in their interaction amongst each other. They may reminisce about previous incidents and accidents; laughing at events in the past renders them safe and cements cooperation and togetherness.

The vocabulary used by boys tended to be different, and those students who used a narrow repertoire of emotions tended to be boys. Emotions mobilised when talking about interaction among boys were embedded in discussions about fun, laughter and jokes. Boys value being 'relaxed' as a quality of a good teacher, a good friend, and good interaction between teachers and students, or among students (cf. Tolonen, 1998b). Not being relaxed conveys possibilities of fear and tensions, and indirectly boys' talk raised the spectre of fear and humiliation, which could be warded off through humour and a relaxed demeanour. Humour is also a device used to cement contact with others, but at the same time it is a way of making difference, or 'whipping others into shape' (Woods, 1990, p. 195). Name-calling, cussing, teasing and bullying are important in the process of 'becoming somebody' and making a space for oneself. Through ritualistic moves some students cement their own centrality, or safety at the very least, whilst others strive to ward off marginalisation.

In London incidents where (hetero)sexual desire and apparent pleasure did appear to be being realised were observed. One example was a young couple (older than our observation group) locked in embrace lying on the playing field, whilst numerous sporting and other activities took place around them. A surprised researcher asked a teacher she was interviewing at the time if that was usual, or even permitted. The teacher shrugged and said 'That's nothing to what they get up to on school trips.' In another instance a young man and woman in our age group were in close physical contact, touching and stroking each other throughout a lesson. But such open expressions of heterosexual desire and activity were rare, despite the constant presence of sexuality, its construction and policing in school, and the existence of heterosexual (and possibly other) relationships amongst the young people.

Linda Christian-Smith (1993) suggests that pleasure, especially female pleasure, can be inherently disruptive in schools. The prototype of pleasure is sexuality, but pleasure is not only and always sexual. Pleasure is easily equated with disruption; it seems to open up spaces for freedom and authenticity. Nevertheless pleasure, too, is socially constructed. Pleasures can provide disappointments and dangers or be productive and an expression of desire.

Every game you play: naming, teasing, cussing and bullying

The official school contains a range of hierarchical relations (Chapter 5). In these hierarchies teachers and other representatives of the official school establish the framework and set the steps and the tempo. In the informal school students are active in hierarchical differentiation. For some students the official school is a place of safety, and its tempo and steps easier; for others the tempo and steps can be too much, and alternative modes of dancing seem safer. Some withdraw to the margins of the dance – or are pushed there by more energetic and aggressive dancers. Control exerted by teachers structures hierarchies in schools, but students, in their own interaction, also construct differences and contribute to the marginalisation of some students. These patterns of interaction are fluid and shifting, often ambivalent, and in complex interaction with the official school. Potential marginalisation is a threat experienced by many students. Although a small minority may occupy marginal places consistently, margins are a constant presence as potential positions and locations to be avoided at all costs for a large majority. Marginalisation is a process which affects social relations in schools well beyond the marginalised minority.

Teasing, naming, cussing and bullying were methods used to position and marginalise the 'other'.[7] Responses to questions about these activities in school varied in the interviews, but ambivalence (about the meaning of teasing; joking or serious, fun or hurtful) and denial (often with a gradual admission of participation) were high on the list. Henna's comment captures some of this feeling: 'it really doesn't feel nice, but I know they don't really mean it when they say it, and then you don't care about it, but it does feel miserable sometimes, but then they get back enough of the same' (FSH). Students were often loth to admit that outright violent bullying was taking place, particularly in their class, or even school:

MAYA: Yeah there's quite, there's probably quite a bit of bullying but I don't think there's anything in this school that's really, really serious. Apart from name calling, I don't think there's violence or anything.

JANET: What sort of name calling goes on do you think?

MAYA: It's just that if there's someone in the class who's different from the rest and they, they have sort of different look to things and always, they're sort of into different things that most people aren't into, they seem, it's like, they sort of take the mick out of those sort of things. But I find, I haven't seen anything really, really violent.... The only things that I've seen that are violent are out of school. Either people from other schools, like bullying some of the people in our school when they see our tie.

(Maya, FSL)

A boy saw quite a lot of bullying, and offers explanations, including noting the similarity of identity and experience between potential bully and potential victim:

KAY: And why do you think people do it?

MAHMOOD: It's 'cause they're lost inside, they haven't got anyone to speak to about their own problems at home or, and around, and that's probably why, and that's, those people can also be victims of it, because of their past life and everything.

KAY: Um, and how about in your own class, is there any teasing or bullying there?

MAHMOOD: Well, I was like sort of er there's this girl, she's like sort of everyone was bullying her, I mean just teasing her, calling her names, but we all, we all thought that we were doing it for a joke, but I didn't exactly do it 'cause I like, I really liked her, and er then she went and told Ms Fraser.

KAY: Um hum.

MAHMOOD: Yeh, but I still, I, I am admitting that I did tease her as well, but I didn't mean it.

KAY: Yeh, it's sometimes quite hard isn't it?

MAHMOOD: Yeh, just trying to fit in, 'cause most people just do it to fit in with their friends and everything, that's the main reasons.

KAY: So what sort of names, I mean you don't have to say who it was, but what sort of names were you calling her?

MAHMOOD: Um, calling her a silly cow and everything, and all this stuff, and we were calling her a slapper and everything, and we like, I mean she was like laughing along with us but I don't think she could, she couldn't hack it after a while, so she just went and told.

(MSL)

Here a boy talks about physical bullying by a group:

PETE: I don't think there's a lot of bullying here. Well every now and then we torture one boy, him we always torture ... it's usually nothing, he just continues to irritate us.

TUULA: If you say you torture him, how does he experience it?

PETE: Well he just laughs and he doesn't get mad, but we get mad at him quickly.

TUULA: You mean sometimes when you do it you are angry, it's not just a joke or ...

PETE: Yes, but he doesn't understand it.

TUULA: How do you torture him?

PETE: I don't know, we put him against the wall or hold him down on the ground under our feet or have our knees on his stomach or something like that.

Students try to protect themselves in many ways. Banding together and moving in crowds, constructing a 'protective layer' around them (Woods, 1990) can offer safety. Many students are on guard, and produce quick retorts if they are subject to verbal abuse. Lasse says that 'generally it's like, if someone calls you names, you call them back immediately'. Although Marjaana says that one should learn not to tease others, knowing how awful it feels, but 'sometimes you end up saying something without thinking, before you think whether it's going to irritate' (FSH). The immediacy of the reactions is nevertheless considered an important form of self-protection.

The dangers of submitting to teasing are clear to students, and one way of handling it is to treat it like a game, thus rendering it safer. In one London school, cussing was interpreted in many ways, one of which was to see it as a form of entertainment: 'I was at an interesting cussing contest. If someone cusses well it's really cool to watch. It's boring when people say the same things when cussing' (Mandy, FSL). Another student said 'Cussing is a joke, but when people cuss others' mothers, fathers, sisters and grandparents about living in dustbins, I think this is nasty and serious' (Robert, MSL). Teasing and name calling can be fun if you are strong and on the winning side.

A variety of reasons for selection for teasing, bullying and cussing were offered, but in general insults were based on difference. You could be for example untidy, lonely, fat, quiet, a pervert, wear glasses, have odd hair, have odd ears and so on. Boys who are considered effeminate are called gay by other boys and by girls; girls who are assertive are called whores by boys; girls popular among boys are called whores by other girls. Teasing of students from ethnic minorities is recounted by many; they have observed teasing and cussing, have been teased themselves, or have themselves been teasers. In one school students had made complaints that they had been cussed on the grounds of ethnic difference, which were taken up by the school. Difference is potentially dangerous; particularly in Helsinki schools students felt that sameness provided safety. In the official school being 'average' was a safe position to be in. In the informal school being 'same as others' provided protection.

MARI: If we sometimes tease someone, s/he'll think it's bullying and submits to it. At least in my opinion there are some people here who think they are victims of bullying and interpret it always in a different way. I think those people are quite irritating, really.

TUULA: But aren't people different?

MARI: Yes, they are. And of course that's good. It would be awful if everyone was the same, but of course there is some sameness in all of us; perhaps it turns out differently when we don't like somebody, so they are always more different than the ones we like more.

(FSH)

One's own group is an important protection, and constructions of desirability of sameness and difference are shifting and fluid; my difference, in alliance with my friends, is positive; your difference, as something distinct from me, is negative. As Valerie Hey (1997) suggests, the badness in oneself is projected onto others and thus safely purged. Shifting, complex alliances are formed, and when someone is being teased, others often join in for their own safety or to remain part of the group; one does not occupy the place of a teaser and the teased simultaneously.

> I mean the main thing is that you don't get teased yourself. You need to belong in the group that teases. Then you don't spend any time with people who are teased, so that you wouldn't be teased yourself.
>
> (Riina, FSH)

A way of dealing with conflicts about hierarchy is to join in in the bullying of someone. In this process the cooperation of the group is cemented at the expense of who is marginalised – and what is marginalised in that process. A student observed that every class has someone who is a 'punch ball'; upon the surface of that, alliances and places of personal safety are formed.

Boys suggest that there is more teasing and bullying among them, and their practices involve more physical action and aggression. Teasing among girls is considered to be largely verbal, but often meaner and more harmful. Though patterns of teasing are complex, and alliances shift, among girls, among boys, and between girls and boys, this notion of the spitefulness of girls is quite strong. Yet boys do recount bitter experiences. The small proportion of students who are subjected to constant, relentless teasing, suffer a great deal; being at school, sleeping at night, going to school in the morning are all difficult. In everyday life at school what is most important is the identification of those who are seriously teased or bullied and, on a more general level, addressing patterns of differentiation through everyday practices of ridicule.

Girls were called whores/slags often by boys, but also by other girls. The potency of this naming was partly its arbitrariness. In the corridors any girl might be called a whore by a boy unknown to her: 'move over, whore'; in these situations 'whore' was used as almost a generic equivalent of a 'girl'. Girls were called whores/slags by boys in situations where boys wanted to exert their hierarchical supremacy; it was a way of trying to ensure that girls occupied appropriate positions in gender relations, and of reiterating and reinforcing sexual difference. This naming was also used in order to challenge girls' sexual behaviour, but among the age group in our study this was less likely.

Girls found this name-calling hurtful, but also puzzling. As their bodies were growing and changing, increasing sexualised name-calling was entwined with wondering about what kind of 'woman' one was becoming. Explicitly sexual name-calling was often said to take place outside school, by older boys and men.

> I mean it's peculiar. If some man comes and says to someone our age, 'hey, let's go and have some fun' and when you don't go, and say no thank you, I'm not going, I'm not going, then they start shouting fucking whore. I mean how is it – how are you a whore when you don't go. I mean I would have thought you were if you did go.
>
> (Asta, FSH)

When young girls are called whores by boys in school, a continuum is established between them and the adult males girls encounter outside the school. Whilst girls often say that 'whore' does not mean anything specific, its sexual nature is nevertheless not forgotten. A majority of girls at this age are not sexually active in relationships; negative references to female sexuality serve to construct appropriate femininity. Sue Lees (1986) suggests that girls are channelled towards having established boyfriends in this way; their agency is curtailed. Girls also called other girls whores, especially those who were popular among boys; in this way appropriate femininity was policed among them.

Many girls gave examples of challenging those who call them whores. One girl, a member of an informal mixed-sex group which gathered together to smoke during breaks, had been called a whore several times, and repeatedly by one particular boy. She explains that she had warned him and would kick him if he would repeat his onslaught: 'I didn't mean to kick him in the head, but he went on and on so accidentally, as I was so irritated with him, accidentally I kicked him in his stomach' (FSH). A boy who is a member of the same group said in the interview that naming was not taken seriously. When he was specifically asked what girls think about being called whores, he admitted that 'some of them can take it a bit – they may come and kick you, or get angry a bit' (MSH).

Boys called others 'homos' or 'queers'. Either these were boys considered to be effeminate, or boys who came too close, who were thought to be different in some way, and whose masculinity was questioned. In interviews boys repeatedly said that sexual naming among boys did not really mean anything, and was not taken seriously. In particular they suggested that naming someone 'homo' or 'queer' did not amount to a suggestion that they were homosexuals; it was a term of generalised insult. But this name-calling, of course, is nevertheless an effective form of policing of boundaries of heterosexuality, and marginalises those boys who are not heterosexual, and they have to live between the dangers of visibility and the painful safety of invisibility (Lehtonen, 1998). By naming women and gays as others, boys expel femininity and homosexuality from within themselves (Mac an Ghaill, 1994). Misogyny and homophobia are clearly linked: 'the dual Others to normative heterosexual masculinities in schools are girls/women and non-macho boys/men' (Epstein, 1997, p. 113). Defining some males as weak consolidates the power of other males, displacing fears and anxieties onto others is a way of protecting one's own fragility (Nayak and Kehily, 1997).

Girls also called boys 'homos' and 'queers'. Generally they explained that this was a form of self-protection. A large number of girls in one class joined together to tease and bully one of the boys; they stared at him, laughed at him, called him 'queer'. Whilst many students disapproved, others said that the boy concerned was a 'pervert' who came too close to girls, touched them inappropriately and brought sexually explicit material to school. We had not seen the incidents to which the girls referred, but did observe the teasing. The teased boy was quiet, withdrawn and shy. It appeared that in this situation a group of girls joined together to assert their unity in tackling male intrusion, but we did not observe incidents where girls constructed such concerted effort round the sexism of more powerful, masculine boys.

The invocation of 'race', gender and sexuality in name-calling/bullying is carefully coded and can be seen as linked to the practices we have discussed in this chapter: negotiation of the informal school, making and breaking friendships, producing versions of masculinity and femininity and resisting adult/teacher perspectives on acceptable behaviour.

Conclusions

Stepping out in the informal school can involve pleasure and pain. Power relations are played out not only in the official school, but within and between groups and individuals in the student cultures of the informal school. Sameness, difference and appropriate normality are constructed, and steps involved overlap, diverge from, move in parallel or opposition to those of the official school. Gender, ethnicity, class and sexuality are implicated in these power plays, and other distinctions which may appear marginal but are possibly central to these basic divisions, are deployed.

Despite a description of the school as 'the desert of the emotions' powerful emotions surge through the relationships of the informal school. The perception of difference and the construction of power hierarchies are crucial in the dance of the informal school, and we have discussed the major mechanism through which these elements operate: teasing or bullying.

There is a striking amount of variation in students' responses when they are asked about teasing and bullying in the school. There are differences in the patterns of naming, teasing and bullying in all of the schools. In both London and Helsinki, in the more local, more working-class school, teasing and bullying is more visible. Teachers do deal with teasing, but their interpretations about what is teasing are broader. In the more middle-class schools where students come from a range of schools besides the local catchment area, teachers are quicker to tackle naming and teasing. Variation within each school is considerable; some students suggest that they never see any teasing and bullying in their school; others say there is a great deal of it. Teasing and bullying can be interpreted in different ways. Some students evidently think about physical aggression, when they say there is very little teasing. Some think about their primary schools, where they have experienced more (or less) student strife. Some are in a powerful, privileged position of not being teased. Some have built protective bubbles round themselves, through secure friendship groups and staying out of trouble. What is the same in all schools is that patterns of teasing are influential in processes of differentiation.

Students' sense of school is largely formed in the informal school in an unwieldy process which most of the time has no particular place to be. The informal movement spreads all over the official steps, but usually intensifies when students move further from the most officially designated places. We continue this exploration in the next chapter.

7
'Strictly Ballroom': the Physical School and Space

Defining space

When the dance is due to begin, the participants are encouraged to arrive punctually and in an orderly manner into the large complex of dance venues. Different steps are practised in different places – break-dancing in the yard, hip-hop in the corridors, and in the various smaller rooms the dancers follow an assigned route from waltz instruction to fox-trot, ballet, mazurka, tango, samba. Some dancers occupy the centre-stage, some take up a lot of space, whilst others dance in the sidelines and the 'wallflowers' watch in the margins. On festive occasions the dancers gather in the hall where performances are laid on.

'Space' and spatiality of social life have been taken for granted. Often space is used in a metaphoric rather than in an analytical way; spatial concepts have been employed to focus analysis on social relations, whilst space itself has remained unexplored (Smith and Katz, 1993). But interest in space has recently increased, particularly in the interstices of human geography, sociology, anthropology, cultural studies, feminist research and lesbian and gay studies. In this vogue space has been understood and defined in a number of ways. We define space as physical, social and mental (Chapter 1).

In the physical school our interest is in space and spatiality as well as bodies and embodiment. We explore space at an institutional level as pedagogies embodied in school buildings and as social organisation of physical space in its possibilities and limitations. We ask how distance and hierarchy are embedded in the social use of space. We trace the micropolitics of space and organisation of control and opportunities for agency by charting time–space paths, their institutionalisation, informalisation and control and agency related to them. Spatial metaphors tend to indicate lack of autonomy experienced by students in schools – but students can hide and escape their limited autonomy in flights of the mind, enacting in the mental, as well as the physical and social space.

Decisions about the use of space include decisions about location and movement of bodies in school; thus schools have a curriculum of the body, as Nancy Lesko (1988) suggests, but also a pedagogy of the body. Students are positioned in multiple ways in schools; these positions are enacted in space, and spatiality is implicated in social, cultural and interpersonal processes of contact, cooperation, differentiation and marginalisation. Gender as well as other social differences are so enduring (though not unchanging), because they are not merely abstract social relations, but played out by bodies in space too. We continue the exploration of movement and stillness and the sound and silence of bodies in Chapter 8.

Spaces limit and shape what is being done in them, as well as being shaped by it, in social and mental processes. We refer to these processes as *spatial praxis*. We understand such praxis as action and practice which can be habitual, but may also be reflective and creative. We act in space, but are more likely to be aware of the action than its location. The school's routinised, organisational framework, embodied in school rules and timetables, is also an arena for enactment, creative ritualisation or redefinition as well as of habituation. In spatial praxis, organisationally defined space is surveyed and regulated, but this control is also negotiated, challenged, ignored or reinvented in bids for autonomy and independence. The ebbing and flowing of routinisation/control and enactment/agency raise questions of differentiation, power and resistance.

Setting the scene: school buildings

School buildings form a physical, built backdrop to the teaching and learning. The buildings embody pedagogical principles and assumptions about ways in which teaching and learning is organised, and about the relationship of the school to its surroundings. For example Victorian school buildings incorporated a hierarchical concept of teaching and learning, and symbolised the separation between school and society. There is a clear demarcation between the area of the school and the outside, with the playground as an intermediary space. The buildings and their layout are rigid, and pose limitations for the

type of activities that can take place. In contrast modern school buildings blend into their environment in a smoother way, and their
internal layout aims to provide more possibilities.

While the school building is usually a physical 'given', building
works have created contrastive spaces in our research schools. During
rebuilding, spaces – classrooms, halls, the library, the gymnasium –
have been reassigned functions; corridors become narrower, parts of
the school expand outwards, eating up outer space, and parts are in-
accessible while building takes place, shrouded, and boarded. These
disruptive changes in the structure of the school offer new opportunities for student resistance, place new demands of control and
discipline on the staff, and construct different relationships between
teachers, students and the physical space. Such different relationships
and practices contribute to a reconstruction of the social space of the
school.

Although schools contain a range of different types of places, when
thinking about school we often visualise classrooms; classrooms
symbolise schools as embodiment of pedagogic practice. Conceptions
about what 'school' as an institution is, assume visible representation
in school buildings. We explore what a 'school' looks like by
discussing the four schools in our ethnographic study, whilst also
making references to other schools in which we have collected data
(including schools in California).

Physical space in schools is not simply 'already there'. It is a social
construction embodying current pedagogic thinking and assumptions
about hierarchy and distance. However, for the teachers, administration, other staff and school students using the building it is 'already
there', presenting 'an appearance of stability and persistence' (Soja,
1985, p. 94). The school is a physical entity which enters into the
activities and processes of those located in school. In these activities
and processes the physical space becomes social space, shaped by
spatial praxis (cf. Soja, 1985). Nevertheless these processes are taken
for granted, and hence difficult to analyse. The buildings of our
research schools in Helsinki are about 100 and 10 years old, respect-
ively. The older school, City Park, is clearly delineated. The borders of
the school yard are formed by the nearby houses. The school is several
stories high. Green Park blends into its environment in the suburb
with less distinguished borders. The school yard continues smoothly
into a park. Green Park is also more horizontal than City Park, less
imposing.

Green Park is built with light-coloured materials and the corridors are light with many windows, as a contrast to the darker but wider corridors in City Park. The narrower corridors are not accidental or incidental. Green Park was built during the beginning of a recession in Finland; a new school building was needed because existing schools were unable to cater for the expanding local population. The planning process was one of rational calculation, and clear guidelines for building were given by the National Board of Education with tight cost control.[1] In rational planning the aim was to maximise efficiency and to waste no space.

The school is already too small to cater for all the local students who wish to attend; the planning was not so rational after all. There are not enough classrooms, some classrooms are crowded, and the ventilation is insufficient. There are few flexible areas in the school, and when a small room was needed for some extra teaching in small groups, a cleaning cupboard had to be converted. In the older City Park there has been more scope for renovation. For example the textile area has been enlarged, and areas in the basement and attic have been reconstructed to enable new and different uses. This has helped to develop more flexible organisation and small-group work, particularly in arts. But City Park, like Green Park, is not able to admit all of the students who would like to come there.

The research schools in London provide a similar contrast; one is very old, and one relatively new. The main building of the newer school, Oak Grove, is 30 years old. But in an expanding school a second, new building was recently finished. The new building can be accessed from the old, and is lighter and brighter, like Green Park. Our oldest school, Woburn Hill, has an old, dark, elongated building. As in City Park, additional building work has taken place over the years. During the research period ancient laboratories and workrooms were being reconstructed and modernised.

As we have said, school buildings embody notions of pedagogy; space is an important constituent of teaching and learning in schools. Although changes in pedagogic practices have been somewhat slower in Finland, and teaching and learning is more teacher-centred than in Britain (Chapter 5), new pedagogic thinking is embodied in Green Park in more extensive storage space and facilitation of the use of a broader range of teaching aids such as audiovisual equipment. Green Park has also more specialised classrooms, for example in computer teaching. City Park was more clearly built for chalk-and-talk type of teaching, though through renovation much more flexibility has been added.

In Oak Grove the two buildings stand in contrast to each other, and to styles of pedagogy and the construction of the student. The old, has long, low and relatively dark corridors, and classrooms furnished and organised in a traditional style, with tables and chairs for the pupils in rows or blocks, largely facing the teacher's desk at the front. The new, brighter and lighter, has a central spacious classroom encircled by a corridor, with further classrooms on the rim of the building echoing the panopticon (Foucault, 1977). The classrooms are activity rooms, for technology (which includes cooking), computer work, dance, music and art. In Woburn Hill these two styles intermingled. Many of the original Victorian classrooms were small and cramped, crowded with old wooden desks and constraining movement; the newer additions and reconstructions were lighter, brighter and more spacious, often containing expensive specialist furniture and equipment.

In terms of the day-to-day life of students, an important shift was the provision of several (individual) toilets for students in our newest school. Individualised toilets provided students more autonomy. In metaphor questionnaires toilets appeared as disliked places. Some students avoided going to toilets altogether in some schools, because they smelled, were messed up, and people smoked in them. This is a severe daily restriction of embodied agency. Individualised toilets were never mentioned as disliked places. Because of increasing individualisation, however, some students have lost an important informal social space where social hierarchies were played out and tested to their advantage, whilst for other students toilets could be truly harrowing places (Lehtonen, 1998).

In Green Park lockers are provided for students, thus giving them a modicum of their own space, and facilitating their movement round the school, unencumbered by their bags and coats, which students in City Park had to carry with them at all times during our main research year. The height of the building with five floors makes the carrying of the bags heavy, and students were delighted when, recently, they were provided with lockers. In Oak Grove, although lockers are provided for students, and are used for storage of some items at some times in the day, it is usual for them to carry bags and wear outer clothing as they move around the school. In Woburn Hill lockers were provided as you moved further up the school, and in the year we were following, some had lockers and some desks in which they could store books and papers. The cloakrooms, for outer clothing and bulkier items, were locked at times, often causing inconvenience to students.

Generally walls, floors, desks and textiles in all the schools were of neutral colours. This was particularly pronounced in classrooms, indicating that activities should be functional, purposeful and of the mind. Teachers themselves often decorated classrooms, some more than others. Generally newer classrooms tended to be neater and tidier. In older schools, with less storage space, side-tables and cupboards could be filled with papers, books and equipment. In the most student-centred school we observed, in California, classrooms were brimming with materials to be used in different projects by students. In Green Park, where textiles, flooring and desks were colour coordinated, least decoration was done by teachers. Whilst the lightness and colour coordination made further decoration less necessary; rational planning also discouraged use of plants and other paraphernalia. In contrast, many plants and objects were placed on City Park's wide windowsills. Paul Corrigan (1987) suggests that school 'names, flags, boards, notifications, and similar paraphernalia.... are part of the general naming of school space as different' (p. 25). Whilst this is the case, other paraphernalia in the classrooms is part of an informalisation of the official: naming of continuities as well as differences. One of the continuities is of gender relations; in many schools there are far more representations of men. Representations also depict white, able-bodied adults. In California schools there were resolutely multicultural pictures and murals, but women remained in the minority.

Different school buildings and classrooms embodying particular notions of pedagogy also promote diverse possibilities for teachers' control. A raised area for the teacher's table still existed in some classrooms in City Park; this displays hierarchy and gives teachers a better view of the whole classroom. The classrooms in Green Park were concise and ordered, and thus easily surveyed by teachers. In Oak Grove, in the new building in the activity classrooms, spaces were such that the students could move around, using the modern and specialised equipment as appropriate to the tasks of the particular lessons, although always under the controlling gaze of the teacher, and with some spaces forbidden to them – typically where supplies are stored and kept. In Woburn Hill new reconstructions provided more space, and more movement was possible, particularly in activity-based lessons, but again still under the control and surveillance from the teachers.

Schools tend to share similar institutional features, such as long corridors, compartmentalisation and institutional differences, and the buildings are recognisable as *schools*.[2] There are, however, differences in ways in which physical space has been constructed and organised in schools. School buildings contain entrance halls, stairs, corridors, classrooms, offices, specialised spaces – such as science laboratories, technology classrooms and art rooms, dining rooms, recreation areas, store rooms, spaces for the maintenance of their infrastructure, such as kitchens and cleaning cupboards. In British schools, as well as in California schools, there is a greater range of different types of places, for example a sculpture area, gardens, and an art gallery. These schools have larger student populations and buildings and can therefore have more facilities, but a pedagogic principle is also involved: the aim is to contain more informal activities in the official school than is the case in Finnish schools.

Notions of hierarchy and distance are embedded in the organisation and compartmentalisation of areas of the school for teaching, planning, administration and recreation. Teachers and students are differentially located in space; singular spaces connote plural spatialities (Keith and Pile, 1993). Chris Shilling (1991) suggests that 'school reflects societal and legal rules which view children as subordinate to adults', and the 'organisation of space and objects within schools is deeply embedded with these meanings' (p. 32). The school is a physical entity which enters into the activities and processes of those located in school. In these activities and processes the physical space becomes social space, shaped by spatial praxis.

Louise (FSL) expresses a strong sense of rationalisation, standardisation and compartmentalisation of schooling, and a sense of being an abstract pupil rather than a student located in a particular way in social relations as a unique individual:

JANET: ... what about the school when you got here, and now even. What do you like about it?

LOUISE: What do I like about it? Erm, the number of resources. The computer room and the library, things like that. I, I really like the library. We, we didn't have a library at my primary school, or anything like that.

JANET: Mm. Right. What about, anything else that you like?

LOUISE: What were you going say?

JANET: Ask about what you dislike? Just to get the other side of the coin.

LOUISE: Dislike? Oh goodness.... *how many rooms there are.*

JANET: Mm.

LOUISE: I really ... [it feels], I don't know, puts me off maybe, the way erm, *everybody's doing the same things, and following exactly the same line of thought.*

JANET: Mm.

LOUISE: D'you understand?

JANET: What, in all the different rooms?

LOUISE: Yeah.

JANET: Yeah, you mean like, like in the same Year group, you'll be doing the same things in different rooms?

LOUISE: Yeah, it's all the same.

JANET: Mm.

LOUISE: Erm, *you're sitting in a geography room and you know that there's another class in the room next to you, another class in the room that way and maybe another class across the corridor, erm, they're all doing exactly the same thing.* Gets a bit, I don't know, boring.

In Louise's comments physical, social and mental space are intertwined.

Students' space and place

School buildings contain various 'stations' (cf. Giddens, 1985), where the use of space is routinised, ordered and controlled. Students are positioned as 'pupils' in these spaces, and expectations of 'professionalism' are conferred upon them. Students' entry into different spaces is controlled, and they lack private space. This production of space is also drawn on as a resource in order to perpetuate domination over students (Shillig, 1991). In everyday life at school use of space is strictly controlled, but it is nevertheless used in a range of ways. We examine this by analysing official time–space paths and their informalisation, which provides a basis for discussing hierarchical relations and differentiation, and questions of power and resistance.

Students were asked in interviews what they thought about school buildings and classrooms, and how they used them. Agency and control were explored by asking questions about movement and immobility and their regulation in the classroom, and about students' own space. In the metaphor questionnaire students were asked what places they liked/disliked in the school. They tended to list spaces in the official school as disliked; for example classrooms (either 'classrooms' in general, or specific classrooms), the staff room, or headteacher's office. The places they liked were often associated with the informal school: corridors, dining room, school yard.

When students described their school buildings in the interviews there was great variation in their responses, although most descriptions were functional. Students in one school might often note its cleanliness, and in another its seemingly endless stairs. But social space was also referred to, either as enabling 'this is sort of, I don't know, quite sort of – in a way – sort of large and kind of free' (Lasse, MSH), or as restrictive 'schools are – well, it's a sort of building of its own type; but otherwise it's fine' (Matti, MSH).

We were often asked what we meant when we asked students if they had any space of their own in schools; the question seemed odd since it problematised notions of space and spatial relations which are taken for granted.[3] Those students who felt they did have their own space mentioned places such as lockers; Jere explained that he used his locker so much that when he went home he tried to open the front door using his locker key. Desks were also referred to as 'own space'. For Aulikki the school feels like a public space belonging to the 'whole world'; but, she adds, there is 'my chair and my desk, and during a lesson it's sort of, "don't shove your elbows onto my desk, it's in my use today" – although I don't think it would be nice to take it home!' (FSH). The availability and safety of their own space to store items was a very real issue for the students in Woburn Hill. Those who had desks resented the fact that others had lockers; the locked cloakrooms were a hindrance and did not guarantee the safety of their possessions.

For some students own space is any space where there are no teachers. Breaks are periods when students can make more decisions about what they do and exercise more agency; spaces seem more open and with greater possibilities. In one London school students could spend breaks in the unlocked classrooms, and enjoyed that facility for spending time with friends.

That space in schools is experienced as restrictive was evident when students described classrooms they disliked. Many students mentioned small classrooms that are dark, cramped and airless. The physical discomfort was reflected in the social construction of lessons in these rooms as more restlessness; it can be 'really wild, everybody's like that – and then the teacher starts to brawl' (Leena, FSH). Space enters into the organisation of teaching and learning, and physical and social combine to establish specific spatialities.

Students do have complex, though often unspoken, notions of space, which incorporate strands of the physical, social and mental. Students tend to prefer classrooms with plants, posters, student work – or large windows with a good view. These are aesthetically interesting, provide material for reading and gazing, or a sense of escape into another mental space.

> [In one classroom] you can see the building opposite ... and there is a sort of – I always look at it ... there is one window there and you can see a fantastic model of a ship. I think it looks great ... I always imagine (*laughs*) what sort of people live in the houses and all sorts of things.
>
> (Julia, SFH)

Many specialised spaces in schools were liked, and often contrasted to classrooms; there were more of these in London (and California) schools than in Helsinki schools. When Finnish students sometimes had textile work in a small space converted from an old flat, they were delighted:

> We always pulled this sofa, it's a sofabed, and we pulled it open. Then we stretched out and knitted – and the sun was shining. That was fun. I like sort of completely forgot I was in school. You know, like it didn't cross my mind that the next lesson would be maths. What happiness that was! Then, you know, next we'd go and sit in some hot seat in some sweaty classroom where the teacher rambles on and all words look and sound the same.
>
> (Auli, FSH)

Students also viewed their classrooms functionally, as mere backdrops to teaching and learning. These students were either disaffected in the official school, or had an instrumental view of education; for them 'classrooms are classrooms' whatever they are like. More important was to have comfortable space where students can relax during breaks, a space untainted by the official school. Many students, however, want these spaces to be supervised; especially those students who are more vulnerable in them. The students' sense of space was often mediated by their centrality or marginality in the informal hierarchies among students. Those central in them had more space available to them, whilst those more marginal students had a more restricted sense of space in school.

In the classrooms the seating arrangements are one way of socially organising space. Seating plans were differentiated on the basis of gender and ethnicity. Patterns varied from group to group, and in different-shaped classrooms too. We drew the seating plan of every lesson we were in, and slowly began to see the variety of patterns that formed – sometimes they were obvious. However, generally boys cluster together, filling up one side of the classroom, one side and the back, sometimes the back and the front. There are various central places in the classroom – sitting by the window, by the wall, at the back and at the front. Sometimes a girl sat among boys; often such girls were marginalised and lonely. Sometimes a boy sat among girls; often such boys were soloists or gender-blenders crossing over rather than being marginalised. Social differentiation is played out in making space in a classroom; this process involves making continuities as well, as friends want to sit next to each other.

Teachers influenced seating plans in the beginning in various subtle ways, although students usually thought that they made the decisions themselves. But after the plan was established, it was difficult to break it. Sitting in someone else's place constituted a challenge. If a teacher wanted to change seating in order to tackle restlessness in a group, this was always a very tense situation which could potentially go wrong if not sensitively handled, as students were likely to complain and challenge an imposed alteration. The seating plan, then, is a microcosm of social relations.

Teachers' space and place

To explore ownership of classroom space, we asked teachers how they feel when an empty classroom fills with students. Classroom space does not seem quite real without students: 'although it's mine when it's empty it's sort of without life; I do like it more when there are pupils there – then it's what it's supposed to be' (Inkeri, FTH). Teachers had different pedagogies, diverse notions of control and varied relationships with students. Some teachers thought that space was automatically shared: 'they are my pupils and it's their space too' (Seija, FTH), but a sense of ambivalence was also expressed, revealing tensions in the control of the space: 'I wish that I could keep everything tidy – it's a bit like at home, when a baby takes the toybox and pours it on the floor' (Katri, FTH).

Many students felt that they had no space of their own in school, especially not in classrooms. Shilling (1991) suggests space is dominated by teachers. But teachers suggest that students can shape space, although there is variation in the extent to which they are prepared to allow that.

the pupils do what they can – they organise desks, pull them together, shift them, somebody comes and picks my chair and wants to sit on it – they do take it as far as they can.

(Ulla, FTH)

Tensions in the classroom can assume a spatial dimension, and in these situations teachers can feel vulnerable and not in control of the situation or the space:

sometimes [the classroom] can be more cramped – you know, you feel you're chased to sit behind the teacher's desk. Then you feel that you can't leave that place, that you [are] safe behind the desk, and that, you know, [the classroom] is smaller with two opposing points with counter-currents between them.

(Kaija, FTH)

When teachers talk about intimacy, companionship and about being cramped, management, control and sharing of space intermingle. They take for granted their duty of maintaining orderly relations in space; that this is hierarchical is also assumed, and potential chaos is always (seen to be) lurking behind the order. Students get little opportunity to exercise spatial agency because a potential descent into chaos makes teachers apprehensive.

When students talked about ideal teachers, they hoped for flexibility in interaction – this included fluidity in spatial relations and use of space. But maintenance of order was seen as important by most students and they share the teachers' sense of potential chaos. They wanted the teacher to ensure a peaceful lesson with room for joking and relaxation too, as 'nobody is happy among a row of statues' (Salli, FSH).

There is space for teachers in the school – staff rooms, department rooms, work rooms – but their space is also limited. In some of our schools teachers found it difficult to find a quiet space to work. Staff rooms were full of people, and teachers often coped by choosing their own places. This choice was not open, as seating arrangements in staff rooms are shaped by habituation and backed up by hierarchical relations. Crucial for teachers was whether they had their own classrooms where they could keep teaching materials and audiovisual aids. Running around from classroom to classroom was hard work for those teachers (lower in hierarchies) who had to do it.

Time–space paths: do the locomotion

Time in schools appears as a variable to be managed and controlled. Patrick Slattery (1995) argues that educationalists are ignorant of the negative impact of the modern conception of time on the human psyche. Learning is a timeless process of becoming, where the past, the present and the future are integrated. Slattery, quoting John Dewey, argues that we always live at a particular point in time, and only by extracting the full meaning of it can we carry it to the future. Smith and Katz (1993, p. 75) note that in geographic representation space is a field, 'a co-ordinate system of discrete and mutually exclusive locations', and suggest that in this definition space and time are unrelated. Time has been defined as change, movement and history; space as the absence of these. Doreen Massey (1993) criticises such conceptions too, and argues that time and space are not separate entities, but form a four-dimensional space–time. Interrelationships do not just occur in space and time, but also create and define space–time. Because of this complexity, space and time have elements of both order and chaos. In schools time and space are interlinked in time–space paths. Movement is organised in particular directions at specific times, and temporally defined locations are mapped: at some point in the day you *have* to be in the computer room, and at another point in the day you may *not* be there (cf. Gordon and Lahelma, 1995). Schools constitute tight limits of space and time. The students are guided into these time–space paths which become routinised through repetition (Gordon *et al.*, 2000d). Giddens (1985) has noted that mapping of daily time–space paths of students and teachers is a useful topological device for charting spatial praxis. Time–space paths are also descriptions of how physical space is socially organised for use. School rules stipulate what is not allowed in the school, including information on how bodies are to be placed in space. Below are examples of the rules of 'Timeland', compiled from the rules of our research schools,

> The school space is formed by the school building and the yards that are surrounded by gates.
> All students in Timeland will be in their seats when the bell rings and be ready to learn. When the lesson ends and the teacher has given pupils permission they leave for the break. The teacher leaves last and closes the door.
> Students in Timeland are not to run in class, halls, cafeteria or patio.

Bags should be carried in an appropriate manner.

School rules vary in their detail, but usually include regulation about movement in the corridors and specifications about when school students are allowed to leave the school area.

Schools also stipulate the school day: when the lessons start, how long the breaks are and when there is lunch or dinner. Timetables given to students are maps to time–space paths; they organise compulsion and exclusion in relation to space; stating when you are supposed to be where. Because of our rusty professional pupil skills it took us longer to learn to follow the time–space paths, but students had difficulties with them too; in the first school weeks waiting for wandering students to find their way to the correct classroom took up lesson time.

Teaching official time–space paths for students entering a new school is a crucial part of the professionalisation of school students. New students represent potential chaos which is to be organised into order; information, control and compulsion are used to carry out this task (Gordon *et al.*, 2000d). They are taught the appropriate manner of movement and bodily comportment, and this process starts on the first school day (Lahelma and Gordon, 1997):

> TEACHER: Do not run, coats on first, then you can go and get your things. Indoors we walk, as there are sharp edges – outside you can run like crazy.

> (ObsH)

Time–space paths are highlighted concretely by locked doors. In the Helsinki schools some of the doors are always locked, while others are locked only at the times when students are not supposed to go there. Doors of classrooms are locked when not in use in one of the London schools and open at all times in the other. The doors to the staff room are normally locked in Helsinki, but not in London schools. Whether the doors are locked or not, students can go to the door and ask for a teacher when they have a reason for that, but they are not allowed to walk into the staff room. Schools employ differing levels of distancing, and sets of rules of access to separate students and staff on the ground which is reserved as 'teachers' space'.

After the initial period of training and exhortation time–space paths become routinised, and at least some students have become professional 'smooth operators'. Through routinisation the size of the school buildings does not seem overwhelming any more, and spatial habituation enables students to concentrate more on other aspects in school, as space becomes taken for granted. For example in practical subjects with more student-centred practices, such as textile and technical crafts and computing lessons, students come in, take out their work and continue from where they had finished in the previous lesson. These lessons can also end without particular rituals; when the time comes, students start packing up and leaving, although this leaving is signalled by the bell.

Often teachers have strict control of time, sometimes students take it – or try to exercise agency. In the beginning of a restless lesson the teacher complains: 'We have already spent seven minutes, and we still haven't come to the point. Henna!!' Towards the end of the lesson Henna puts her hand up: 'It's five to already, we'll be the last to eat again.' The teacher remarks that this is because time was wasted at the beginning.

Time–space paths become routinised and students become habituated to them, but routinisation repeatedly breaks down. 'When do we have an exam?', 'will there be many more of those?', 'will we have a break?', 'have we got a double-lesson?', 'can we leave yet?', 'can I stay in for the break?' (ObsH) were questions recorded during one lesson.

A process of informalisation and diversification of these paths is also taking place. Bronwyn Davies (1983) emphasises that students are active in negotiating the order in the classroom; part of this negotiation addresses time–space paths. As well as negotiation, students use inquiries, requests and trade-offs; they plead, beg, test, resign themselves, step aside, ridicule, challenge, disrupt and resist. Below are two examples from lessons:

> *Students want to go and eat, and the whining starts again, 'let us go'.*
> *Now they are starting to go to dinner, girls are already getting up.*
> TEACHER: No, you won't go anywhere without writing down your homework.
> GIRLS: There are queues there, we want to go and eat.
> TEACHER: All right, go then.
>
> (ObsH)

> Sara is leaving:
> I can't take it, I'll lose my mind …
> I promise that I'll get a top mark for the next exam if I can go now …

Can I leave?

(ObsH)

The teacher allowed Sara to leave a little early; the daily life in schools is marked by small victories gained by students. The metaphorical torture was at times an explicitly expressed sensation.

A boy: When does this lesson end?
Teacher: 15 more minutes.
Jere: Let us go a bit earlier (*the teacher does not reply*).
Heikki and Pete get up and are about to leave.
Teacher: 'We aren't stopping yet. Sit down.'
She tells them to take their exercise books.
[*The boys protest*]: 'NNNOO!!!' 'Don't torture us!!'
Jere starts to sing 'What a wonderful life'.
Teacher: That's the right attitude.

(ObsH)

Here students negotiate, test and dramatise the situation. The teacher relents to the extent that she lets them go just a little before the end of the lesson. Situations where teachers call for '*patience*' and students plead '*torture*' are symbolic representations of positions that develop when students no longer wish to be professional smooth operators. They want more agency, but not outright confrontation. They turn the teacher's demand for patience back to her; she has to handle their suffering whilst they negotiate for a fast exit.

Students also negotiate for *more* time – to stay in during break to finish their knitting, writing, or drawing. These requests often meet the same fate as pleas for leaving early – such a diversion from time–space paths is often not possible, as in many schools students are not allowed to stay in classrooms without the teacher, and teachers need or want their breaks, either for a brief respite from their own time–space paths, or for chores such as gathering materials for the next lesson.

Time–space paths regulate presence and absence, but they are not absolute. There are situations when the students have legitimate reasons to make exceptions such as going to the dentist, or to rehearsals for a school play, to a music lesson. Sidestepping time–space paths, for whatever reasons, can give students pleasure, as a boy explained to his friends: 'I had a great day yesterday. I was thrown out of the Swedish lesson, we didn't have home economics and I didn't go to art. I just came in to eat' (ObsH). For the students, trying to hide in the corridors or going to the nearby shop during breaks when they are supposed to stay in the schoolyard is a means of exercising agency (and possibly resistance) through evasion. A hole in the fence through which students escaped to the forbidden shops was a constant focus of critical attention and attempted control by teachers, both physically at the fence and verbally in assembly and class. For the teachers, responsibility for ensuring that students spend their breaks where they are supposed to is one of the least enjoyable of duties.

When the use of space and time is tightly ordered and controlled, students seeking visibility or interested in disrupting school practices find it easy to do so through diverging from the required paths or by using them in different ways. If running is forbidden, to run becomes a way of displaying defiance (Gordon, 1996). When order is so finely tuned, a sense of chaos is easily produced. This partly explains the coexistence of routinisation and unpredictability in schools. Teachers said that they never knew what was going to happen in the course of the school day; this experience was shared by the researchers.

Ways of inhabiting time–space paths are related to differentiation and forms of enactment, and this is particularly clear in the case of gender differentiation. Generally boys are more active in negotiations and testing, they tend to leave the classroom more quickly for example: often those who leave last are girls. During the first two weeks when students were positioning themselves in the classroom, some boys quickly assumed visibly active styles, becoming soloists and jokers (Gordon *et al.*, 2000d). Such a position was harder for girls to acquire, particularly at the beginning, but both girls and boys adopted a range of styles of operating which could vary in different situations.

A few students seemed to step aside, but not necessarily into the margins; with great social skills they managed to construct more flexible use of time and space. Their actions became noticeable only after a long period of observation. Barry was observed throughout an entire maths lesson to undertake no work whatsoever, accomplished through judicious use of movement around the classroom collecting or depositing perfectly legitimate materials or sitting quietly at his desk. Such students were less subject to control. Wexler (1992) found that particularly high-achieving students had more leeway in the high schools he studied. In our schools those active in student councils, some socially skilful working-class girls and several working-class boys, managed to negotiate more space for themselves.

Whilst some students were subject to *less* control than others, some were subject to *more* control – control also exerted by students. Girls' absences seemed to be particularly noted by boys. When teachers checked the register at the beginning of lessons, some boys were likely to shout for example that Nelli and Irina were 'skiving'; sometimes they speculated on the reasons for absence. These speculations were often sexualised as when some boys shouted that Nelli was 'having an abortion'. Such teasing had differential effects; Nelli was always determined to challenge boys' comments assertively and not to be marginalised, but Irina, who could not speak Finnish very well and was isolated in the classroom, was further marginalised through such comments.

The kind of control described here could lead to girls using time–space paths in less diverse ways than many boys; but many girls want to start lessons punctually and peacefully. Girls tend to have a greater interest in schooling than boys; it has been argued that girls, particularly from minority ethnic groups, see a clear connection between qualifications and their chances in the labour market (Mirza, 1992; Fuller, 1980).

The spatial praxis of students is constructed in a context of habituation, acquired through an intensive induction when entering the school, and maintained through routinisation. Despite this strong framework, spatial praxis can also be reflective. Time–space paths are diversified and informalised by student activities. Students are also active in exerting control over each other in the process of making differentiations:

> I know that there is a place in the attic and quite a few students go there. I did go there once and there was this gang there and they said, go away,... they were from our form – but they said they had something important going on, so I sat down on the stairs.
>
> (Lotta, FSH)

Some students are skilful in sidestepping regulations. Manu described how he conducted himself when he did stay in – as Heikki suggested above:

> I'll go over there, downstairs, and I just say that I'm going to the toilet and I ... just stay sitting, yeah, I got a sore foot, I'm not well enough to go out, I have a headache, whatever.
>
> (MSH)

We have emphasised that boys use more space and their time–space paths contain more informalisation and diversification. An interesting, invisible example was provided by a group of rather quiet, high-achieving girls creating their own routes; they tended to sidestep routinisation in adventurous ways. They did not try to stay in during breaks, but broke another rule – they left the schoolyard, and did so without getting caught. They climbed out through a window in an area which was assigned male, and explored the area surrounding the school, for example having fun in a carousel in a nearby children's playground, or discovering old buildings. These girls were not subjected to strict control, as they rarely caused trouble. They were skilled in their actions and exercised agency quietly, for their own pleasure.[4]

Spatial praxis and resistance: everybody dance now

Students can acquire more autonomy in relation to time and space at school, but unless students are happy to disengage from the official school, this is limited. The organisation of time–space paths constructs the social use of school buildings and they are fundamental in shaping spatial praxis in school. The control exerted by the required time–space paths is overwhelming and a focus of criticism by students, despite the existence of negotiation and informalisation. Time–space paths are an organisational feature which incorporates power, and outright resistance to such power is difficult to maintain – hence the modes of diversification which the students employ described here.

Space, spatiality and spatial praxis are taken for granted, rendering them hard to bring within the reach of analysis. Using space in a way that is different from the habitual and sanctioned can have many different meanings. Students may aim to alter, hinder, ritualise and dramatise, or remain unaffected, as well as to oppose or challenge. These practices may or may not be related to resistance, and resistance can be located in the gaze of the researcher. Siiri and Manu offer interesting possibilities for interpretation.

Siiri's behaviour in one of the schools could be seen as illustrating hidden resistance. She usually sat quietly and did nothing that could be classed as audible or visible resistant activity in the classroom. Our observation of her posture and demeanour suggested withdrawal and hostility. When we conducted a questionnaire, Siiri sat quietly and answered the questions, but after many of her answers she added:

'what the fuck has this to do with you!'. She agreed to be interviewed, but in the interview was quiet and rather curt. Whilst in school she mostly occupied a mental space of her own, and for a great deal of the time she absented herself from the spatial praxis of the school altogether by staying away.

Manu's spatial praxis could be seen as creative and active. He is habitually late, he frequently walks about during lessons (when the students should be still), he hides under desks and talks with people through the window. Often when he acts in a manner required of a professional student, he dramatises and ritualises his own activities and, implicitly, the official praxis in the classroom. But could this be seen as resistance? The Finnish researchers conducted their ethnographic research cooperatively and had all met and observed Manu. It was hard to decide whether Manu was resisting, stepping aside, using irony, ritualising, dramatising or protecting his autonomy. When Manu sat on the table in the home economics class and said 'I've got my periods – the table is getting wet', this was open to a myriad of interpretations not conveyed by simply labelling it as resistance; Manu could also be regarded as engaging in a process of challenging and controlling girls in the group. He expressed little interest in teaching and learning in school and his standing in the official school hierarchy of achievement was low. But he was accepted as the joker in the class, and (as we saw above) teachers did not often enter into a confrontation with him, nor he with them. In an idiomatic and spatially metaphoric way we can say that Manu, as well as those dealing with him, occupied 'the line of least resistance'.

A third example refers to a lesson in which students at the end of a long day seemed to react to a teacher talking about what they regarded as self-evident. The description here reflects the experiential sensations of the researcher which were recorded as part of the observation material. She too was tired, stiff and wanting to go home. During the lesson somebody drummed on the desk with her fingers. Another student joined in by slapping her knees rhythmically; another by tapping her foot on the floor. The variety of voice and sound increased, though the noise was not overwhelming. Instead of the line of least resistance, this is an example of power used by students in a subtle way, in the sense of working towards a desired result by 'multiplying a number by itself a certain number of times' (cf. 'power' in mathematics).

The framework of power relations was highly visible in Californian schools which we visited. Some schools had police officers in the campus area; in some there were hefty male supervisors, whose demeanour was friendly and relaxed, but whose presence exhibited embodied authority (cf. Wexler, 1992).

Gendered differentiation is evident in spatial praxis. Boys use more space than girls, although it is important to note within-group differences. Quiet boys who are not perceived to fill the place of a confident male, can be subject to a considerable amount of surveillance and regulation by other boys and, though to lesser extent, by girls too. Girls can use space in active, embodied practices, but mainly in such groups where they form the majority. Girls who are immobile in space may nevertheless be spatially active mentally. Such immobility could also be regarded as resistance within accommodation (Anyon, 1983). The girls may be carefully observing the practices of boys and other girls, thus forming an understanding of the social dynamics of the group, an understanding which helps them to steer their way in the school. They may be day-dreaming, engaging in pleasurable fantasies, thus tapping into their own desire, and perhaps developing a sense of autonomy and independence and an understanding of spatial possibilities beyond the here and now.

Spatial metaphors and spatiality

The journey into adult citizenship and the construction of independence is fraught with complexities for young people. Their responsibilities in the construction of their own lives are emphasised in individualistic cultures, yet the scope they have for decision-making in their daily lives is limited. Although the process of teaching and learning is a negotiated and contested process where students are active participants, as Bronwyn Davies (1990) emphasises, their personal autonomy is rather narrow in schools. The routinisation of school time and space, teacher-centred classroom practices and often fragmented curricular knowledge constitute a considerable incursion into the autonomy of students.

We discuss metaphors students used when they completed the sentence 'School is like ...'. We collected these in many schools in Finland and in Britain so the analysis is not solely based on metaphors from our research schools. Metaphors referred mainly to the physical school, and often to the time–space paths, particularly in Finland; in Britain metaphors also referred to the informal school.

There were often interesting contrasts in students' talk. They might describe their school as having positive features, teachers overall were competent, school friends were important; yet many of their school metaphors referred to total institutions, like prisons or madhouses. Some of the students explained this apparent contradiction:

TUULA: You have sounded fairly satisfied when you have talked about this school – so how come a prison? Isn't prison quite negative?

JERE: It is negative, although I do talk quite positively about school – but there are negative things here because there isn't very much freedom and so on – that's why I thought about prison. Because we haven't got much freedom in most lessons – on the other hand sometimes it's quite good that there's no freedom, so you can learn as well.

(MSH)

Expectations of education are embedded in cultural understandings in complex ways – students frequently expressed their desire for agency, whilst also asserting the necessity for control. They often operate with the same order/chaos conceptualisation of school as teachers.

Tommi said that school was like a prison where 'you have to circle round from classroom to classroom and obey all those people who are there – so there isn't a lot of difference – but you *can* get out from here' (MSH). Tommi is a high-achieving student – negative metaphors were not only produced by students who are not succeeding. Sinikka's grades are excellent, but for her, too, school is a prison 'because you can't get away from here – if you don't want to be here, you can't get away, you have to be in school. And then you have to be good or at least I'm like that, I want to do well at school, I have to be there' (FSH).

An explicit sensation of capture is expressed by the metaphor of a 'mousetrap': 'you get trapped in it and there's no way out. *Oh no!!!*' (FSL). Other total institution metaphors were for example 'hell', 'mental asylum', 'torture chamber'; school can be like a 'nightmare', 'being buried alive' a 'bitter lemon' or a 'rotten apple'. These metaphors contain a great deal of humour and wit – but also capture pain and frustration.

Cultural constructions and representations of individuality which are encountered by students can be contradictory with their experiences of the control exerted over them in everyday life at school, and this may explain the negative metaphors for school which they produce. Metaphors both hide and reveal (Lefebvre, 1991; Gordon and Lahelma, 1995; Gordon *et al.*, 1995) – whilst they tell one story, often one that is difficult to express with words, they omit another. Thus they represent moments both of clarity and of obfuscation.

Finnish metaphors relate overwhelmingly to the physical, whereas British metaphors were more likely to refer to the informal school; school was seen as a 'second home', a 'playground', 'a youth club'. These terms referred to the organisation of sociality. School was also more frequently described through metaphors of travel and movement, such as 'a busy train', a 'vehical [*sic*] which takes you from being an ignorant child to a responsible adult', or a 'straight road which leads nowhere'. These metaphors reflect a greater integration of official and informal school compared with Finland. Students' experiences of the physical school were more embedded in the official and the informal in Britain; demarcations between the different levels were more blurred than in Finland. This could also provide more opportunities for inculcating the official view of the school and its activities. British metaphors tended to be more positive, but references to the informal school could also take the form of a 'crowded cattle auction', where sociality is restricted by space and function.

The analysis of metaphors suggests that the social organisation of physical space can seem unbearably limited: following correct paths at correct times, and pausing at correct stations, can become unendurable. Students have a number of options. They can exit time–space paths by not coming to school, either for a day, or for longer periods. They can come to school, but not adhere to time–space paths; be late, skip a lesson, or leave early. They can redefine their space through various activities such as eating and drinking, grooming themselves or each other or applying make-up – all forbidden activities requiring dexterity and subterfuge to avoid discovery. Students can try to physically stretch the contours of space available to them by tapping their pencils, drumming their feet, throwing items across the room: scraps of paper (often with messages), pencils, rubbers and other small items of equipment, often with the excuse of lending them to other people. Students can try to distance themselves from their everyday school experiences by preventing the school from impinging on them, keeping their main interests firmly outside. Finally, they can stretch the limits of their space in their minds. Whilst sitting at their desks students can, in their minds, be far away, inhabiting wide vistas of endless possibilities. Mental flight may not be purposeful.

For example during a biology lesson sometimes ... I haven't got the energy to listen at all ... well, I don't really talk in biology lessons at all, I just watch and then I sort of notice that I haven't been – sort of listening at all – that I've been thinking about my own things.

(Heli, FSH)

Drifting, though pleasurable, can be troublesome.

Sometimes when you come late to school having overslept and then, you know, the teacher talking can tire you into such a deep hypnosis that virtually the whole day is spoilt.

(Santtu, MSH)

We suggest from our observations of facial gestures and bodily posture that girls in classrooms engage in the activity of 'mental flight' more often than boys (Gordon and Lahelma, 1996). Mental flight can take place because movement which is not part of teaching and learning is so visible in the classroom. In lessons where they are expected to sit still, some students move around more than others. Girls are more likely to remain seated, and in interviews and discussion they argued that their movement is more controlled that that of boys. They suggested that they were more often reprimanded for movement than boys, even for a movement as slight as turning round in their seat. Those girls who were more mobile were particularly conscious of restrictions imposed on them, and freedoms granted to boys:

When teachers say to them, 'go to your own place', they say 'I'll go very soon', then it's 'well, you can stay there for a little while, come soon'. It's just like that you know, if they don't do something, it's 'do it a bit later if you don't want to do it now' … you know [when it's] somebody wild, they can't be bothered to tell them off all the time, they just say 'do it a bit later'.

(Netta, FSH)

Generally in observation boys were more likely to move around the classroom, and in interviews they did not seem to be aware of the extent of their movement. This suggests that they were less likely to be confronted with reprimands when mobile. Girls were more likely to be aware of the compulsion to be still. It takes confidence to stand up and walk about in a still classroom. Many students do it only to sharpen their pencils, fetch paper and equipment, and may be self-conscious even then, as movement is more likely to be watched than is remaining still.

Boys use more space and also tend to have a sense of having more space. Physical space is also social, and its sociality is also relative. The meanings of the same space differ for girls/boys. The school yard can be bigger for boys than girls, the corridors wider, the classrooms more spacious, and the space round their bodies more extensive (Gordon, 1996). Whilst clear gender differentiation is observable and experienced as such, differences between girls and boys are not absolute. Some girls do move about a great deal, and some boys move around very little and inhabit very tight spaces. In one British school, in the metaphor questionnaire most boys mentioned a section of the school yard as a place they liked, because they could play football there. Most girls mentioned this same section as a place they *dis*liked, because 'it is loud and footballs fly everywhere', but a couple of boys also mentioned this as a place they disliked. Boys who are peripheral in space that is central for other boys can be particularly marginal if they do not measure up to modes of masculinity predominant in the school. Invisibility accomplished through immobility can provide greater safety.

The sheer physicality of schools (discussed further in Chapter 8) is so visible partly because of the pent-up energy generated by sitting still. We were particularly aware of the issue of movement and of the effects of sitting still, since we ourselves had difficulty maintaining immobility in school. We often developed stiff backs, necks and shoulders – particularly from writing copious notes. Teachers were not particularly aware of the difficulty of sitting, as they tended to move about in the classrooms, and their time–space paths were more diverse than those of students. Teachers were, of course, also constrained by these paths, and their daily lives were often characterised by busyness and a sense of rushing here and there.

Centres and margins: social relations as spatial

Spatial relations create difference, and difference is constituted in spatial relations. Spatial metaphors illustrate the importance of space as a constituent of social relations, as well as being a stage on which these unfold. The following extract from an interview illustrates an extensive use of expressions which spatialise social relations; the discussion concerned the rule about staying within school boundaries:

> I think that overall it's a good rule, although sometimes it's really detestable or loathsome to follow, because you have to be *in some*

sort of box inside some lines. But you know, *if there weren't any limits*, everybody would *go wherever*. And during the day teachers are responsible for pupils – and we have pupils with a sense of adventure, and they would go *anywhere* and cause problems.

(Salli, FSH)

Spatial demarcations are often used to describe relations between girls and boys:

> Sure girls and boys are in different groups, but that's nothing special. We speak to them often. It's like that in normal life too, there's a sort of border there. It's not very big, but it's not very small either.
>
> (Matti, MSH)

> This border between girls and boys has opened up. As a matter of fact I assumed that girls would come and talk in the secondary school.
>
> (Leo, MSH)

Elin described the social composition of her class (with a female majority) by concentrating on the girls; when asked how she would describe the boys, she explained that they were in an 'in-between space'.

Social hierarchies were also expressed through spatial metaphors. Spatially active students were perceived as central in the class, whilst those who were less active in space were perceived to be more marginal. Salli describes her form as having three groupings; first the 'active', 'open' ones, secondly the 'quiet' ones and thirdly those who are 'quiet' and 'do not greatly bring themselves forward', but 'don't huddle in the corner either'. Activity, openness and location in centre–margins, spatially and metaphorically, were used to describe differentiations among students.

Sensitive observation of spatial demarcations and limits is important for students when interacting with others. The appropriate 'personal' space around a body is culturally constructed, so that the distance people prefer to place between themselves and others varies from country to country and social group to social group. Incursions into that space surrounding other people are potentially hazardous and can become conflicts about power and hierarchy. Reading the spatial limits accurately is both useful and important.

if you have a friend whom you really know, you know that you can [tease] her/him, sort of, because you know where the limit is.

(Lotta, FSH)

Competence is required in reading borders and limits and deciphering demarcations. Uncertain students may therefore search for safety in marginal places, in order to ensure that they do not accidentally make unwelcome incursions into other people's space; especially spaces of those students who are particularly intent on defending them.

Well on the first day I did go away from the crowds. I went to a sort of – there's a sort of roofed shelter over there, so I went there for a quite a while, but then things started to turn out all right.

(Harri, MSH)

Students who use physical space visibly and actively, particularly in classrooms, have to learn to judge the borders and limits in relation to the official as well as the informal school, and to teachers as well as other students. This is particularly the case if they are not interested in challenging teachers and do not want confrontation, but are more interested in side-stepping restrictions and acquiring more space for themselves. In these situations sussing out teachers is important (Chapter 5). Not only do students need to suss out differences between teachers, but they need to learn to be sensitive to situational and temporal shifts and changes in particular teachers. Lassi described a teacher who 'sometimes has a really strict lesson and then sometimes it's like, you know, there's no limit anywhere' (MSH). Spatially mobile students, who do not behave in an oppositional way, learn to acquire space. Those students, often boys, who are more resistant to teacher control and take an oppositional stance to school may not learn that they should not intrude into other people's space, and their agency may be exercised at the expense of the agency of others. A classroom can support soloists if most of the students blend in; it can support movers and talkers, if most of them sit still and quiet.

Victoria Foster (1996) analyses the space which girls have to enter in order to pursue equal rights as citizens in schools, calling it 'transpositional mediating space', and referring to psychic experience embedded in space. This space incorporates asymmetrical gender relations and constructs girls as lacking masculine learner subjectivity. Foster suggests that girls' desires are easily judged as trivial and confused (cf. Hey, 1997). Gender relations are asymmetrical; and so all girls as *girls* and all boys as *boys* are positioned in a particular way. But we have emphasised that other axes of difference intersect gender relations, and a range of culturally and socially constructed femininities and masculinities can be constructed. Moreover, specific girls and specific boys have more space in negotiating these positions. The difficulties experienced by quiet girls (and some quiet boys) often go unnoticed (cf. Walkerdine and Lucey, 1989). But not all quiet girls (or boys) are victims of the more boisterous; many of them may be competent, bored, active in their minds, wanting to study.

Although space is taken for granted, the use of spatial metaphors demonstrates an implicit sense of the spatiality of social relations, also revealed in the ready discussion of space in school which emerged in the interviews. Our analysis also suggests the complexity of control and agency in schools. Opportunities for exercising agency, while limited for students (as they are for teachers), do exist, and action and inaction are constantly folding over space. Difference and marginality are played out in space; space which both constitutes them, whilst also being constituted by social relations of differentiation and marginalisation. This has pedagogic implications; if unequal relations of difference are to be addressed, attention must be paid to agency in spatial praxis.

Conclusion

Physical space becomes social space when teachers organise and re-organise its use, and allocate and re-allocate students into it. Students respond by practices of accommodation, conformity, negotiation, stepping aside, challenge and resistance. Both teachers and students have power here, and each is able to control the other. The power of teachers consists of the ability to do or act – they are granted authority and are invested with rights to discipline. Students have an ability to do or act and are able to exercise control over others – but they are not invested with rights to discipline, or granted authority. Whilst the relationship between teachers and students is strictly hierarchical, there is no clear division between powerful teachers and powerless students.

Giddens (1985), in his discussion of time–space, criticises approaches which overemphasise regulation and control. The idea that every limitation is at the same time an opportunity for enactment is borne out in our analysis of everyday activities in schools. In spatial praxis students are inscribed into particular subject positions. But they are able to experiment with ways of locating themselves in those positions – although it is unlikely that they can escape them altogether. By experimenting with these positions they can work towards agentic, embodied spatial praxis. But exercise of agency is also a site for making difference. Some students can claim more space than others; those pushed into margins have less space and less autonomous bodies. Those students with more space to exercise control are likely to be boys (but not all boys) and those with less space to do so are likely to be girls (but not all girls). Patterns of student agency are embedded in complex ways in social dimensions of inequalities. A boy who is able to exert control over some boys and possibly most girls may in turn be in a vulnerable position in the official school in terms of hierarchies constructed round achievement; these may provide more powerful sites for some of those students over whom he is able to exert control.

Our dance metaphor contains control, agency and resistance. In some spaces there is more concentration on the formal steps of the dance than in others. There is a difference between dancing on a polished ballroom floor, or on the grass at an outdoor rock concert. Space is used differently by different individuals, couples or groups – some take over the central area in the ballroom. These same dancers may or may not take over the grass in the rock concert – if they do, they may be joined by others who remain on the sidelines in the ballroom. Those on the margins may be bored, or may watch others. They may comment on the steps taken by dancers, praising or ridiculing. Whether the dancing is 'strictly ballroom' or not, both centre and margin wield differential positions of power and influence.

8
'Twist and Shout': Bodies in the Physical School

Introduction

The dance is always bodies in movement, and in the school many forms of dance can be represented, and legitimate and illegitimate steps (from the most constrained to the most extravagant movement) can be found. For any observer entering a school in a break between lessons a major impression is of movement and sound, and of a large number of young bodies interacting in a relatively confined space. The sense of embodiment, of the physicality of what happens in schools, is strong. Students walk, run, play, mill around, talk, shout, laugh.[1] They rush into play areas to play energetically at break, or in sports lessons, and return hot and flushed to their lessons. Movement and sound surrounds the observer. This tumult contrasts with the stillness and quiet which descends once lessons have started; sounds are muted, confined to the individual classrooms, and controlled within these (Gordon and Lahelma, 1996). Distant shouts may be heard from the outside sports areas, but the corridors are hushed and calm.

Change and development in the teenage years are marked heavily on the body – it is a period of bodily change second only to the drama of early childhood. Bodily changes assume social significance.

> Anne, the outstanding 'swot' of the class, had previously had a very straight classical image, but over the weeks approaching her thirteenth birthday had shed her glasses for contact lenses, worn her hair loose, and a short skirt. In the sports changing room she spent a long time examining herself in shorts in the mirror, clearly intrigued by the newly emerging body.
>
> (ObsL)

165

In an interview a boy pointed out that he was having a physical spurt: 'Like it's quite weird like, you usually look up at them. Suddenly you're looking down.' It is, as a girl remarked in an interview, 'a time when you're growing in all kinds of places'. When a young woman makes such a comment, we are likely to think about the increasing femininity of her body; she herself included her brain as being a place for growth. Bodies change shape and size with rapidity as physical development gets into its stride. This bodily unruliness, this imbroglio, is part of what the school must control, constrain and channel.

But definitions of adolescence as troublesome and stormy are also social constructions with implicit assumptions about gender. Sinikka Aapola (1997) notes that the discourses of adolescence have social consequences for young people. Though empirical studies do not 'unequivocally verify the perception of a chaotic adolescence' (p. 53), notions of unruliness encourage focus on problems and crises. The gendering of adolescence means that young girls are reminded of biological femaleness and of the demands of femininity, and boys of maleness and the requirements of masculinity, and each of their positions in the heterosexual order.[2] Growing bodies and embodiment are significant elements in the secondary school and all those taking part in the dance are participants in producing and maintaining the cultural constructions linked with such growth and change.

The material body and its social construction are entwined in complex and contradictory ways which are difficult to disentangle in practice. A social constructionist approach enables one to avoid the pitfalls of biological essentialism, but need not lose sight of human embodiment. There is indeed no conceptual dualism which will allow us to distinguish the material, physical body from the social meanings, symbolism and social management of the socially constructed body. What we focus on here is how the processes and practices of the school contribute to the way in which social categories, in this instance particularly gender, are inscribed on the body. We examine movement and voice in particular, arguing that control, resistance and negotiation all have embodied aspects, that 'taking place' is spatial and embodied.

The embodiment of teachers tends to be neutral, and they often dress in subtle tones. They are aware of students watching them. The school is characterised by control and surveillance – the teachers gaze upon the students, and the students upon the teachers, and each gaze upon their own group. Many school rules and practices relate to aspects of bodily comportment and much resistance to school discipline has a physical, embodied manifestation.[3] If the task which society demands of the school is dual, regulation and emancipation, in relation to the body there is very little emancipation. Appropriate bodily control and comportment surveyed and policed by the school is an important element in the progress from unruly adolescent to responsible adult, from 'pupil' to 'citizen'. Students learn what is acceptable and appropriate in relation to their bodies, voice and movement in school contexts, 'sit up straight', 'don't use that tiny voice, like a mouse', 'silence, speak only when I say you can', 'you do not talk when I am talking', 'shut up and get on with it', 'I will wait for you to be quiet', 'walk, don't run', 'wipe that smile off your face'. Some accept the constraints of the school, encoded in rules and experienced constantly in practice, and others stretch the boundaries, in ways which can be very visible and obvious transgressions, or more subtle and discreet. Both the control exerted by the school and laid down in the rules (for example about no running, eating, loud noises in unacceptable places, gum chewing, wearing of forbidden garments, bodily decoration and embellishment), and the flouting, skirting or playing with this control by the students in undertaking all of these activities, are gender-differentiated practices, although some are undertaken by both girls and boys. This differentiation is generated both by the rules themselves, and the expectations embedded in them, and by the responses of the students, imbued with their own gendered expectations, embodiment and practices. This chapter focuses largely upon gender and embodied practice, but as we have discussed earlier, school practices and processes accomplish and support many other distinctions, for example in relation to age, 'race' or ethnicity, able-bodiedness and sexuality, and some of these will be touched on in the discussion.[4]

What to wear and how to wear it

Dressing for the dance of the school operates under different constraints in Finland and England/Wales. In Finland there is no school uniform, although there are requirements about what kinds of clothing can be worn in particular contexts (sports outfits, indoor and outdoor clothing) and students themselves develop dress codes. In Britain school uniform has a long history, the basic argument in favour being that it irons out differences, for example, of class or income, which might be revealed with free choice of clothing for school, and that it creates an image and identity for the school. In

some schools the uniform is merely a specification of colour to be
worn, and types of clothing appropriate for different activities. In the
light of recent marketisation in education, and the concomitant
requirements of image creation for schools, many schools which did
not have uniforms are adopting them. Each of the schools in the study
in London had a school uniform, and the teachers were obliged to
enforce its correct use (as set out in the school handbook).

> *Teacher asks Hadi to do up his top shirt button.*
> HADI: I can't sir, it hurts. I've got a fat neck.
> TEACHER: Good, no pain, no gain. Do it up.
> HADI: But sir [*doing up top button, mock pleading*].
>
> (ObsL)

Students were obliged to have the appropriate garments for both
summer and winter, and outdoor garments were not to be worn in
school. The uniform differentiated the genders in relation to, for
example, the use of skirts for girls only and blazers for boys only. Girls
were allowed to, and did, wear trousers in both schools. Length of
skirt, and height of heel of shoe, was specified in each school for girls,
and trainers were strictly forbidden to be worn within the school,
although they were required for certain sporting activities.[5] Sports
clothing was gender-differentiated. Apart from small studs or sleepers
in the ear, earrings and particularly multiple earrings were disallowed,
as were other items of jewellery. Make-up was against the rules (cf.
Gordon *et al.*, 2000c).

All of these rules were transgressed by many of the students, and
from observation it was clear the disciplinary focus in each school
tended to be on one or two aspects of uniform rule breaking. In one
school the wearing of trainers was of particular concern, to the confusion of one researcher, who on the first day in school could not
understand why the teacher was creeping around looking under desks
at students' feet at the beginning of the lesson. Boys were the trainer
transgressors, and often wore black, rather subtle-looking trainers
which could confuse the teachers. Shirts hanging out were the major
problem in one school, and boys again were the major transgressors
here, largely due to their greater activity; for example, more expansive
actions in the classroom, rushing around the school, and into classes
after strenuous activity in breaks on the playing fields or tennis and
basketball courts. But girls were also caught breaking this rule; here a
girl comments: 'guess the rules are alright. Except for one, we have to

keep our shirts tucked in 'cause I never do, I find I can never keep my shirt tucked in and get told off many times for that' (SFL).'

Some girls made changes to their uniforms in terms of length of skirt (very short) and height of shoe heel (too high) and wore make-up and jewellery. The make-up was sometimes very obvious, for example highly coloured nail varnish, although there was also subtle use of make-up, which was often hard to detect. Girls often groomed each other and themselves in the classroom and in breaks. Teachers did comment on this, but not always. One male teacher commented 'Maya, we are in a biology lesson, not having your hair done.' A female teacher said to an African–Caribbean girl who was wearing expertly applied light makeup and an intricately constructed hair-style, and had forgotten her book for the lesson:

It might be better if you spent a little more time in the morning getting your books together, and a little less time making yourself beautiful.

(ObsL)

In observation we noted:

Many of the girls wear rings and earrings and a few wear makeup and nail polish on a day-to-day basis. Mr. Norris has asked Penny and Lita to remove their rings. Bridget has commented on the fact that she often wears nail polish but is never reprimanded for this. Mandy and Annette apply makeup during class. Mandy wears high length black fashion boots. Annette wears black, slip-on shoes with a heel and strap at the back.

(ObsL)

Much of this decorative effort by the girls can be seen as part of the process of the construction of femininity (see below). They are creating an image as feminine, fashionable, and distinguishing themselves from bods or boffs, identifying themselves as members of a particular group within the school or class.

Some of the students felt that transgressions by the boys were more often picked upon by teachers than those of girls:

Most of them [the rules] are like necessary but about school uniform, this school seems to have a lot of school uniform but it's like, girls have to wear black shoes and no heels ... but a lot of people don't obey them. But the school doesn't seem to do anything about it so it's – there's no point in writing a rule and sort of not going by it.... The teachers say 'tuck in your shirts', they don't say anything about trousers or jumpers ... they seem to go harder on the boys than they do on the girls [*shrugs*].

(Rita, FSL)

School uniforms are not used in Helsinki schools, rules do not include stipulations about clothing and trainers are regularly worn by many students, both girls and boys. Generally 13–14-year-old students during the time of our study were able to combine comfort and fashion. Girls and boys tended to wear trousers, often loose ones, jeans, and flannel shirts or loose tops. Students do not seem to emphasise gender difference – sometimes the dress of girls and boys could be almost identical. Despite this, students were able to make fine distinctions on the basis of the width of trousers, looseness of tops and colours chosen.

When girls were asked why they did not wear skirts more often, they referred to comfort – trousers were more comfortable particularly in cold weather, and skirts were not that fashionable. But girls also were wary of skirts, because diversion from the normal dress code might be commented on by other students. Tarja Tolonen discovered that among older students boys might lift up skirts. Wearing trousers and loose clothing was sexually safer. Gender neutrality served as a protection against sexual harassment. There were some differences between the two schools in Finland. Students in the performing arts tended to dress slightly more flamboyantly. Girls wore skirts more often, either long or short, or shorts.

Whilst there was no official regulation about the type of clothing to be worn in Helsinki, clothing was nevertheless a disciplinary issue causing debate, because there were regulations on how to dress inside the classroom. Disputes and negotiations were mainly between teachers and boys among whom baseball caps or woolly hats in the winter were very popular. Disputes and negotiations about wearing hats and caps started on the first school day and continued throughout – these are comparable to disputes and negotiations about shirts and trainers in London schools. The cap discussions were constant, ritualistic and dramatised. In one biology classroom a model of a skeleton stood near the door. Boys in one teaching group were in the habit of throwing their caps on the head of the skeleton as they walked in, thus creating a small everyday performance by disrobing themselves and robing the skeleton. Students were allowed to wear make-up and jewellery. Many girls wore jewellery, but not particularly conspicuous items, and some girls wore make-up in moderation. Those few girls who wore more makeup tended to have a reputation for being 'hard' (see discussion of Mandy, below).

Hair was an interesting area of gender differentiation. Girls were allowed to wear long, even very long hair (an acceptable indication of gender) which could be loose, except in science and technology lessons. Such hair required frequent grooming, and fads of particular types of hair decoration or restraint could sweep the class and the school. Many of the boys adopted fashionable hairstyles (following pop stars, footballers and other perhaps unsung heroes and role models associated with their immediate groups or community) as part of their identity construction and presentation of self. As the caretaker in one school said:

> I am surprised that at the school they focus so much on uniform, they go for uniform but not on hair. You get all sorts of weird and wacky hairstyles which they do not seem to be bothered about.
>
> (Andrew, MSSL)

Whilst dress styles among students were similar in Helsinki schools, hairstyles were more differentiated between girls and boys as well as among girls and boys. Few girls had short hair, and the styles they adopted were more feminine than their clothing. Most of the girls had hair which was shoulder length, and many girls had adornments in their hair – combs, ribbons, and ties. Boys tended to have short hair, but many had fashionable cuts. Some boys did have long hair, but length of hair could signify (or be read to signify) transgression in relation to masculinity. Some students dyed their hair and a few had some patches of (often changing) colour in their hair. The importance of hairstyles was recognised in the official school too, when a boy was asked to take his cap off – he refused saying that his hair was in a mess, and on this occasion the teacher withdrew the demand, anticipating a potential conflict with a self-conscious but determined young man.

Hairstyle was also differentiated by ethnic identity. In one London school some of the African–Caribbean girls wore elaborate plaited hairstyles, possibly with additional hairpieces, and boys either cropped/locks combinations, or cropped hair with patterns or symbols cut into the hair. Ethnic styles were less elaborate in the other school. As with smoking behaviour (Holland *et al.*, 1996), deployment of the uniform and bodily embellishment were used as part of identity construction and signs of group membership by the students, and as such resistance to the dictates of the school in these processes may be merely one component.

The gaze of fellow-students, informal control by peers (especially boys but also other girls) and fear of being sexualised (Lees, 1986) curtail girls' embodiment more than official regulation. This was evident, for example, in one interview in which a girl criticised the wearing of body-hugging polo-neck jumpers by some female students. Bodily comportment, including dress, style and movement, is implicated in spatial praxis. We have argued (Gordon *et al.*, 2000d) that the school as a form of total institution may require the student to disrobe, dismantle, to leave outside the classroom elements of the informal school and outside world, as part of taking on the role of the abstract pupil. This metaphor may capture the use of power in the process of producing docile bodies from the unruly bodies with which the school can be confronted in its task of normalisation. But it is argued that the docile bodies of Western society are gendered, and the disciplinary practices of the institutions in those societies engender the docile bodies of women more docile than those of men (Bartky, 1990; Ramazanoglu and Holland, 1993). The blind eye which is turned to the feminisation of the uniform and gendered bodily embellishment among girls in the London schools could be seen as part of that process of gender differentiation. It could also be seen as a moment in which agency, embodiment and power are simultaneously constituted (see, too, the discussion of sport, below).

Femininity, masculinity and sexuality

The control function of the school is particularly apparent in relation to sex and sexuality, as has been illustrated in Britain in the struggles around sex education and the injunction on the 'teaching' of homosexuality (Thomson, 1995; Epstein and Johnson, 1998, Chapter 5). Sex and sexuality must be particularly constrained, controlled and channelled. It has been argued that the school is a prime site for the construction of gender difference (Delamont, 1990) and normative heterosexuality (Epstein, 1994), and many recent ethnographic studies have provided evidence of the ways in which these are produced and reproduced in the school. They have also argued that these processes take place within a broad framework of the requirements of hegemonic masculinity (Carrigan *et al.*, 1985; Connell,

1987), itself constructed in oppositional relation to femininity and subordinated forms of masculinity, particularly homosexuality. And it is on and through the body and its deployment that these processes are enforced, realised, resisted, or subverted.

In the discussion of dress code above, it is clear that the schools (in London) differ in what they require of boys and girls in adhering to uniform, and in the policing of these differences, and in Helsinki a more informal control is exercised by the peer group. The changes which some girls make to the uniform, pushing against its constraints to varying degrees, are associated with presenting a feminine and a sexual image. Young women are under pressure more generally in society to construct their material bodies into a model of femininity which is inscribed on the surface of their bodies, through such skills as dress, make-up and dietary regimes. They must manage their appearance very carefully in order to stay on the right side of the slippery boundary between being acceptably attractive and overly sexualised. They must also be vigilant against fat, spots and surplus hair, evidence of menstruation – against anything which might break up the smooth surface of the feminine body (Prendergast, 1995; Holland *et al.*, 1998).

There was, then, a sense in which girls in London schools who were dressed in a more feminine way were enabled to do so partly because such expectations of gender display were culturally more typical, but also because they felt they were more at ease in displaying their bodies in skirts, as a skirt was part of the uniform. Shortening the skirt was a way of individualising one's dress, and a more sexual appearance was a form of stepping aside, challenge and resistance. Girls in Helsinki were less interested in such displays of femininity. Those interviewed by us and by Tarja Tolonen (1998b) often stated that they disliked pink, lace and frills (which they had been made to wear as children). On one hand dressing up was likely to elicit comments from others, and on the other hand girls thought they did not need to dress like a girl or a woman, and enjoyed this lack of compulsion.

The neutrality in dress was therefore partly chosen by students and partly imposed upon them; not having to be feminine was both an opportunity and a constraint. Finnish gender politics emphasise neutrality more than British ones; welfare state policies have attempted to develop social citizenship, so that as participants in the labour market Finnish women are less gendered in state practices. Generally, young people are likely to be more uniformly dressed. They are not as actively 'making gender' through their clothes, but they are also less likely to adopt conspicuous individualistic displays than are girls and boys in London, where the British liberal legacy has placed stronger emphasis on the desirability of individualism. That Finland is more homogeneous culturally than Britain is observable in dress.

Boys have to negotiate masculinity. Their embodied styles were mostly masculine. There were, however, some gender-blenders in each of the Helsinki schools, both female and male. Holly Devor defines gender-blenders as people who 'indisputably belong to one sex and identify themselves as belonging to the corresponding gender while exhibiting a complex mixture of characteristics from each of the two standard gender roles' (1989, p. vii), meaning female and male. Eetu presented a somewhat ambiguous style whilst placing himself firmly among the boys; he usually interacted with boys, and did not make any great overtures to girls, though sometimes in lessons he sat among the girls. His hair was long when he started school, and he let it grow throughout the three-year period in the secondary school, sometimes combing and often stroking it during lessons. There were frequent occasions when his masculinity was questioned and he was called a girl or gay, by other boys. He joined in this banter by fluffing up his hair and participated in the speculations about femininity though not about homosexuality. He was active in sports both in school and outside. He dressed in clearly male attire (and denim jackets) and managed to steer a course through the teasing, apparently unscathed.

Tero was a gender-blender, although he dressed in masculine clothes and had short hair. His embodied style consisted of a mixture of characteristics of female and male. He moved gracefully and lightly, but was not particularly interested in sports or physical education at school. He interacted with boys and girls, and was at ease with both of them. He had considerable social skills, was able to get on with adults as well as with people of his own age, and interacted actively with the researchers. He negotiated a place for himself in his class and in the school, seemingly by refusing to address putative questions about the ambivalence of his style. He was called 'homo' (Chapter 6) on occasions by girls and by boys, but he carried on regardless. His conversational skills, curiosity and friendliness helped him to find a space for himself, despite the fact that he skirted limits and borders of appropriate heterosexuality.

In one London school Annette presents a threat to the model of appropriate femininity in a number of ways for both boys and girls, since she has no desire to conform to the 'look' [approved presentation of femininity in the group – a modern, fashionable style; the other girls see her as emulating 1970s fashion, label her a 'hippy'; the boys label her a 'tart'] she threatens the boys and girls simultaneously. Annette produces anxiety because her 'bad taste' look reveals a femininity that is not natural but a hyper-femininity which is performed rather than embodied. In performing camp, Annette threatens masculinity [and femininity] because she reveals how arbitrary the sex–gender equation can be.

(ObsL)[6]

One girl seems to fall into the trap which Lesko has seen as the sexualisation of deviance, where the lower-status girl is seen as 'loose', 'wild' and 'hard' and this is equated with sexual pollution (Lesko, 1988, p. 124). The teachers perceived Mandy as a major disruption in the classroom with a range of undesirable traits, she was well known as a truant, who smoked during breaks, refused to do her work, talked consistently through class, walked around the classroom, chewed gum, wore make-up and long black boots, combed her hair during class, drew pictures and sang songs. They objected to her deep, husky voice which she defended, arguing that 'the teachers don't like the way I act like a boy. I've been sent to a child psychologist but there is nothing wrong with me, my voice is normal, it's a cockney accent.' She was characterised (by teachers) as being like her mother, 'promiscuous'. In each of these cases the girl has stepped beyond the bounds of acceptable femininity, creating problems for both teachers and students caught in the process of construction of normative femininity and masculinity.

Intricate steps: movement in space

The students' time–space paths dictate permitted movement in the spaces of the school, but the physical space may disrupt or provide them with opportunities for 'inappropriate' movement, for example exaggerated 'milling about', pushing, making a lot of noise, bodily contact, at narrow, congested junction points where time–space paths cross. Within the classroom this movement and flux comes to a sudden halt, and bodies are frozen into immobility in many lessons.

There were constant tensions between immobility and movement. Sitting still for prolonged periods was hard for many students. Sanna explained what it felt like to be immobile in your desk: 'my arse gets numb – I get all sweaty'. The strong embodied sensations of having to endure stillness were expressed by many students. Asta explains: 'I get this feeling that – oh hell what am I doing here – I could be at home eating chocolate and watching *The Bold and the Beautiful* (*laughter*) video.' Elisa explained that at times sitting still at your desk was difficult:

> when you try and listen to something and you have such a hard seat, you know. Some of them are so uncomfortable, because they've all been made in the same mould, and you can't find a comfortable position. You know, as everyone is shaped sort of differently.... And I think it's tedious at least in the spring, when it's warm outside and the ventilation doesn't work. And then it's really stuffy.
>
> (FSH)

Most students referred to at least occasional or periodic frustration with sitting still; nevertheless, girls move about less than boys during lessons.

When students were asked what they do when they get frustrated, examples of a range of activities were given: drawing, fetching hankies, paper and equipment, sharpening pencils, washing hands, having a drink, just sitting, trying to concentrate, looking out of the window, lying on the desk, snoozing, sleeping, checking the time, looking around, fidgeting, imagining things, letting your thoughts wander, going to the rubbish bin, talking, doing some extra writing, changing position, stretching, leaning back, swinging on the chair, shoving chairs and desks, standing up, asking for the lesson to finish earlier. No systematic gender differentiations were found in what students said they did.

Our observation notes indicate that students undertake even more movement than they say they do when the tensions between movement and immobility overcome them: fiddling with equipment – for example trying to balance a pen on the ruler and then adding the eraser (and failing), dropping equipment, swinging and tapping feet, rubbing eyes, clapping hands, waving fingers, fetching books, looking at each other's work, shifting desks, opening classroom doors, opening windows and curtains, switching lights on and off, doing dancing movements, shoving others with pens and compass, throwing things, trying to make an excuse to leave the classroom, picking up a desk and laying it on your lap, hiding under the desk, rolling around on teachers' wheeled chairs, playing ball with a racket, knocking the wall and more. As we move down this list, the activities mentioned are more likely to be engaged in by boys than girls.

Many students try to find ways of moving which appear legitimate and part of the official activities during the lesson. For students who wanted to stand out inappropriate movement provided an easy way of putting on a show. Where many girls (and boys) tried to cover their movement, some boys could jostle for position by exhibiting a withdrawal from official school through movement. Various kinds of show could be witnessed in the classroom. For example Matti gets up: 'Teacher, can I beat that guy up, he's a political opponent' (ObsH) – or he asks to borrow a pencil, and when Kalevi lends it to him, Matti kneels in front of him with theatrical gratitude. Even when movement was part of the normal activities of the classroom, some boys would make every opportunity to play-act – for example walking with swinging, jutted hips in a sexualised macho manner. Such sexualised display was unlikely to be witnessed among girls in mixed-gender settings.

Our classroom observations often record boisterous boys and still girls. Of course all the boys did not move – for some boys space was particularly restricted and movement was curtailed (Chapter 7). However, when some boys move, the impression formed is of boys moving. The tendency for gendered differentiation is easily exaggerated and generalised, and in such ways gender differences are constantly made and remade. Hille notes that 'girls sit still you know, and boys move about wherever' (FSH).

Many girls are concerned to do well at school, either by achieving good grades or by forming good relationships with other students and often with teachers too. They invest a fair deal in their schooling, and so these girls are less likely to move around in ways that hamper their concentration – or the appearance of it. But if they do move, their movement is more likely to be noted and controlled, by other students and by teachers. Heli explains:

> If I turn towards a friend and sort of look in that direction, that is commented on, even if you are listening … or if you're really tired and keep your eyes closed, it's 'you're not allowed to sleep during the lesson' and you have to sit more or less with a straight back – or something like you're not allowed to lean against the wall – I mean I think that's a bit, sort of, if you sleep, you only harm yourself … or lean against the wall, it's you yourself who gets a bad

posture (*laughs*) – I mean it's more than just being brought up or educated.

(FSH)

Her comments indicate tensions between agency and control; the sense of autonomy and personal responsibility, and embodied regulation.

In our experience some teachers in Helsinki are aware of the problems of sitting still, and allow brief activity periods including stretching and jumping. The students shriek as the movements impinge on their sore shoulders and necks (the researchers present have also felt like screeching, but exhibited stronger self-control as the prototypes of the ideal professional pupil).

Teachers move about during lessons a great deal more than students; indeed some of them hardly stand or sit still throughout the lesson. They are not always aware of the extent of the difficulties immobility can cause. We have observed and experienced the problems of the sensations of compulsory stillness, and found them reiterated in the negative metaphors for the school which students produced (Chapter 7). The attempts to try to cater for all students can be draining for teachers; in some lessons and during some activities many students want constant help. Some of them patiently put their hand up, possibly remaining unnoticed as more forward students call for immediate assistance. In the hustle and bustle of a busy lesson it is difficult for teachers to see to everyone, and often quiet students remain unnoticed – some of them can remain alone in their difficulties and perhaps switch off from the task at hand; others may help each other.

There are lessons in which movement and noise are allowed, within clearly defined parameters (negotiated or exploited as ever by some students). Here a teacher explains the ground rules for the disruption of school rules in a drama lesson:

> He does relax uniform rules – shirts out, ties off, top button of shirt undone, blazers off. But students cannot leave the room like that. When they arrive they should move chairs and tables to the side of the room, to provide space for movement. And when called upon to move in the pursuit of objectives of the lesson they can move freely. But when the teacher calls out 'freeze' they should hold the position they are in (and stop talking to attend to the next requirement). When he calls out 'stop' they should stop whatever they are

doing, including talking. In addition to calling out 'stop', 'I'll raise my hands up like that [hands up palms to the front].' 'You do not talk when I am talking'. He explains that there are two useful elements for acting 'voice and body' and here they are clearly being given permission to use both within agreed constraints. When they leave the room, everything should be as it was when they arrived, the space in the room, and their presentation of self in the school at large.

(ObsL)

It takes some time in this lesson for the students to respond to the teacher's requirements as he wishes, and he admonishes them for their failures, which usually involve the use of voice and body when required to stop. But most of the students enthusiastically take part in the exercises, some of which include bodily contact, and a considerable amount of movement, and noise.

Having and using voice

In Finnish the word 'ääni' incorporates a number of meanings – 'sound', 'voice', 'having a voice', and these meanings are all included in the way that we are using 'voice' here. We have seen that sound is a large part of what takes place in school, and it comes in many forms in the interactions between students and between teachers and students: chatting, arguing, negotiating, commenting, asking, yelling. It can be part of the formal or informal school. The school bell and headteacher's information through the loudspeaker may penetrate through all spaces and disrupt both official and informal actions. In some lessons the teacher takes control, and s/he may use most of the voice and space in the classroom.

Very fast paced lesson. Teacher directed, felt quite breathless and on the edge of my seat, as if questions could come to me any minute ... in her quick fire methods of inclusion, felt that there was no escape from her gaze.... Frequent use of individual names, seeing class members as named individuals rather than anonymous, or boys or girls. Frequent use of 'hands up' to answer questions, combination of hands up to respond to the volunteers, and to bring in quieter members – usually managed to elicit a public verbal response from every class member in each lesson.

(ObsL)

The most audible action which attracts attention of the teacher, as well as the researcher, comes from the boys. They can compete with each other for the teacher's attention, shouting answers without raising their hands. Both boys and girls ignore the 'handsup' rule and call out answers, and teachers themselves can be variable in their enforcement of it, or use different question-and-answer techniques, but it is largely boys who call out without a hand up when it is required.

We did try to hear multiple voices and pay attention to gendered conflicts to get beyond the more apparent surface noise. We observed boys challenging the less quiet girls and competing with them for attention, as in the following extract:

> Henna protests that the teacher asks Juuso for an answer after he
>   has shouted.
> The teacher asks Henna not to shout.
> Lasse shouts again grumbling 'Henna is wrong', 'Henna is shouting.'
> Marjaana shouts, teacher says laughing: 'Do not scream.'
> Soon after this, Juuso screams 'because they also [girls] scream'.
> HENNA: Teacher, come now and take this ink paperball from Lasse.
> [Laughing, Lasse acts as if he would throw something.]
> TEACHER: Henna, do you want to change place? [so that Lasse
>   cannot tease her].
> [Henna changes place ...]
> Soon Henna shouts: 'Teacher, he is trying to throw again!'
> [Henna and Lasse argue across the room, Lasse play-acts throwing.]
> HENNA: If my pullover gets dirty you'll have to go and buy me a
>   new one from France.
>
> (ObsH)

It is almost a truism of classroom observation that similar behaviour from boys and girls is interpreted differently. Boys may be critical and boisterous, but be regarded as active individualists, and/or fishing for the teacher's attention. When girls are boisterous or dominate the audible space they are more frequently interpreted as behaving inappropriately, or as resisting the teacher. Their boisterous use of voice challenges the teacher, the girls' informal culture interrupts the official teaching.

Here a bunch of noisy, boisterous girls is regarded as behaving uncharacteristically (by both researcher and teacher) and chastised (by the teacher):

The girls are a bit punchy today, lively, talkative, especially on the far table (from where I am sitting). I later discovered that there was a change in friendship lineup going on. The teacher of this class also reported the whole class, but especially the girls, for being misbehaved.

(ObsL)

This was in a lesson when the boys immediately in front of the observer had played ever more elaborate games involving considerable movement and noise, with the classroom equipment. Whilst girls may chat quietly if seen to be performing the lesson tasks, their voices may be interrupted if they are regarded as disrupting the lesson, as in the next example:

At various points in the lesson, Jatta hums, drums the back of a chair quietly, and waves her feet around.
TEACHER: Jatta, that is disruptive.
Jatta stops humming and drumming with her fingers. She waves her feet again.
JATTA: Everybody here is Maths crazy.
Jatta hums very quietly.

(ObsH)

Girls were shouting in a basketball game, and the researcher observed:

I realised that I had never before heard the girls shouting. The teacher interjects that this high-pitched squealing 'is enough to make people feel sick. It's a sports court not a playground for young children'. Anja did a fake squeal, the teacher said 'out!' and stood with arm pointing to the door. Anja is sent out of the gym.

(ObsL)

In the conflict discussed earlier, Henna was reprimanded for her language more often than Lasse:

Lasse hoots in a shrill voice every time somebody answers incorrectly. Henna says 'buuu' or 'jeee' when somebody answers correctly.
TEACHER: This is not a place for buuing.
Suddenly Henna turns backwards and asks Erkko why he cannot take the cap from his head.

LASSE: He says that his hair is from arse [laughing, Erkko does not laugh] he said it himself, I only repeat.
Henna repeats laughing: From arse!
TEACHER [angry] to Henna: Do not use such language!

Critical girls, and girls who participate in classroom discussion, can find space in the official school, as in this summary of a discussion of a story about mother/daughter interaction set in the past in a Finnish lesson where girls are in the majority in the group:

> When the story finishes, there is a lively discussion, and I did my best to record it, including lots of quotations of girls' talk. Girls criticise corporal punishment and the mother. Others point out that the mother did not want to punish the daughter in such a way. Lotta notes the historical period, and refers to the idea that children won't learn without punishment. Salli notes that the mother felt under social pressure to conform to contemporary customs. Noora keeps criticising the mother, saying that a child who is hit becomes withdrawn. Asta notes that the girl was a dreamer. Heli notes that she did not get a lot of opportunity for playing. The discussion is complex, with many different strands – it is initiated by Asta, who starts talking immediately the tape finishes, without waiting for the teacher to indicate what should be done next, or how the discussion should proceed.
>
> (ObsH)

bell hooks (1989) refers to the process of 'talking back'. It means speaking as an equal to an authority figure, daring to disagree, or it can just mean having an opinion. To speak when one is not spoken to is an act of risk and daring, defiance of the 'right speech of womanhood'; talking back, bell hooks suggests, can be empowering. Valerie Walkerdine (1992) has criticised the idea of 'giving a voice' to marginalised groups, as there may be no voice to be found if speech has been suppressed. Talking back may be necessary in developing that voice.

The quietness of girls can be disturbing for teachers, and they often suggested that problems are easier to sort out with boys since they say what is on their minds, whereas girls do not. Silence can be disconcerting when the ideal aim in lessons is suitable speech. We explore the way in which suitable speech is negotiated by focusing on a group of 'bold, beautiful and brainy' girls. Their speech was subject to both approval and scrutiny. Teachers welcomed their 'activity' in speech, but controlled their talking back. Noora provides an example:

> Once we had a test, or the teacher had decided that there'll be a test. There was nothing about it in the test list, and she hadn't said anything. We thought that we won't start the exam, and – well, she started to criticise us endlessly. Everyone was completely quiet and she looked at us really contemptuously, so I said to her that it's not a very nice way to start a day, having her shouting at us, you know, this is not anyone's fault, you don't need to shout at us. And Sinikka also said don't rage at us, and she was completely hysterical, 'Get out, get out!'
>
> (Noora, FSH)

Discussions with the girls suggested that their 'talking back' was likely to cause anxiety and internal conflict: 'What gets me into trouble is – my big mouth!' (McLean Taylor *et al.*, 1995, p. 39).

Suitable speech of girlhood/womanhood was also controlled by boys. Sonja explains that 'mostly girls are not really able to shout very much – if they could shout like the boys, fingers would be pointed, you know, that's not feminine at all' (Sonja, FSH). Sonja is more quiet than she would like to be, although she does prefer a peaceful environment in the classroom so that she can concentrate on her work, and she can be irritated by noisy boys. Talking back to boys requires energy and commitment. Nelli talks about noisy boys whom she considers to be fun, but she gets annoyed when boys criticise her. Unlike Sonja, Nelli does talk back to boys, but she explains that when you do so, boys come up with new retorts. It is an endless circle.

But not talking back can be costly too. Elli, who describes herself and her friends as quiet girls, explains:

> We are sort of those who are quieter, but we're not quiet. We understand that you have to treat teachers like human beings and not shout or swear or lie, so we're in every way sort of angels and saints. But we're not angels and saints because we're not completely flawless.
>
> (Elli, FSH)

She explains that whilst loud girls 'say what they think', she and her friends 'think what they say'. Their carefulness is also indicated when Elli talks about school rules, saying that she does not know them, nor needs to, as she would never break them anyway. This is unlike another girl who explains that she does not know the rules and expects that she breaks them quite often. Elli's consideration for others is commendable, but her silence is costly, because it provides her with a limited range of options. She finds school boring and the subjects superfluous, apart from practical activities like cooking and sewing. At home she does a great deal of housework and child-rearing. She praises domestic femininity, but at the same time finds domestic duties hard work.

Our examples demonstrate both the danger and importance of talking, as silence can marginalise as well as cause pain. Talking back can also provide pain, as adults are teaching young girls the 'right speech of womanhood'; girls are to strive towards individuality but, as we have suggested earlier, the position of a soloist or a joker is not easily open for girls and, if they succeed, the process of gaining it can be fraught. In order to be a full citizen, however, a person must occupy a subject position and possess a speaking voice (see Chapter 1).

Boys' talk is also controlled, but less as 'boys'; more differentiation among boys is expected and accepted. They can also be soloists and jokers. The process of becoming an individual is not so fraught for boys, or it is fraught in different ways. A particular boy's speech can be controlled – a barrage of laughter and comments accompany the talk of those boys whose masculinity is in question. Such laughter is often heard at tense junctures when hierarchical relations among boys are undergoing change.

In some ways the quiet girls – and boys – are not noticed, there are few references to them in our notes and in the midst of visible and audible action they are at times taken for granted. At the same time they are being ideal students, or researchers may see them as such. When nothing 'really happens', during stillness and silence in the classroom, researchers would often use their time making notes about the classroom space or the embodiment of the teacher or the students. They focus more on less visible and audible action and non-events. There are moments when the researchers decided to concentrate on girls, and then stillness and silence were recorded. This can reveal aspects of the internal dynamics of girls' relationships, which otherwise would go unnoticed.

We have discussed how activity has been recorded and interpreted in the researcher's gaze (see Gordon *et al.*, 1998). The opposite of visible and audible activity is stillness and silence; it is not necessarily passivity. Being active, according to the *Oxford Advanced Learner's Dictionary*, means among other things being in the habit of doing things, lively, or having an effect. Doing things in schools is not only visible and audible; the dictionary gives 'an active brain' as an example. In school research, however, activity is often related to its physical (visible and audible) signs. Although European social thought emphasises the importance of mind over body, reason over emotions, nevertheless the possibility that a bodily 'passive' student is active in her mind is ignored. We as ethnographers had difficulties in recording stillness and silence in the lesson.

Movement in the curriculum: sport

In one London school girls are required to wear short skirts for games, as part of the school uniform. Boys can wear shorts and tracksuit bottoms when warming up. The girls are, however, permitted to wear tight, cycling shorts beneath their skirts, so preserving their 'modesty' by not revealing their knickers should they engage actively in games, but highlighting the school's insistence on gender differentiation in this regard, and its role in the construction of gendered identity and heterosexuality. Some girls, particularly those from certain ethnic groups, maintained a high degree of modesty in the changing rooms. In Finland, girls must change their clothes for PE, but there are few specific stipulations about clothing beyond comfort and ease – girls wear tracksuit bottoms, shorts or leggings.

In Britain there has been considerable debate about gender differentiation and segregation in games, with powerful arguments being put forward both for and against (Flintoff, 1990; Scraton, 1992; Evans, 1993). One school in the study segregated for some activities but taught others together. The other had entirely segregated sport, but this was an issue and was likely to change, as young teachers favoured non-sex-segregated sport. The solidarity between boys and their male teacher generated through sports carried into the classroom in this school, where sports teachers also taught other lessons. The teachers would know the boys better and in a different context, and this would carry into the more academic lesson, to the detriment of attention for the girls, whom they knew only in the context of the academic lesson. The observer muses in a maths class taught by one of these teachers:

> Effect of using football anecdotes to illustrate probability, asked class if anybody had seen rugby or football, only boys chipping in with responses.
>
> (ObsL)

In Finland sport is normally taught in gender-separated groups. Girls have a female teacher and boys a male teacher. This can be seen as providing girls with a safe feminine space within the school; and boys an arena of embodied masculinities. We have noticed continuities and moments of solidarity and closeness between girls and their female sports teacher, and between boys and their male sports teacher (Gordon *et al.*, 2000d). Gender separation in sports is not complete, and sometimes meeting places within girls' and boys' sports paths emphasise gender difference. In sports courts, swimming pools and skating areas girls and boys do sports close to each other, but they have different teachers and usually different programmes. Generally girls resisted the male gaze, objecting to incursions into their dressing room by male teachers, and to boys looking into the gym through the windows while they are playing there. The responses of girls varied in mixed sessions. Some girls performed a 'modest' feminine, less active, even an ineffectual role – refusing to run or exert themselves, or running as if in high heels for a bus. Other girls, however, participated actively and energetically and were commended by both male and female teachers for their athletic prowess. The presence of the former ('feminine' girls) in mixed teams generated in these lessons are objected to by the boys; the presence of the latter is often desired by both boys and girls because of their skill and power.

Good sportswomen are valued in interschool and other local and regional competitions. There were some very athletic, powerful girls in the groups followed in each school, and some who had little interest and did not engage. This is also true of the boys. In terms of the construction of hegemonic masculinity, lack of engagement was more of a problem for the boys. Mac an Ghaill (1994) has pointed out that a male bod/boff can compensate in retrieving his masculine identity by being good at sport (see too Redman and Mac an Ghaill, 1997). Football was an area of separation between the sexes in Britain. Girls often wanted to play, and in each school had asked to be able to, but it never quite seemed to work out. In our Helsinki schools girls do play football in sports lessons, but football does not have the same importance for boys as in British schools. Ice hockey is very popular and boys play it in the winter, often with considerable speed, skill and pleasure. Girls seldom play ice hockey.

In London there was an occasion when the reverse of the male gaze was observed. Girls and boys were in training for an approaching sports day on adjacent open all-weather pitches. The boys were practising various race lengths running around their pitch. The boys, given an opportunity, would stand at the fence between the two pitches, watch the girls, and comment on their performance in hurdles or sprint. But at another point girls came to the fence to watch the boys' performance, commenting favourably or unfavourably, and encouraging members of their own class in the competition.

Those students who did not make particular efforts to compete in the official hierarchies based on achievement, constructed their space and deployed their bodies in different ways. Embodied micro-politics of space, in which masculinity and ethnicity are involved, are of interest here. One example is a boy who came to one of the schools from an African culture some years earlier. He was relatively large, fit and athletic, and took an interest on his arrival in basketball, which he had never played before. A sports teacher saw him as a 'natural talent' who 'did not need to think' to perform.[7] Staff in general saw him as a basketball fanatic. He carried his basketball with him at most times, sometimes spinning it on his finger whilst walking. In this way he diversified and informalised official time–space paths and his bodily comportment in them, and symbolically inserted one space (to do with sport and his own bodily power) into another space – the school corridors and classrooms.

The second is a case of a boy of African origin from a European country, Anton. He could not speak English on his arrival, but spoke another European language, which some teachers understood, and attempted to speak to him in it. But, as was the practice in the school, he was to learn English by being immersed in it in lessons and in interaction with his peers. His method to create an identity and a place for himself in this new environment, and to communicate with his peers, was through his athletic prowess. This he took to extremes, and not only on the playing field. In any lesson he would use anything to hand to 'play' physical activity, a game. For example the dough to make a pie was employed as many different types of ball in play-acting various sporting activities (basketball, baseball, tennis), culminating with dropping it from a height, and catching it momentarily before it hit the ground. He also play-acted 'fighting' with other boys, ducking and weaving, throwing punches, grappling them to the ground. In a games lesson there was a beautiful example of his use of this construction of identity, and the role it played in his relationship with both teachers and peers. The teacher invited the boys each to suggest a warm-up exercise, demonstrating it in front of the class, who would then perform it. The exercises suggested reflected the athletic skill, and desire to perform, of the participants. Some were very gentle, some slightly more energetic. When it was Anton's turn he performed a number of press-ups, pushing himself up into the air and clapping his hands after each one. The class, teacher and observer collapsed laughing at the thought that any of us would be able to follow that performance.

Physical exercise lessons are the ones that disrupt the routinised time–space paths and the immobility of bodies. Then students are expected, required, to move, and immobility is regarded as passivity. Students' bodies are surveyed in different ways than they are during other lessons. Sport also enlarges their paths. In the Helsinki schools only some of the sport lessons take place in the school area. Students often walk some distance to a sports or skating field, or they take a bus to a swimming pool or to another sports hall. Sports lessons also bring unexpected situations; unpleasant weather changes plans to have a lesson outdoors, and some of the groups have to have a health education lesson due to insufficient space in the sports hall.

Bodies in authority

Students make bodily contact for a range of reasons; they can be creating connections (grooming, playing together, making sexual contact) or hierarchy. We have discussed this in the chapters on the official and informal schools. Here we discuss teacher contact with students. An important rule about movement and the body in schools is that of contact. There should be no physical contact between teachers and students, particularly contact which could be interpreted as aggressive, violent or sexually motivated by the teacher; teachers said 'We are not supposed to, we are given directions that we should not make any physical contact.' The exceptions to this rule are if students are fighting, when you should interpose your body (the researchers were also told to do this in that school) or if there is a danger that students will hurt themselves. This is a sensitive issue from both student and teacher perspective in Britain, but not discussed so much in Finland. In Britain there has been rising student violence towards teachers, coupled with an increased awareness of student and parental 'rights' in the educational context. This can create the paradox of a teacher who has been threatened, or even struck by a student, and who has responded by physical restraint and removal of the student from the classroom, being reprimanded or disciplined. Whilst the guidelines seem clear, in practice these interactions are fraught with difficulty for the teacher, and teachers may have little support for their actions.

One teacher to whom this happened castigated himself for moving into the pupil's space and provoking a confrontation:

> I made the mistake of walking up to him and saying, do this, I shouldn't have done that, I should have kept, I should have stayed at my desk and thought well, what do I want out of the situation. If I step up and walk towards him, that's you know, entering like an arena where there could be more confrontation, because sure enough, he pushed me ... he pushed me a couple of times and I just put my arms round him and grabbed him, took him to the door, took him out of the classroom. And that was inappropriate, because I shouldn't have entered into the initial confrontation of walking up to him.
>
> (Jeremy, MTL)

A further paradox is provided by those subjects in which contact is perhaps inevitable – types of physical exercise, sport, dance and drama. The guidelines remain, in particular in relation to male teachers and female students. But one small female teacher used her physical presence and power, and the latitude on physical contact afforded by these disciplines, to control male students, often much larger than herself. She was prepared to be physically assertive and to make bodily contact, and reported a time when a group of boys used physical aggression to challenge women teachers:

> I think a lot of aggression came out, I don't know where that came from, there was a lot of challenging of female teachers and challenging their authority and who they were. I think also there was a challenging of how much the girls in the class would put up with that sort of behaviour as well.... And testing their physical persona as well with the older boys.
>
> (Katherine, FTL)

And her way of dealing with it:

> I am little and quite tough and because I have worked in some very rough schools, then I suppose ... I did exert physical force on some people. I did pull them about and shove them against the wall and throw them out of my room, bodily, literally bodily, whereas other people possibly wouldn't but I did. I did handle the children.[8]

While physical contact between teachers and students is problematic, it is common for some teachers to put their hands on the shoulders of a restless student, in order to calm her or him down. This seems to be a means to maintain order in the classroom without having to use time for reprimands. One teacher used bringing his face very close to the pupil as a rather aggressive form of control, usually coupled with a sarcastic remark. Other teachers, in a more supportive physical deployment of their own body, sat on desks/tables, knelt or crouched at the side of students to talk to them, bringing themselves to the physical level of the seated student.

Contact does take place between teachers and students but, particularly in England/Wales, teachers must beware of confrontation and misinterpretation. Considerations of good practice, the security of both teachers and students, and allowing students their space and some autonomy arise in these situations.

Conclusion

Delicate and intricate steps and movements are undertaken by both students and teachers in the dance of the school, and while a fundamental requirement is for control of bodies, and adherence to the formal steps of the dance, some students improvise, or create their own steps, and can talk back. Our examination of bodies in the physical school has demonstrated, however, that gender is integral to the dance, and while both boys and girls are controlled, and their bodies often subjected to an irksome immobility, the control is often gender-specific. Girls are expected to move and speak out less, to take up less space, to sit in stillness and silence, and so they do, or most of them often do. Even aware researchers, gazing with the eye of the ethnographer, have difficulty tearing the gaze from the sound and movement of the boys' dance, to the stillness and silence of the quiet girls, attending to the required tasks of the school.

And the students control each other, creating gender and within-gender hierarchies, and helping to construct gendered and sexualised identities. While in the London schools apparel and adornment is strictly controlled by the use of the school uniform, and in Helsinki no such obvious control is apparent, in each country appearance is deployed in the construction of group membership, and individual identity, often to enhance or display appropriate sexuality. This was particularly marked in the London schools, where some of the girls adjusted their uniforms to enhance their femininity. This gendered display, although contrary to school rules, was not hounded with such devotion to duty by the teachers as in the case of other uniform transgressions. In this, as in the expectations of greater movement, noise and the taking of space by boys, we have seen the complicity of the school in the construction of gender and sexuality.

9
Who are the Wallflowers?

Many expectations are placed on education systems. At the broadest level they are expected to regulate and maintain the *status quo*, to produce citizens for the society in which they are located. These citizens should know how to operate as responsible adults, and how to exercise their political and civic rights and obligations. But schools are also expected to emancipate and to produce social change, and to contribute to the construction of a just, equitable society, where individual aptitudes and interests can be realised. These expectations can overlap, but they are often contradictory, and the latter can be cast aside when strong right-wing ideologies hold sway.

We have demonstrated that, in everyday practices in schools, regulation and emancipation can be discerned as tensions between control and agency. School students are habituated in the time–space paths of the school; they are taught to take correct steps in correct places. But they are also encouraged to take responsibility for their actions, to work out the correct steps, and to personalise their styles, albeit in a way that fits the official agenda. In this context students set out to make spaces for themselves, and to integrate the demands of both control and agency. It is in these processes that differentiation of abstract pupils takes place; students exercise agency in different ways, and become professional and competent to varying degrees. For many the desire is to be 'normal' or 'ordinary', and not to stand out – but at the same time they need to construct an acceptable degree of individuality. In this situation a minority of soloists and jokers can flourish, although they must have considerable social skills in order to benefit from the advantages educational competence and everyday professionalism can offer. Some students lack those skills, or are reluctant to develop them. In the context of the dance we can ask: who are the wallflowers, and how do they occupy the margins?

We have explored these processes by focusing on the official, the informal and the physical school. Schools are complex institutions, where socially shaped relations of power intersect to produce hierarchical relations; these include diverse social positions, gender and age relations, ethnicity, sexual orientation, and able-bodiedness or impairment. The analytic differentiation between these intertwined levels has helped us to focus on these multilayered elements. In various spaces of the school – in classrooms, dining areas, corridors and school yards – many simultaneous processes of making difference and binding connections are taking place. Through differentiating between these levels we have been able to crystallise our focus on spatiality and embodiment, but conducting the analysis through these layers can also pose constraints. An activity can take place in the official school and the physical school at the same time, and many informal processes have embodied dimensions. In this chapter we focus in a different way by thinking both within and across the categories of the official, the informal and the physical school. We turn to our central concepts and review what we have found in relation to them. We consider questions raised in the initial comparative, crosscultural analysis, where we examined educational policies, concentrating particularly on questions of equality and social justice. Implications of what we have discovered about everyday processes at school are related to debates on the directions of schooling.

Our crosscultural focus and ethnographic approach has in many ways collapsed differences between schooling in Britain and in Finland. We have demonstrated everyday processes and practices, and looked at the range of ways in which control and agency are exercised in schools. Differences between the schools and between different systems of schooling have often moved to the background. Having described and illustrated the basic processes of the secondary school we are now in a position to move on to examine difference. Crosscultural educational research, beyond comparative research with systematic, often quantitative data, is rare. The reasons are clear – sustained and constant cooperation is required across language and cultural barriers; in ethnographic research extensive familiarisation with the data is necessary. This requires a considerable amount of travel and a great deal of time, and makes massive demands on researchers – although the rewards are great. In comparing our data and experiences, we have constantly been sensitised to taken-for-granted processes in schools.

We now summarise and remind ourselves and readers of some of the central differences between the countries we have studied, and their education systems. At the time when New Right policies were born in the USA, the school institutions of Finland and Britain were very different. The restructuring of education gave more curricular autonomy to Finnish schools and teachers, who did not have the tradition of curriculum development and control. At the same time the curricular autonomy of schools and teachers in Britain, which had been used both in ways that promoted and challenged inequalities, was curtailed. The education systems of these two countries are now more similar than before restructuring. Choice, accountability and competition are emphasised in the official rhetoric of both countries, but in school practices the different traditions of teachers have their impact on how the reforms are implemented, and on what meanings are given to these terms.

The essential dimensions of difference that we have tried to analyse in this book are gender, ethnicity, and social class. The contexts in which the schools have to challenge these differences vary in each country.

Are girls leading the dance?

In Finland a majority of women work full-time. The Nordic welfare state model has extended the social citizenship of women, and has broken down some traditional gender differences, whilst also maintaining some and introducing others. It is easier for Finnish women to support themselves, and this is reflected in their extensive participation in the labour market, the higher incidence of cohabitation, as well as the larger percentage of single women. Finnish women have more opportunities to try to construct independent lives. On the other hand, some of the gender differences are driven underground, and an emphasis on gender neutrality and extensive rhetoric of gender equality makes it difficult for Finnish women to raise questions about gendered inequalities.

Gendered divisions are more traditional in Britain, where social citizenship is less developed, particularly after the long period of Conservative rule. In this period traditional values, the family and women's responsibilities within the home were emphasised, and these ideals were reinforced by lack of child-care and limited maternity leave. But the stronger tradition of liberalism and emphasis on individuality has led to a more heterogeneous society in which women are constructing a variety of different paths through their lives, and the women's movement has also been more vocal in raising the issue of women's subordination.

In the USA there is less emphasis on women's place in the home than in Britain, but there is insufficient infrastructure to support them when they work. The labour market is structured in such a way that being in work is not necessarily enough to keep poverty at bay. The rudimentary US welfare state does not provide sufficient support, and there are many obstacles for women who attempt to construct independent lives. The focus on 'race' in California schools has left gender somewhat mute, though racial groups contain gendered divisions.

Our analysis suggests the complexity of gendered patterns in secondary schools. Gender is more a muted category in Finnish than in British educational policies and documents. The myth that gender equality has already been achieved in Finland has led to 'gender-neutral' policies that do not challenge self-evident, dichotomous assumptions about gender difference.

London schools embraced anti-sexist, as well as anti-racist and anti-bullying policies, which raised awareness of both students and teachers to issues of difference and equality. Principles of gender and ethnic equality arose in lessons and in the discourse of both teachers and students in interviews. Some students used the school policies to enable them to make formal (or less formal) complaints about behaviour and practices they saw as contravening the policies. In Helsinki schools gender was not often addressed. Although some of the teachers were sensitive and aware of gendered imbalances, others were not. Some teachers regarded gender as a natural category that explains, for example, differences in behaviour and fields of interest; these were, then, not regarded as pedagogic challenges. Gender or equality issues were sometimes discussed during lessons in Helsinki schools, but seldom in ways that would help the students to challenge stereotypical assumptions. We suggest that a formal policy of equal opportunities is important in schools; it sensitises teachers in their everyday work, although it by no means ensures equality.

With or without written policies of gender equality, schools still cannot change gendered patterns in the society, and differentiation on the basis of gender could be observed in the activities and processes of the school. In most of the groups that we followed, some of the boys used most of the time, space, voice and movement that was granted to or taken by students in the classrooms, while most girls and the rest of the boys were located in the margins. There were girls who tried to take place and voice in the classroom, and were successful especially in the group where girls were in a majority. In some other groups boys made constant efforts to silence outspoken girls. For some of the teachers 'bold, beautiful and brainy' girls were difficult to *get along* with. Centres and margins in classroom contexts are not, however, simple locations of inclusion or exclusion. Although some of the students suffered from being positioned in the margins on whatever basis, others could use the margins and their own marginality effectively – studying, learning and using the school for their instrumental aims. Several girls, for example, who did not use voice or take place in the lessons, achieved well in schools and constructed themselves as competent girls. They also helped other girls in situations where teachers concentrated on noisy boys. On the other hand, being positioned and positioning themselves in the centre of classroom interaction seemed to be a trap for some (often working-class or black) boys whose lack of concern for academic achievement was not challenged. For some other (often middle-class or white) boys this centre was a beneficial position on the route towards individual citizenship.

Our book provides examples of the impact of the informal and physical school in the construction of gender relations. Although there were some cross-gender friendship relations in the classes we followed, only seldom did a girl name a boy as a friend or vice-versa. Interaction during lessons and breaks also took place most often in single-gender groups. We have recorded girls' supportive acts towards each other; yet in the interviews conflicts among girls were regularly mentioned. Boys often said that they are all friends; yet conflicts and bullying among them was often observed. These contradictions suggest that girls and boys interpret their relations in different ways, and the general observation that girls tend to be more exclusive towards each other than boys are, needs further consideration. Sexual relations and dating were not common in this age group; sexuality, however, was present especially in jokes and name-calling with sexualised connotations. Sexuality, then, was a form of informal inclusion and exclusion.

In Finnish educational debates, boys' underachievement has been on the agenda since the early 1980s, whilst this discussion has begun in Britain more recently. In the Finnish context girls have often been blamed for some boys' failures – girls achieve 'too' well; it is only in the latest British debates that the impact of male 'lad' cultures have been questioned. Boys still are in the centre more often than girls in the official, informal and physical layers of the school. But this does not mean that all boys are in the centre, or that being in the centre is good for all boys. Certainly it does not help girls to construct themselves as competent, individual citizens. There are wallflowers among girls and among boys.

Multicultural rhythms

Finland has been more monocultural than most European states. There have been minor changes towards less restrictive principles in recent years, but in school it is still rare to find children who come from different national cultures. Resources are in short supply for such children's needs – the new situation has emerged in parallel with restructuring, and the need for special resources for immigrant children, for example, competes with other needs in a situation of economic cutback. Finland's recent membership of the EU is a further change with a potential impact on our understanding of citizenship and difference.

Britain has a long history as a multicultural society, with immigrants from former British colonies entering the country with citizenship rights. A series of regressive immigration acts has increased restrictions and reduced these rights. In Britain, schools have had to take into account the diverse ethnic and cultural backgrounds of their students, particularly in urban areas, although often they have been regarded as a 'problem'. In London schools many teachers and students claimed that students from different ethnic backgrounds were not treated differently by teachers, but such differentiation did occur. Tensions amongst pupils from different ethnic groups were also apparent in both the official and informal school. Cussing and name-calling was often based on such differences and in the official school (in teachers' distinctions and expectations) and the informal (in students') both class and 'race' factors could lie behind what were ostensibly other differences brought into play. What is clear is that there is considerable awareness of the issues, and the anti-racist and anti-bullying policies of the schools can provide a resource for both students and teachers. Again, both teachers and students were aware of the shortcomings of both policies and practice in dealing fully with some of the problems which could arise through processes of making the difference in schools.

The schools in Helsinki did not have coherent policies to handle language problems and racist comments that we saw in everyday life.

Although some teachers talk in ways which indicate that for them difference means diversity, for some of them 'race' is still a self-evident category, and difference is taken for granted. They may cite particular examples of assertive students who have become skilful in dealing with any ethnocentric remarks they confront, but do not always themselves challenge these. We observed situations when foreign cultures were discussed in eurocentric terms. Teachers often point to lack of policies, guidance and in-service training; the *Framework Curriculum* emphasis on tolerance, integration and understanding has not materialised sufficiently in particular policies and back-up.

Still more diverse than in London is the situation in California, a 'melting pot' where the majority of school students will be non-white by the beginning of the next millennium. In the schools that we visited we saw numerous examples of teachers' efforts to challenge inequalities that are embedded in cultural differences, and attempts to reinterpret them as diversity. An on-site police officer in several of the schools indicated the difficulties that these schools have to handle; racial tension and the ensuing conflict are imbedded in the society and will not be eliminated by teachers' efforts alone.

Citizenship and individuality

Our aim was to explore the construction of citizenship in schools, but citizenship is an abstract concept which we needed to operationalise. We decided to do that through an exploration of nationality, of being Finnish/British. To examine what kind of expectations are placed on an adult citizen as a citizen of a particular nation state, evocations of nationality seemed an appropriate avenue to pursue. On the surface nationality is universal, but like citizenship it is riddled with difference. We realised that notions of nationality produced rich insight into expectations, differences and marginalities, and into the process of making spaces. We shall continue to explore these questions in a followup study.

The notion of citizenship is much more developed, and more central in defining the relationship of the individual to the nation state in Finland and other European countries than it is in Britain. The link between citizens and individuals is most weighted towards individuality in the USA, and especially so in California, where the importance of the nation is constantly in tension with the rights of the individual.

The production of individual citizens takes place simultaneously in the official, the informal and the physical school. In the official school students are constructed as knowing citizens; national curricula define what a citizen should know. The official level also includes the inculcation of ways of being for citizens as responsible adults, ready to step into the world of work and the (heterosexual) family. But the individual citizen should also be autonomous, critical and unique. So the official school does not require automatons, although students should be good-mannered and well behaved; a degree of informalisation of the official activities is a negotiated, but a desired, end. Students should be active in the process of negotiating the classroom order, although this activity does not include all the processes in the informal school. The informal school is, potentially, also a space where the responsible citizen is criticised. A citizen exists alongside other citizens, and is able to cooperate with them; in the physical school the emphasis is on the well-ordered conduct of crowds, in an organised, predictable manner. The citizen is thus placed in space in particular ways. Healthy citizens' bodies are a necessary resource; bodies should be both fit and presentable. These processes are negotiated, ordered and controlled by teachers and other staff, and by the rules and ethos of the school, but also by the students themselves. Complex, overlapping and intertwined practices contribute to the making of citizens. All this takes place in space which contains various representations of the sphere of the citizen – school halls, corridors and classrooms contain symbolic condensation of the acceptable, admirable and diverse citizen, through cultural and artistic representations of the knowledge and interests of the citizen, as well as desired and desirable knowledge.

It is the combination of these many elements that produces conceptions of particular types of citizens in different countries and in different schools. In California multiculturalism and individuality are represented, encouraging diversity, along with flags and portraits of American leaders, producing a tension between emphasis on the nation and emphasis on the individual citizen. In Helsinki a school of performing arts depicts Finnish presidents, whilst also including large art displays, which emphasise culture and individual as well as collective effort in the production of these displays. The potent symbol of the national flag was not so apparent in the London schools, although it might be found amongst the flags of many nations depicted in foreign-language classrooms, or dissected into its subnational components for a discussion of the separate countries of the union.

Citizenship, then, is in a shifting dynamic relationship to individuality. Euro-American nation states share many similarities, but there are also differences between them, one of these being the relationship between the individual and the state. But in all countries this relationship is gendered. Women are less likely to be represented and discussed as unique individuals. Women are still seen in the context of their relationships to other people, they can be abstractions, and at the same time remain concrete. Men are seen as abstract individuals, as carriers of rights. These categorisations do not completely determine people's lives and the ways in which individual women and men construct themselves; but they construct and are constructed by power relations, which confer more privileges on those named men than on those named women.

The way in which individuality has been perceived is crucial in shaping citizenship and one's access to the status of a citizen, beyond formal rights. Being named as part of a group determined through gender, age, ethnicity, sexual orientation and impairment, defines differences in hierarchical ways.

Different ballrooms

Unlike Britain and the USA, Finland does not have a strong tradition of elitist private schools, and since comprehensive reform in the early 1970s almost all students attend the schools in their catchment areas. In addition, as a result of rapid structural change from an agrarian to an industrial/post-industrial society in the 1960s, towns in Finland do not have traditional working-class areas comparable to the inner-city areas of London. One of the underlying ideologies of comprehensive reform in Finland was that of equality of opportunity: the same curriculum and equal resources must be provided for everyone. Although the principle of equality has never been as evident in everyday policies as in policy texts, it has brought about a very centralised curriculum and rather similar schools in different parts of the country. In Britain, as well as the USA, schools have varied much more in relation to the social background of students, resources and the curriculum – although centralised achievement tests have led to a more unified system in practice.

Compared with Finland, the more diverse school system in Britain has contributed to the maintenance of education inequalities in relation to social background. But, at the same time, more extensive autonomy for teachers and schools has provided the possibility of developing curriculum and teaching. In many schools these possibilities have been used to produce a more inclusive curriculum which challenges issues of gender, ethnic and social inequality. This area of work was a target of attack for New Right policies in the 1980s.

In both countries we had one school with students from a more middle-class, and another with a more working-class, background. Teachers in both of the London schools saw their pupils as 'different', 'exceptional', that the school in some way had a unique set of students. In Oak Grove the difference was couched around the type of background from which they came (working-class, different ethnic groups, recent immigrant, refugee) and the problems which might flow from this. In Woburn Hill difference was seen in terms of ability, motivation, and expectation, 'we are training the elite', the next generation of lawyers and doctors. Teachers in City Park school in Helsinki, as well, regarded their students as 'exceptional'; as especially motivated, high-achieving young people. This was not equally evident in the perceptions of teachers in Green Park, some of whom emphasised that theirs is a school with 'ordinary' pupils. Although we want to emphasise that these were all good schools with skilled teachers, it seemed that the more middle-class schools in both countries could provide students with more chances to construct themselves as competent, individual citizens. In a follow-up study of these young people we will return to this issue.

The New Right policies in both countries already have broadened differences between schools in Britain (and in the USA). In Finland the new education legislation (1998) provides opportunities for similar developments. Educational debate on the challenges for the idea of comprehensiveness has started – hopefully not too late.

Who are making spaces?

Teachers and students often operate with a range of understandings about difference, for example in terms of ability, achievement, personality and family background. In these characterisations, we suggest, social differences are played out whilst they are also muted. Complex processes of marginalisation are taking place round gender, social class, race/ethnicity and sexuality, though often explained through other terms. Questions about centres and margins are complex. Whilst few students are clearly marginal at many levels, most of the time marginality is not a characteristic of individuals, but of social processes. We need to ask not simply *who* are marginalised, but *what* is marginalised. Many students move in and out of the margins in their everyday lives at school, but some more so than others, and those with fewer exits often occupy multiple marginalities which are spatially played out in embodied ways.

The group of wallflowers occupying the margins has then a shifting constitution, though some students find themselves there more often than others. Margins as well as the centres are multilayered and offer changing opportunities for making spaces; though being central in the informal school is different from being central in the official school. An opportunity for enactment in the physical school does not necessarily provide opportunities for enactment in the official school. These shifting constellations of margins and centres have power relations embedded in them; power, then, is complex, at times clearly visible, at other times well hidden.

Operations of power in schools interact with societal patterns. In Finland emphasis has been placed on a comprehensive education system, and differences between schools are far smaller than in Britain and in the USA. In these two countries equality-of-opportunity policies at the school level are resources drawn upon to counteract inequalities. Democratic schooling is strived for in different ways, on a national level or in particular districts or schools. We suggest that in Finland discussions on equality need to be brought into the everyday life of schools; in Britain and in the USA more democratic educational systems are needed, as well as continued development of school-based policies.

The democratic educational tradition in all these countries has focused on social differences and emphasised equal access. This tradition has remained mute on several levels. If social class has been addressed, gender and race/ethnicity may have remained silent. Whilst New Right policies have been effective, both in similar and diverse ways, in all these countries we find no golden age to return to. But we do want to retrieve ideas of democracy and equality from the Right that has snatched these away from us. We want to re-emphasise social citizenship, and broaden citizenship further by including cultural and sexual citizenship. This implies huge challenges for schools; teachers and students should be provided a base for doing this. Resources and facilities are required, whilst these alone are not enough. Schools, supported by the societies and localities they find themselves in, should turn their attention to official, informal and physical everyday practices.

Learning should be interesting (whilst requiring effort and

determination too). Listening to students, the message is that they want well-ordered, well-organised environments which are also flexible and sympathetic, and allow all students to make spaces for themselves. Whilst all the dancers in the school are involved in the process of making differences, adults in schools and at all levels of educational endeavours should aim to ensure that no one is assigned to the margins as a wallflower. Gender is too important a category to be muted in education. The diversity amongst girls and boys is often visible in schools; this may hide difficulties many girls have in making spaces, since centrality is not easily afforded to women and girls. Attention to gender in its intersections with other social categories enables us to ask 'which girls?' and 'which boys?' when we focus on marginality.

Appendix: Methods in Use

The basis for the cooperation of the authors was laid during the 16 years that Tuula lived and conducted her initial and postgraduate studies in London. She also undertook research in schools in England and worked with Janet Holland on the 'Girls and Occupational Choice' project. Tuula Gordon and Elina Lahelma began their association in 1985 when Tuula first planned to move back to Finland, and had in mind some of the basic ideas for a piece of research that has materialised in this project. Tuula's and Elina's joint work continued in Finland in the context of the network 'Gender and Education' (later called 'EDDI': Education and Difference) which they initiated together in 1987. In this network the basic ideas for this project were discussed and elaborated, and the Finnish project team was established.

Some of the concepts and methods that we use in this research were initially explored in the 'Physical School' project, conducted by the Gender and Education research group in Finland, from 1992 to 1994. Tuula was the coordinator of the research group, with Elina and other members of the Finnish research team here major participants. During the planning phase of this research Elina conducted pilot research in eight schools in England (winter 1992–3), and Tuula visited one of them. During this time Elina and Janet met regularly and discussed the study, reflecting on the project plans made initially by Tuula.

Both project teams met regularly, discussing the observation experience and records in great detail. This process was of considerable value in interpreting what was observed, and the collective work enabled the development of a shared language and focus for observations and interpretation. Discussion between London and Helsinki took place by email, telephone, and face-to-face contact. Both within and between the London and Helsinki teams, a practice of *analysis through discussion* was generated, with particular interactions, incidents or trends chosen for joint focus, with the aim of grasping both generalities and particularities. These processes have been full of analytical insights, and it has proved to be very challenging, and at times impossible, to try to develop ways of writing such analyses.

A comprehensive observation schedule was developed for each layer of the school, the official, the informal and the physical. This was to direct the gaze of the researcher onto as many relevant aspects of those layers as possible. In Finland there were, particularly in the beginning, often two researchers observing any one lesson (sometimes more) and so the gaze of each could be directed towards specific aspects.

Each researcher had her own specific class to follow in each school, although they did observe in the classrooms of the other researchers. The method was to follow the class throughout the day, observing and participating, and taking extensive notes. In Britain each observer was alone in the classroom, and tried to cover each layer of the school, although at different times and in different lessons the emphasis may be on one or other aspect of the classroom and the processes taking place there. Feedback sessions were held regularly after observation. The Helsinki team followed together more than 900 lessons and several other occasions in the schools, for example staff meetings, parents' evenings, extra days, discos. The London researchers followed about 320 lessons, plus assemblies and other events in the school, and elsewhere occasionally when the class was on the move.

Our aim was to interview all the students in the classes that we followed, teachers who taught 'our' classes, and teachers significantly placed in hierarchies (heads, deputy heads, heads of years and departments) and some members of the support staff. From the Finnish schools we have 96 student interviews (51 girls and 45 boys), 44 teacher interviews (34 male and 10 female) and 4 support staff interviews (1 male, 3 female). In the London schools we have 71 student interviews (39 girls and 32 boys), 16 teacher interviews (10 male and 6 female) and 3 support staff interviews (1 male, 2 female). In Helsinki Tuula conducted altogether 69 and Elina 50 of the interviews. Tuija conducted 16, Tarja Palmu 5, Tarja Tolonen 2 and Pirkko 2 interviews that we used. In London Janet conducted 52, Kay 33 and Nicole 5 of the interviews. In one London school we were able to conduct very few student interviews, but do have many informal discussions with the students in our observation notes.

In student interviews we asked for their memories of the primary school and starting secondary school. We asked students' opinions on various issues in the official school; for example teachers, subjects, lesson content, working methods, school rules. We discussed their relationships in school, friendships, teasing, and hobbies, and their homes and families. Questions on space and embodiment were included, and we also asked questions addressing difference and marginality in schools. In teacher interviews we asked many of the same questions as in the student interviews. We also discussed, for example, teachers' work, their own school, school space, curriculum and their own subject, students in our research groups, and their world views. We also sought their perceptions of gender, nationality and ethnicity. In the support staff interviews we asked questions similar to the teacher interviews. In all interviews we were trying out ways of getting at difficult issues and concepts, such as 'difference' and 'marginality'.

Students and teachers completed a short 'metaphor questionnaire' which involved questions about what they did in the lunch break, spaces around the school that they liked or disliked, and required them to produce a metaphor for the school, 'School is like ...'. The association questionnaire had the following prompts: school, teacher, pupil, girl, boy, child, young person, British/Finnish, researcher. In general these responses provided illuminating access into ways in which the students, teachers and support staff thought about these issues.

The use of these methods was supplemented by participant observation, informal discussions and documentary evidence such as school records, teaching materials and students' work.

Reading, interpreting and writing

For analysis, the observation notes were word-processed, and in Britain the major coding and analysis was undertaken from the written notes. But brief descriptions of the observed lessons, couched in the descriptive and conceptual codes of the analysis, were word-processed. All of the lesson notes were read, but in each case a time period was selected from the large number of lessons observed for detailed analysis. The material had three analytic readings. The first was thematic – where we looked for the major themes emerging from the data; the second was conceptual/interpretive – where we made interpretations on the basis of concepts we had developed; and the third was extractive – where we drew out illustrations of themes and concepts.

Everything was coded in terms of the descriptive and analytical codes employed for the physical, official and informal school. These concepts are employed in the chapters presenting the data, and included, for example: for the physical school – space, time, voice, movement, bodies; for the official – pedagogic relationship, hierarchy, distance, closeness, power, knowledge; and for the informal – resistance/accommodation, friendship, teasing/bullying/cussing, lurking, tension and fear, pleasure.

For the interviews the process of analysis and interpretation included several readings. First we did an overall reading of the interview, highlighting areas of interest within the framework of the study. This was followed by a selective reading, writing a summary of each interview, to which we added a summary of other information available about the student (for example, background, grades, choice of subjects). On a further selection an 'I' analysis was undertaken, based on the work of Carol Gilligan's team (McLean Taylor *et al.*, 1995) which involved highlighting any statements in which the word 'I' occurred. When these statements are then read through, certain themes, regularities and patterns begin to emerge, which can throw light on the individual. We were able to observe gender differences between hesitant girls and determined boys who used statements such as 'I plan', 'I want', 'I won't'. But within-gender differences were evident too. For example, whilst Noora (Chapter 1) used frequent, assertive 'I' statements, one quiet, shy boy used very few 'I' statements – he used 'we' and frequently talked in the passive.

This was followed by an interpretive, conceptual reading, from which we generated files referring to marginality, difference, individuality and nationality. A further content analysis was undertaken by the Finnish researchers to generate a set of descriptive codes based on the interview content, and these were used to code the interviews on NUD*IST. While these codes were essentially descriptive, some of them intersected with, and were incorporated into, the more thematic and conceptual codes developed in other readings. The researchers in London added some of the more conceptual codes to the NUD*IST analysis of the interviews.

Our method of working for this book was very dependent on international conferences and email. We have produced a number of papers for conferences, each writing sections and passing them back and forth by email, producing the results of our separate data from the specific analyses being undertaken, and integrating the comparative data into the whole. Fortunately for the British author we work in English, which involves extra effort and difficulty on each side – in translating the Finnish data, and in editing the English. When we met at the conferences, dotted through the years, to present papers we would spend many hours sharing experiences, checking progress and process, and planning the next phases of the research. We also took the opportunity, where available, to visit each others' schools in the two countries. On one occasion the Finnish researchers replicated their method of (mass) observation in one of the London schools, with three Finnish researchers and one British observing lessons separately or together in a number of classrooms. We joined the intricate dance of the school to understand the complex and multilayered steps everyday life there involves. We have gone on to learn and share yet more difficult movements in order to present the account in this book.

Notes

Notes to the Introduction

1. Words and music by Sting, © 1983; reproduced by permission of EMI Music Publishing Ltd/Magnetic Publishing Ltd, London, WC2H 0EA.
2. Tuula Gordon and Elina Lahelma visited five schools in California, in the San Francisco Bay Area, in two education districts, spending one day in each school, and attending evening activities in two schools (one elementary school, three middle schools and one high school); we visited some of these schools with Barrie Thorne and her research group.

Note to Chapter 1: Individual Citizens

1. We identify quotes from individuals by a pseudonym, plus gender (M/F), whether a student, a teacher or a member of the support staff of the school (S/T/SS), and whether in Helsinki or London (H/L). We have marked fieldnotes ObsH and ObsL.

Notes to Chapter 2: Space and Place for Markets

1. The term United Kingdom covers England, Wales, Scotland and Northern Ireland. In terms of education, Northern Ireland is largely similar to Britain, but with differences which are specified in the 1989 Education Reform Order; Scotland has a different education system. In this book we use the term England/Wales, since the education system and legislation to which our study refers is that of England/Wales. When speaking more generally we may use the term UK, or Britain.
2. Feminist consideration of the marketisation of school education was discussed at a Conference at the Institute of Education in London in 1995. Papers from the Conference were published in *Discourse*, Vol. 17, No. 3, 1996, edited by Jane Kenway and Debbie Epstein.
3. In Finland, equality of opportunity in relation to region and place of residence has been emphasised; this is linked to Finland's geopolitical and historic development, including the involvement of the agrarian Centre party in the 'social-democratic' comprehensive school reform (cf. Antikainen, 1990).
4. Cf. Green's (1990) comparative historical study on the impact of centralisation/decentralisation on the development of national education systems.
5. In Britain this polarisation has occurred, and one response of the New Labour government to schools falling below a specified level of performance is to follow the previous government and 'name and shame' them. This policy has, however, received considerable criticism.

6. But see Rendell (1985) on struggles to keep education out of the Equal Opportunities Act.
7. Educational legislation and policy in both Finland and England/Wales is in a process of change, including new plans for the curriculum to be implemented in the year 2000. In England/Wales the new National Curriculum is likely to include citizenship and democracy, and sex education, and working groups were meeting in the late 1990s to formulate the content.

Notes to Chapter 3: Curricula for Nations

1. Hannu Simola (1998) has studied Finnish educational texts. He argues that the Finnish state educational discourse has created an abstract, universalistic, non-historical and decontextualised concept of pedagogy.
2. In 1985 the proportion of foreigners in Finland was 0.3 per cent of the population, in 1995 it was 1.3 per cent. Finland has Gipsy and Saami minority groups, and 6 per cent of Swedish-speaking Finns. Finnish and Swedish are the official languages, and Swedish-speaking children have a constitutional right for education in their own mother tongue.
3. The Finnish documents that we have analysed are the *Framework Curriculum for the Comprehensive School* (NBE, 1994) and a series of booklets published by the National Board of Education for schools and teachers. In Britain, we have examined the Dearing version of the *National Curriculum* (DFE, 1995), *Curriculum Guidance*, 8: *Education for Citizenship* (NCC, 1990) and 'Education for Adult Life: the Spiritual and Moral Development of Young People' (SCAA, 1996). In both countries we have also reviewed secondary sources, and commentaries on the documents where necessary.
4. In Britain a government Task Group has been set up to consider Citizenship and Democracy for inclusion in the curriculum in 2000.
5. The extracts from the Framework Curriculum are from the official translation of the document. By using an exclamation mark (!) we have noted the systematic use of 'he' and 'man' in the translation. Here the sexist language sounds absurd: what is 'equality among men with no respect to sex'? The Finnish language does not differentiate between 'he' and 'she', and in the Finnish text in this extract uses 'human being' instead of 'man'.
6. In Britain a considerable amount of material has been produced by academics, practitioners and commercial publishers providing ideas for implementing the National Curriculum and cross-curricular themes, and some of this does provide examples of ways in which teachers can realise equal-opportunities aims with respect to gender, ethnicity, citizenship and nationality within the framework of the National Curriculum (Osler, 1995; File, 1995; Allen, 1996).
7. Use of the term 'flocking' in the context of the tiny proportion of minority groups actually in Finnish schools has unfortunate resonance with right-wing arguments in Britain that immigrants were 'flooding' our shores.
8. 'Innate' is the term used in the official translation; we would translate the word as 'inner'.
9. Now transformed into the Department for Education and Employment.

10. In the curriculum of handicraft 'equality' means that students who have chosen textile handicrafts (girls) and those who have chosen technical handicrafts (boys) have a few lessons on the other subject. Gendered choices are not challenged.

Notes to Chapter 4: Invitation to the Dance

1. Our thanks are due to Kay Parkinson for suggesting this metaphor.
2. Consider the horror caused by 'unacceptable' steps and movements in ballroom dancing in the film 'Strictly Ballroom'.
3. The methods of data collection and analysis are described in detail in the Appendix.
4. Luckily enough, we are going to meet the students again in the future; we are planning together to conduct a follow-up study called 'Tracing Transitions' in England and in Finland.
5. The Finnish team had been collecting metaphors for the school since the earlier study under the aegis of the Gender and Education Network (Gordon and Lahelma, 1996; Gordon *et al.*, 1995; Lindroos and Tolonen, 1995). Finnish metaphors were also collected by Tapio Aittola's research team (see Laine, 1995). In Britain, to supplement the metaphors provided by the students in the two schools under detailed study, the author tapped into networks of researchers that she knew were working in schools, to obtain a wider sampling of metaphors. Our thanks are due to Valerie Hey, Gaby Weiner, Debbie Epstein and Shereen Benjamin in this connection.

Notes to Chapter 5: One Two Three, One Two Three

1. The situation has now deteriorated and there is a lively public debate on the issue.
2. The Finnish team had an exceptional opportunity to follow the process through which pupil professionalism for secondary school was taught and achieved during the early days and weeks after students' arrival in their new school. See Lahelma and Gordon (1997), and Gordon *et al.* (2000d).
3. Academically oriented students were called 'bods' or 'boffins'.
4. There are more examples in Lahelma and Gordon, 1998.
5. We adopt this term from Connell *et al.*, 1982.
6. As well as the researchers' gaze, as we have argued in Gordon *et al.*, 1997.

Notes to Chapter 6: Stepping Here, Stepping There

1. We thank Mary Kehily for suggestions on this chapter.
2. The persons concerned with the students' social, mental and physical welfare.
3. In Finland 68 per cent of teachers in comprehensive schools were female in 1995; somewhat more in primary schools and in the cities than in secondary schools and in the countryside. Need for male teachers has been

an issue publicly discussed; for example the Minister of Education has expressed concern about the 'feminisation' of the teaching profession. The reasons given for the need for more male teachers have been diverse and often contradictory in public discussion, as in our teachers' interviews. Students in interviews emphasised the need for good teachers, with fewer references to gender.
4. Jokes reported to us were in bad taste.
5. Shirley Prendergast describes the tightrope which girls see boys as negotiating with 'friendly' punches. A misplaced, misjudged or misinterpreted punch can result in a 'flash fight' – an instantaneous, aggressive, fighting response. (In discussion at the BSA Conference, 1998.)
6. Máirtín Mac an Ghaill in a seminar in Finland, 1996.
7. 'Bullying is defined as any action that makes someone feel unhappy or uncomfortable because of their gender, sexual orientation, race, religion, culture, appearance, ability or disability. Verbal bullying is name-calling; non-verbal bullying is offensive written comments or physical harassment' (from the anti-bullying policy of one London school). In one school some students were unwilling to use the term bullying, preferring teasing. In the other the more general term employed was 'cussing', although bullying was also used. The term 'cussing' has its origins in black street language, and contains an element of performance and skill.

Notes to Chapter 7: 'Strictly Ballroom'

1. If more spacious schools with more varied facilities were built, such extras were not financed by the National Board of Education.
2. We have studied the plans of our research schools as well as those of several other schools that we have visited
3. Exceptionally, one student asked whether the researcher referred to mental space, and explained that there was enough mental, but not enough physical space. Nevertheless, her metaphor for school was a prison, and she explained this by emphasising restrictions.
4. The researchers had not noticed these adventures till the girls told about them in interviews.

Notes to Chapter 8: 'Twist and Shout'

1. This impression of embodied activity is not quite so strong in Finnish schools: schools are smaller, the students start at age 13/14 years, so the youngest age groups (11–13 typically in English/Welsh schools) are absent.
2. Aapola (1997) argues that adolescence in boys is linked with irresponsibility, but white, middle-class boys are seen to be on the road towards increasing autonomy and individuality.
3. See too discussions of school rules in Chapter 7.
4. See the discussion in, for example, Mac an Ghaill (1994), Epstein (1994), Mirza (1992), Gillborn (1993), Thomson and Scott (1992).
5. In one school, during the period of research, due to pressure from students

the rule forbidding the wearing of Doc Marten boots was changed to allow them.

6. Interpretation and comments on observation notes (Vitellone, 1995). See Butler, 1990; Holland *et al.*, 1994.

7. This teacher made a distinction between 'natural' talent, which did not need thought (associated with basketball) and the more 'intellectual' approach needed in, for example, tennis. In this school African–Caribbean boys played basketball and white (or at least non-African–Caribbean boys) played tennis (cf. Nayak, 1997; Hall, 1997).

8. In fact, in January 1998 government guidelines on physical contact were being revised, to allow teachers to make physical contact (to push or to move a student) when required for reasons of discipline or control. Teachers are not allowed, of course, to strike the student.

References

Aapola, Sinikka (1997) 'Mature Girls and Adolescent Boys? Deconstructing Discourses of Adolescence and Gender', *Young*, vol. 5, no. 4, pp. 50–68.

Abercombie, Nicholas, Hill, Stephen and Turner, Bryan (1986) *Sovereign Individuals of Capitalism* (London: Allen and Unwin).

Acker, Sandra (1988) 'Teachers, Gender and Resistance', *British Journal of Sociology of Education*, vol. 9, no. 3, pp. 307–23.

Aittola, Tapio, Jokinen, Kimmo and Laine, Kaarlo (1995) 'Young People, the School and Learning Outside the Classroom', in Tapio Aittola, Riitta Koikkalainen and Esa Sironen (eds), *Confronting Strangeness* (Department of education, University of Jyväskylä, Finland 5/1995), pp. 43–56.

Alapuro, Risto (1988) *State and Revolution in Finland* (Berkeley: University of California Press).

Allen, Beryl M. (1996) 'Gender, Methodology and the Curriculum Process', *Teaching History*, no. 83, pp. 14–16.

Antikainen, Ari (1990) 'The Rise and Change of Comprehensive Planning: the Finnish experience', *European Journal of Education*, vol. 25, no. 1, pp. 75–82.

Anyon, Jean (1983) 'Intersections of Gender and Class: Accommodation and Resistance by Working-class and Affluent Females to Contradictory Sex-role Ideologies', in Stepen Walker and Len Barton (eds), *Gender, Class and Education* (Lewes: Falmer Press).

Apple, Michael W. (1992) 'Constructing the Captive Audience: Channel One and the Political Economy of the Text', *International Studies in Sociology of Education*, vol. 2, no. 2, pp. 107–31.

Apple, Michael W. (1993) 'Thinking Right in the USA: Ideological Transformations in an Age of Conservatism', in Bob Lingaard, John Knight and Paige Porter (eds), *Schooling Reform in Hard Times*, Deakin Studies in Education Series 9 (London and Washington, DC: Falmer Press).

Arnesen, Anne-Lise and Ní Chartheígh, Dearbhal (1992) 'Pathways to Change: Gender and Curriculum Development in Teacher Education', *Series on Equal Opportunities and Teacher Education in Europe*, vol. 1 (Sheffield: ATEE and Pavic Publications).

Arnot, Madeleine (1991) 'Equality and Democracy: a Decade of Struggle over Education', *British Journal of Sociology of Education*, vol. 12, no. 4, pp. 447–65.

Arnot, Madeleine (1992) 'Feminism, Education and the New Right', in Madeleine Arnot and Len Barton (eds), *Voicing Concerns: Sociological Perspectives on Contemporary Education Reforms* (Wallingford: Triangle Books).

Arnot, Madeleine and Gordon, Tuula (1996) 'Gender, Citizenship and Marketisation: a Dialogue between Madeleine Arnot and Tuula Gordon', *Discourse: Studies in the Cultural Politics of Education*, vol. 17, no. 3, pp. 377–88.

Arnot, Madeleine, David, Miriam and Weiner, Gaby (1996) *Educational Reforms and Gender Equality in Schools* (Manchester: EO Commission).

Arnot, Madeleine, David, Miriam and Weiner, Gaby (1997) 'Educational

Reform, Gender Equality and School Cultures', in Ben Cosin and Margaret Hales (eds), *Families, Education and Social Differences* (London and New York: Routledge, in association with the Open University).

Aronowitz, Stanley and Giroux, Henry (1986) *Education under Siege: The Conservative, Liberal and Radical Debate over Schooling* (London: Routledge and Kegan Paul).

Atkinson, Paul (1990) *The Ethnographic Imagination* (London and New York: Routledge).

Bartky, Sandra L. (1990) *Femininity and Domination: Studies in Phenomenology of Oppression* (London: Routledge).

Bernal, Martin (1991) *Black Athena: The Afroasiatic Roots of Classical Civilisation* (London: Vintage).

Bhabha, Homi K. (1990) 'Introduction: Narrating the Nation', in Homi K. Bhabha (ed.), *Nation and Narration* (London: Routledge).

Billig, Michael (1995) *Banal Nationalism* (London: Sage).

Blum, Lawrence A. (1996) 'Antiracist Civic Education in the California History–Social Science Framework', in Robert K. Fullinwider (ed.), *Public Education in a Multicultural Society: Policy, Theory, Critique* (Cambridge: Cambridge University Press).

Bowles, Samuel and Gintis, Herbert (1976) *Schooling in Capitalist America* (London: Routledge and Kegan Paul).

Bracey, Paul (1995) 'Developing a Multicultural Perspective within Key Stage 3', *National Curriculum History, Teaching History*, vol. 78, pp. 8–10.

Brenner, Johanna (1996) 'The Best of Times, the Worst of Times: Feminism in the United States', in Monica Threlfall (ed.), *Mapping the Women's Movement* (London: Verso).

Brophy, Jere E. and Good, Thomas L. (1974) *Teacher–Student Relationships: Causes and Consequences* (New York: Holt, Reinhart and Winston).

Burr, Vivian (1995) *An Introduction to Social Constructionism* (London: Routledge).

Butler, Judith (1990) *Gender Trouble: Feminism and the Subversion of Identity* (London: Routledge).

Butler, Judith (1991) 'Imitation and Gender Subordination', in Diane Fuss (ed.), *Inside/out: Lesbian Theories, Gay Theories* (London: Routledge).

Carrigan, T., Connell, R. W. and Lee, J. (1985) 'Toward a New Sociology of Masculinity', *Theory and Society*, vol. 14, no. 5, pp. 551–604.

Christian-Smith, Linda (1993) 'Sweet Dreams: Gender and Desire in Teen Romance Novels', in Linda K. Christian-Smith (ed.), *Texts of Desire: Essays on Fiction, Femininity and Schooling* (London: Falmer Press).

Clifford, James and Marcus, George E. (eds) (1986) *Writing Culture: The Poetics and Politics of Ethnography* (Berkeley: University of California Press).

Cohen, David (1990) 'Governance and Instruction: the Promise of Decentralization and Choice', in William H. Clune and John F. Witte (eds), *Choice and Control in American Education*, vol. 1: *The Theory of Choice and Control in American Education*, Stanford Series on Education and Public Policy (London, New York and Philadelphia: Falmer Press).

Connell, Robert W. (1987) *Gender and Power: Society, the Person and Sexual Politics* (Cambridge: Polity Press).

Connell, Robert W. (1989) 'Cool Guys, Swots and Wimps: the Interplay of

Masculinity and Education', *Oxford Review of Education*, vol. 15, no. 3, pp. 291–303.

Connell, R. W., Ashenden, D. J., Kessler, S. and Dowsett, G. W. (1982) *Making the Difference* (Sydney: Allen and Unwin).

Corrigan, Paul (1987) 'In/Forming Schooling', in Henry A. Giroux and Paulo Freire (eds), *Critical Pedagogy and Cultural Power* (London: Macmillan).

Crawford, June, Kippax, Susan, Onyx, Jenny, Gault, Una and Benton, Pam (1993) *Emotion and Gender: Constructing Meaning from Memory* (London: Sage).

Dale, Roger (1992) 'Recovering from a Pyrrhic Victory? Quality, Relevance and Impact in the Sociology of Education', in Madeleine Arnot and Len Barton (eds), *Voicing Concerns: Sociological Perspectives on Contemporary Education Reforms* (Wallingford: Triangle Books).

Dale, Roger and Ozga, Jenny (1993) 'Two Hemispheres – Both New Right?: 1980s Education Reform in New Zealand and England and Wales', in Bob Lingaard, John Knight and Paige Porter (eds), *Schooling Reform in Hard Times*, Deakin Studies in Education Series 9 (London and Washington, DC: Falmer Press).

Darmanin, Mary (1993) 'More Things in Heaven and Earth: Contradiction and Co-optation in Education Policy, *International Studies in Sociology of Education*, vol. 3, no. 2, pp. 147–72.

David, Miriam (1992) 'Parents and the State: How has Social Research Informed Education Reforms?', in Madeleine Arnot and Len Barton (eds), *Voicing Concerns: Sociological Perspectives on Contemporary Education Reforms* (Wallingford: Triangle Books).

Davies, Ann Marie, Holland, Janet and Minhas, Rehana (1992) 'Equal Opportunities in the New Era', *Hillcole Group Paper 2*, 2nd rev. edn (London: Tufnell Press).

Davies, Bronwyn (1983) 'The Role Pupils Play in the Social Construction of Classroom Order', *British Journal of Sociology of Education*, vol. 4, no. 1, pp. 55–69.

Davies, Bronwyn (1989) *Frogs and Snails and Feminist Tales: Preschool Children and Gender* (Sydney: Allen and Unwin).

Davies, Bronwyn (1990) 'Agency as a Form of Discursive Practice: a Classroom Scene Observed', *British Journal of Sociology of Education*, vol. 11, no. 3, pp. 341–61.

Davies, Bronwyn and Harré, Rom (1991) 'Positioning: the Discursive Production of Selves', *Journal for the Theory of Social Behaviour*, no. 20, pp 43–63.

Davies, Bronwyn and Hunt, Robyn (1994) 'Classroom Competencies and Marginal Positioning', *British Journal of Sociology of Education*, vol. 15, no. 3, pp. 389–408.

Davies, Paul, Mabbott, Ann and Thomas, David (1992) 'Equal Opportunities within the National Curriculum', in Geoffrey Hall (ed.), *Themes and Dimensions of the National Curriculum: Implications for Policy and Practice* (London: Kegan Page).

Delamont, Sara (1990) *Sex Roles and the School* (London: Routledge).

Delamont, Sara and Atkinson, Paul (1995) *Fighting Familiarity: Essays on Education and Ethnography* (Cresskill, NJ: Hampton Press).

Denzin, Norman and Lincoln, Yvonne (eds) (1994) *Handbook of Qualitative*

Research (London: Sage).

Devor, Holly (1989) *Gender Blending: Confronting the Limits of Duality* (Bloomington and Indianapolis: Indiana University Press).

DFE (Department for Education) (1995) *The National Curriculum* (London: HMSO).

Donald, James (1992) *Sentimental Education: Schooling, Popular Culture and the Regulation of Liberty* (London and New York: Verso).

Donald, James (1996) 'The Citizen and the Man about Town', in Stuart Hall and Paul Du Gay (eds), *Questions in Cultural Identity* (London: Sage).

Education Group, Centre for Contemporary Cultural Studies (1981) *Unpopular Education: Schooling and Social Democracy in England Since 1944* (London: Hutchinson).

Epstein, Debbie (1994) *Challenging Lesbian and Gay Inequalities in Education* (Buckingham: Open University Press).

Epstein, Debbie (1997) 'Boyz Own Stories; Masculinities and Sexualities in Schools', *Gender and Education*, vol. 9, no. 1, pp. 105–15.

Epstein, Debbie and Johnson, Richard (1998) *Schooling Sexualities* (Buckingham: Open University Press).

ERA (1988) *Educational Reform Act* (London: HMSO).

Evans, John (ed.) (1993) *Equality, Education and Physical Education* (Lewes: Falmer Press).

Feintuck, Mike (1994) *Accountability and Choice in Schooling* (Buckingham and Philadelphia: Open University Press).

File, Nigel (1995) 'Surviving the National Heritage Curriculum', *Multicultural Teaching*, vol. 13, no. 3, pp. 23–5.

Fine, Michelle (1988) 'Sexuality, Schooling and Adolescent Females: the Missing Discourse', *Harvard Educational Review*, vol. 4, pp. 29–53.

Fish, Stanley E. (1989) 'The Young and the Restless', in Veeser, H. A. (ed.), *The New Historicism* (London: Routledge).

Flintoff, Ann (1990) 'Physical Education, Equal Opportunities and the National Curriculum: Crisis or Challenge', *PE Review*, vol. 13, no. 2, pp. 85–100.

Foster, Victoria (1996) 'Space Invaders: Desire and Threat in the Schooling of Girls', *Discourse: Studies in Cultural Policies of Education*, vol. 17, no. 1, pp. 43–6.

Foucault, Michel (1977) *Discipline and Punish: The Birth of the Prison*, translated by A. Sheridan (London: Penguin).

Foucault, Michel (1980) *Power/Knowledge* (London: Harvester Wheatsheaf).

Fuhrman, Susan H. (with assistance from Patti L. Fry) (1990) 'Diversity Amidst Standardization: State Differential Treatment of Districts', in William H. Clune and John F. Witte (eds), *Choice and Control in American Education*, vol. 2: *The Practice of Choice, Decentralization and School Restructuring*, Stanford Series on Education and Public Policy (London, New York and Philadelphia: Falmer Press).

Fuller, Mary (1980) 'Black Girls in London Comprehensive Schools', in Rosemary Deem (ed.), *Schooling for Women's Work* (London: Routledge & Kegan Paul).

Fullinwider, Robert K. (1996) 'Multicultural Education: Concepts, Policies, and Controversies', in Robert K. Fullinwider (ed.), *Public Education in a Multicultural Society: Policy, Theory, Critique* (Cambridge: Cambridge University Press).

Garside, Ross (1995) 'Whose Heritage, Sir? and Other Issues: the New English National Curriculum', *Multicultural Teaching*, vol. 13, no. 3, pp. 6–8.

Gewirtz, Sharon, Ball, Stephen J. and Bowe, Richard (1993) 'Values and Ethics in the Education Market Place: the Case of Northwark Park', *International Studies in Sociology of Education*, vol. 3, no. 2, pp. 233–54.

Giddens, Anthony (1985) 'Time, Space and Regionalisation', in Derek Gregory and John Urry (eds), *Social Relations and Spatial Structures* (London: Macmillan).

Gillborn, David (1993) *Race, Ethnicity and Education: Teaching and Learning in Multiethnic Schools* (London: Unwin Hyman).

Gillborn, David and Gipps, Caroline (1996) *Recent Research on the Achievements of Ethnic Minority Pupils* (London: HMSO).

Goodson, Ivor (1994) *Studying Curriculum: Cases and Methods* (Buckingham: Open University Press).

Gordon, Tuula (1986) *Democracy in One School? Progressive Education and Restructuring* (London, New York and Philadelphia: Falmer Press).

Gordon, Tuula (1991) 'Onko kasvatus "naisten käsissä"?' (Is Education 'Controlled by Women'?) *Kasvatus* (*The Finnish Journal of Education*), vol. 22, no. 3, pp. 205–11.

Gordon, Tuula (1992) 'Citizens and Others: Gender, Democracy and Education', *International Studies in Sociology of Education*, vol. 2, no. 1, pp. 43–56.

Gordon, Tuula (1993) 'Citizenship, Difference and Marginality in Schools – with special reference to gender', a research proposal.

Gordon, Tuula (1994) *Single Women: On the Margins?* (London: Macmillan).

Gordon, Tuula (1996) 'Citizenship, Difference and Marginality in Schools: Spatial and Embodied Aspects of Gender Construction', in Patricia F. Murphy and Caroline V. Gipps (eds), *Equity in the Classroom* (London and Washington, DC: Falmer Press).

Gordon, Tuula and Lahelma, Elina (1995) 'Being, Having and Doing Gender in Schools', in *Gender, Modernity, Postmodernity – New Perspectives on Development/Construction of Gender*, Universitetet i Oslo. Senter for Kvinneforskning. Arbeitsnotat, 2/95.

Gordon, Tuula and Lahelma, Elina (1996) '"School is like an Ants' Nest" – Spatiality and Embodiment in Schools', *Gender and Education*, vol. 8, no. 3, pp. 301–10.

Gordon, Tuula, Holland, Janet and Lahelma, Elina (2000a) 'Friends and Foes: Interpreting Relations between Girls in Schools', in Geoffrey Walford (ed.), *Genders and Sexualities: Studies in Educational Ethnography*, vol. 3 (Stamford, Conn.: JAI Press).

Gordon, Tuula, Holland, Janet and Lahelma, Elina (2000b) 'From Pupil to Citizen: a Gendered Route', in Madeleine Arnot and Jo-Anne Dillabough (eds), *Gender, Education and Citizenship: An International Feminist Reader* (London: Routledge).

Gordon, Tuula, Holland, Janet and Lahelma, Elina (2000c) 'Moving Bodies/Still Bodies: Embodiment and Agency in Schools', in Linda McKie and Nick Watson (eds), *Organising Bodies* (Basingstoke: Macmillan).

Gordon, Tuula, Holland, Janet, Lahelma, Elina and Tolonen, Tarja (1997) 'Hidden from Gaze: Problematising Action in the Classroom', paper presented at the British Sociological Association Annual Conference.

Gordon, Tuula, Lahelma, Elina, Hynninen, Pirkko, Metso, Tuija, Palmu, Tarja and Tolonen, Tarja (2000d) 'Learning the Routines: Professionalisation of Newcomers to Secondary School', *Qualitative Studies in Education*.

Gordon, Tuula, Lahelma, Elina and Tarmo, Marjatta (1991) 'Gender and Education in Finland – Problems for Research', *Nordisk Pedagogik*, vol. 11, no. 4, pp. 210–17.

Gordon, Tuula, Lahelma, Elina and Tolonen, Tarja (1995) '"Koulu on kuin ..." metaforat fyysisen koulun analysoinnin välineenä' ('"School is like ..." Using Metaphors in Analysing Physical School'), *Nuorisotutkimus* (*The Finnish Journal of Youth Research*), vol. 3, no. 3, pp. 3–12.

Graham, Duncan (1993) 'The First Three National Curricula and the Millennium', *Educational Review*, vol. 45, no. 2, pp. 119–24.

Green, Andy (1990) *Education and State Formation: The Rise of Education Systems in England, France and the USA* (London: Macmillan).

Hall, Stuart (1997) 'The Spectacle of the "Other"', in Stuart Hall (ed.), *Representation: Cultural Representations and Signifying Practices* (London: Sage in association with Open University).

Halpin, David, Power, Sally and Fitz, John (1997) 'In the Grip of the Past? Tradition, Traditionalism and Contemporary Schooling', *International Studies in Sociology of Education*, vol. 7, no. 1, pp. 3–20.

Harvey, David (1975) *Social Justice and the City* (London: Edward Arnold).

Haug, Frigga (1987) *Female Sexualization: The Collective Work of Memory* (London: Virago).

Haywood, Chris and Mac an Ghaill, Maírtín (1995) 'The Sexual Politics of the Curriculum: Contesting Values', *International Studies in Sociology of Education*, vol. 5, no. 2, pp. 221–36.

Hey, Valerie (1996) 'A Game of Two Halves – a Critique of Some Complicities: Between Hegemonic and Counter-hegemonic Discourses Concerning Marketisation and Education', *Discourse*, vol. 17, no. 3, pp. 351–62.

Hey, Valerie (1997) *The Company She Keeps: An Ethnography of Girls' Friendships* (Buckingham and Philadelphia: Open University Press).

Hill, Dave (1990) 'Something Old, Something New, Something Borrowed, Something Blue: Schooling, Teacher Education and the Radical Right in Britain and the USA'. Hillcole Group, Paper 3 (London: Tufnell Press).

Hillcole Group (1991) *Changing the Future: Redprint for Education* (London: Tufnell Press).

Hirvi, Vilho (1994) 'Vapauden ja tasa-arvon herkkä suhde' (The Delicate Relation of Freedom and Equality), *Kasvatus* (*The Finnish Journal of Education*), vol. 25, no. 2, pp. 207–12.

History – Social Science Framework for California Public Schools (1987) (Sacramento: California Department of Education).

Holland, Janet, McGrellis, Sheena and Arnold, Sean (1996) 'Protective Factors in Adolescent Smoking', report for the Department of Health.

Holland, Janet, Ramazanoglu, Caroline, Sharpe, Sue and Thomson, Rachel (1994) 'Power and Desire: The Embodiment of Female Sexuality', *Feminist Review*, vol. 46, pp. 21–38.

Holland, Janet, Ramazanoglu, Caroline, Sharpe, Sue and Thomson, Rachel (1998) *The Male in the Head: Young People, Heterosexuality and Power* (London: Tufnell Press).

hooks, bell (1989) *Talking Back: Thinking Feminist, Thinking Black* (Boston: South End Press).

Husu, Liisa and Niemelä, Pirkko (1993) 'Finland', in Leonore Loeb Adler (ed.), *International Handbook of Gender Roles* (Westport, CT: Greenwood Press).

Hynninen, Pirkko (1998) '"Juicy Henna" and a Boy in a "dress"': Sexuality Lurking in School Counseling', paper presented at the NFPF Congress.

Jackson, Philip (1968) *Life in Schools* (New York: Holt, Reinhart and Winston).

Jakku-Sihvonen, Ritva and Lindström, Aslak (eds) (1996) *Is Equality a Reality in the Finnish Comprehensive Schools?* (Yliopistopaino, Helsinki: National Board of Education).

Johnson, Richard (1976) 'Educational Policy and Social Control in Early Victorian England', *Past and Present*, no. 49.

Jones, Kathleen (1990) 'Citizenship in a Woman-Friendly Polity', *Signs*, no. 41, pp. 781–812.

Kaarninen, Mervi (1995) *Nykyajan tytöt: Koulutus, luokka ja sukupuoli 1920–ja 1930–luvun Suomessa* (Modern Girls: Education, Social Class and Gender in Finland in 1920–1930) (Helsinki: Suomen Historiallinen Seura).

Karakasidou, Anastasia N. (1997) *Fields of Wheat, Hills of Blood: Passages to Nationhood in Greek Macedonia, 1870–1990* (Chicago: University of Chicago Press).

Kehily, Mary (1997) 'Agony Aunts and Absence: an Analysis of Sex Education Lessons', paper presented at British Sociological Association conference, University of York.

Kehily, Mary and Nayak, Anoop (1996) 'The Christmas Kiss: Sexuality, Storytelling and Schooling', *Curriculum Studies*, vol. 4, no. 2, pp. 211–27.

Kehily, Mary and Nayak, Anoop (1997) 'Lads and Laughter: Humour and the Production of Heterosexual Hierarchies', *Gender and Education*, vol. 9, no. 1, pp. 69–87.

Keith, Michael and Pile, Steve (eds) (1993) *Place and the Politics of Identity* (London: Routledge).

Kenway, Jane (1990) *Gender and Education Policy: A Call for New Directions* (Victoria: Deakin University Press).

Kenway, Jane (1995a) 'Feminist Theories of the State: To Be or Not To Be?', in Maud Blair and Janet Holland with Sue Sheldon (eds), *Identity and Diversity: Gender and the Experience of Education* (Clevedon, Philadelphia and Adelaide: Multilingual Matters in Association with the Open University).

Kenway, Jane (1995b) 'Having a Postmodernist Turn of Postmodernist *angst*: a Disorder Experienced by an Author Who is Not Yet Dead or Even Close to it', in Richard Smith and Philip Wexler (eds), *After Postmodernism, Education, Politics and Identity: Knowledge, Identity and School Life*, Series 3 (London and Washington, DC: Falmer Press).

Kenway, Jane (1995c) 'Masculinities in Schools: Under Siege, on the Defensive and under Reconstruction?', *Discourse: Studies in the Cultural Politics of Education*, vol. 16, no. 1, pp. 59–79.

Kenway, Jane and Epstein, Debbie (1996) 'Introduction: the Marketisation of School Education: Feminist Studies and Perspectives', *Discourse: Studies in the Cultural Politics of Education*, vol. 17, no. 3, pp. 301–14.

Kenway, Jane and Fitzclarence, Lindsay (1997) 'Masculinity, Violence and Schooling: Challenging "Poisonous Pedagogies"', *Gender and Education*, vol. 9, no. 1, pp. 117–33.

Kenway, Jane, Blackmore, Jill and Willis, Sue (1996) 'Pleasure and Pain: Beyond Feminist Authoritarianism and Therapy in the Curriculum', in Patricia F. Murphy and Caroline V. Gipps (eds), *Equity in the Classroom* (London and Washington, DC: Falmer Press).

Kenway, Jane and Willis, Sue with Blackmore, Jill and Rennie, Léonie (1998) *Answering Back* (London: Routledge).

Knight, John, Lingard, Bob and Porter, Paige (1993) 'Restructuring Schooling towards the 1990s', in Bob Lingard, John Knight and Paige Porter (eds), *Schooling Reform in Hard Times*, Deakin Studies in Education Series 9 (London and Washington, DC: Falmer Press).

Kozol, Jonathan (1992) *Savage Inequalities: Children in America's Schools* (New York: Harper Perennial).

Lahelma, Elina (1992) *Sukupuolten eriytyminen peruskoulun opetussuunnitelmassa* (Gender Difference in the Curriculum of the Comprehensive School.) (Helsinki: Yliopistopaino).

Lahelma, Elina (1993) *Policies of Gender and Equal Opportunities in Curriculum Development – Discussing the Situation in Finland and Britain*, Research Bulletin 85, Department of Education, University of Helsinki and ERIC database.

Lahelma, Elina (1994) '"But the School Likes to Mix Us", Sukupuoli brittikoulussa' (Gender in the British school), *Nuorisotutkimus* (*The Finnish Journal of Youth Research*) vol. 12, no. 1, pp. 21–8.

Lahelma, Elina (1996) 'Vallan haastamista? Opettajien kokemuksia oppilaiden sukupuolisesta häirinnästä' (Challenging Power? Teachers' Experiences on Pupils' Sexual Harassment), *Kasvatus* (*The Finnish Journal of Education*), vol. 27, no. 4, pp. 478–88.

Lahelma, Elina and Gordon, Tuula (1997) 'First Day in Secondary School: Learning to be a "Professional Pupil"', *Educational Research and Evaluation*, vol. 3, no. 2, pp. 119–39.

Lahelma, Elina, Gordon, Tuula and Holland, Janet (1996) 'Curricula for Nations: the Construction of Citizenship and Difference in Finnish and British Schools', paper presented at the European Conference of Educational Research.

Lahelma, Elina and Gordon, Tuula (1998) 'Gränsöverskridande – om kön i läroplaner och i sklans praxis', in Anne-Lise Arnesen (ed.), *Likt og ulikt. Kjønnsdimensjonen i pedagogisk tenkning og praksis*, HiO-rapport no. 2 (Oslo: Høgskolen i Oslo) pp. 115–36.

Laine, Kaarlo (1995) '"Pakollinen aivojenkasvattamispaikka" Nuorten metaforia ja kuolukokemuksia' ('"Involuntary Centre for Brain Moulding" – the School Metaphors and School Experiences of Young People'), *Nuorisotutkimus* (*The Finnish Journal of Youth Research*), vol. 13, no. 3, pp. 21–32.

Lees, Sue (1986) *Losing Out: Sexuality and Adolescent Girls* (London: Hutchinson).

Lefebvre, Henri (1991) *The Production of Space* (Oxford: Basil Blackwell).

Lehtonen, Jukka (1998) 'Young People's Definitions of their Non-Heterosexuality', in Helena Helve (ed.), *Integrated or Marginalized Youth in Europe, Nuorisotutkimus*, 2000, 6/98 (Helsinki: Nuorisotutkimusseura ry).

Lesko, Nancy (1988) 'The Curriculum of the Body: Lessons from a Catholic

High School', in Leslie G. Roman and Linda K. Christian-Smith, with Elizabeth Ellsworth (eds), *Becoming Feminine* (London: Falmer Press).

Lindroos, Maarit and Tolonen, Tarja (1995) 'Koulu on kuin hullujenhuone' (School is like a Madhouse), *Nuorisotutkimus* (*The Finnish Journal of Youth Research*), vol. 3, pp. 13–20.

Lukes, Steven (1973) *Individualism* (London: Basil Blackwell).

Mac an Ghaill, Maírtín (1994) *The Making of Men* (Buckingham: Open University Press).

Markkola, Pirjo (1990) 'Women in Rural Society in the 19th and 20th Centuries', in Päivi Setälä (ed.), *The Lady with the Bow: The Story of Finnish Women* (Keuruu: Otava).

Marshall, T. H. (1963) *Sociology at Crossroads* (London: Heinemann).

Massey, Doreen (1985) 'New Directions in Space', in Derek Gregory and John Urry (eds), *Social Relations and Spatial Structures* (London: Macmillan).

Massey, Doreen (1991) 'Flexible Sexism', *Environment and Planning: Society and Space*, vol. 9, no. 1, pp. 31–57.

Massey, Doreen (1993) 'Politics and Space/Time', in Michael Keith and Steve Pile (eds), *Place and the Politics of Identity* (London: Routledge).

McKiernan, D. (1993) 'History in a National Curriculum: Imagining the Nation at the End of the 20th Century', *Journal of Curriculum Studies*, vol. 25, no. 1, pp. 33–51.

McLean Taylor, Jill, Gilligan, Carol and Sullivan, Amy M. (1995) *Between Voice and Silence: Women and Girls, Race and Relationships* (Cambridge, MA: Harvard University Press).

McRobbie, Angela (1996) 'Looking Back at the New Times and its Critics', in Chen Kuan-Hsing and David Morley (eds), *Stuart Hall: Critical Dialogues in Cultural Studies* (London: Routledge).

McRobbie, Angela (1997) 'The Es and the Anti-Es: New Questions for Feminism and Cultural Studies', in Marjorie Ferguson and Peter Golding (eds), *The Cultural Studies in Question* (London: Sage).

Metso, Tuija (1999) 'Kodin ja koulun suhteita – kasvatusprosessien kohtaamisia ja erojen rakentumisia' (Relations between Home and School: Meeting of Educational Processes and Construction of Differences), unpublished manuscript.

Meyer, John W. and Baker, David P. (1996) 'Forming American Educational Policy with International Data: Lessons from the Sociology of Education', *Sociology of Education, Extra Issue*, pp. 123–30.

Middleton, Sue (1992) 'Equity, Equality, and Biculturalism in the Restructuring of New Zealand Schools: a Life-History Approach', *Harvard Educational Review*, vol. 62, no. 3, pp. 301–22.

Mills, Martin (1997) 'Towards a Disruptive Pedagogy: Creating Spaces for Student and Teacher Resistance to School Injustice', *International Studies in Sociology of Education*, vol. 7, no. 1, pp. 35–56.

Mirza, Heidi S. (1992) *Young, Female and Black* (London: Routledge).

Molloy, Maureen (1995) 'Imagining (the) Difference: Gender, Ethnicity and Metaphors of Nation', *Feminist Review*, no. 52, pp. 94–112.

Morley, David (1997) 'Theoretical Orthodoxies: Textualism, Constructivism and the New Ethnography in Cultural Studies', in Marjorie Ferguson and Peter Golding (eds), *Cultural Studies in Question* (London: Sage).

Murphy, Patricia (1996) 'Defining Pedagogy', in Patricia Murphy and Caroline

V. Gipps (eds), *Equity in the Classroom: Towards Effective Pedagogy for Girls and Boys* (London and Washington, DC: Falmer Press).

Nayak, Anoop (1997) 'Tales from the Darkside: Negotiating Whiteness in School Arenas', *International Studies in Sociology of Education*, vol. 7, no. 1, pp. 57–80.

Nayak, Anoop and Kehily, Mary Jane (1997) 'Masculinities and Schooling: Why are Young Men so Homophobic?', in Deborah Lynn Steinberg, Debbie Epstein and Richard Johnson (eds), *Border Patrols: Policing the Boundaries of Heterosexuality* (London: Cassell).

NBE (National Board of Education) (1994) *Framework Curriculum for the Comprehensive School 1994* (Helsinki: Painatuskeskus).

NCC (National Curriculum Council) (1990) *Curriculum Guidance, 8: Education for Citizenship* (London: HMSO).

NCC (National Curriculum Council) (1991) *Circular 11: Linguistic Diversity and the National Curriculum* (London: HMSO).

Norris, Nigel, Aspland, Roger, MacDonald, Barry, Shostak, John and Zamorski, Barbara (1996) *An Independent Evaluation of Comprehensive Curriculum Reform in Finland* (Helsinki: National Board of Education, Yliopistopaino).

Nummelin, Raija (1997) *Seksuaalikasvatusmateriaalit – Millaista seksuaalisuutta nuorille?* (Sexuality Education Materials – What Kind of Sexuality for Adolescents?) (Helsinki: Stakes, Reports 206).

Osler, Audrey (1995) 'Does the National Curriculum Bring Us Any Closer to a Gender Balanced History?' *Teaching History*, no. 79, pp. 21–4.

Palmu, Tarja (1998) 'Koulun salin monet kasvot' (The Hall as an Example of School Space), *Nuorisotutkimus* (*The Finnish Journal of Youth Research*), vol. 16, no. 1, pp. 12–18.

Pateman, Carole (1988) *The Sexual Contract* (Cambridge: Polity Press).

Popkewitz, Thomas S. (1991) *A Political Sociology at Educational Reform: Power/Knowledge in Teaching, Teacher Education, and Research* (New York: Teachers College Press).

Prendergast, Shirley (1995) 'With Gender on my Mind: Menstruation and Embodiment at Adolescence', in Janet Holland and Maud Blair (with Sue Sheldon) (eds), *Debates and Issues in Feminist Research and Pedagogy* (Cleveland: Multilingual Matters in association with the Open University).

Probyn, Elspeth (1993) *Sexing the Self: Gendered Positions in Cultural Studies* (London: Routledge).

Ramazanoglu, Caroline and Holland, Janet (1993) 'Women's Sexuality and Men's Appropriation of Desire', in Caroline Ramazanoglu (ed.), *Up against Foucault: Explorations of some Tensions between Foucault and Feminism* (London: Routledge).

Redman, Peter and Mac an Ghaill, Máirtín (1997) 'Educating Peter: the Making of a History Man', in Deborah Lynn Steinberg, Debbie Epstein and Richard Johnson (eds), *Border Patrols: Policing the Boundaries of Heterosexuality* (London: Cassell).

Rendell, Margherita (1985) 'The Winning of the Sex Discrimination Act', in Madeleine Arnot (ed.), *'Race' and Gender: Equal Opportunities in Education* (Pergamon Press: Oxford).

Riddell, Sheila I. (1992) *Gender and the Politics of the Curriculum* (London and New York: Routledge).

Roche, Maurice (1992) *Rethinking Citizenship: Welfare, Ideology and Change in the Modern Society* (Cambridge: Polity Press).

Roman, Leslie (1993) 'Double Exposure: the Politics of Feminist Materialist Ethnography', *Educational Theory*, vol. 43, no. 3, pp. 279–308.

Ruddock, Jean (1994) *Developing a Gender Policy in Secondary Schools* (Buckingham and Philadelphia: Open University Press).

Runnymede Trust (1993) *Equality Assurance in Schools: Quality, Identity, Society* (London: Trentham Books).

SCAA (School Curriculum and Assessment Authority) (1996) 'Education for Adult Life: the Spiritual and Moral Development of Young People', *SCAA Discussion Papers* no. 6.

Scraton, Sheila (ed.) (1992) *Shaping up to Womanhood: Gender and Girls' Physical Education* (Buckingham: Open University Press).

Sharp, Rachel and Green, Tony (1975) *Education and Social Control: A Study in Progressive Primary Education* (London, Henley and Boston: Routledge and Kegan Paul).

Shaw, Jenny (1996) *Education, Gender and Anxiety* (London: Taylor and Francis).

Shilling, Chris (1991) 'Social Space, Gender Inequalities and Educational Differentiation', *British Journal of Sociology*, vol. 12, no. 1, pp. 23–44.

Simola, Hannu (1998) 'Constructing a School-free Pedagogy: Decontextualization of Finnish State Educational Discourse', *Curriculum Studies*, vol. 30, no. 3, pp. 339–56.

Singh, M. Garbutcheon (1990) *Performance Indicators in Education* (Geelong: Deakin University Press).

Skeggs, Beverley (1991) 'Challenging Masculinity and Using Sexuality', *British Journal of Sociology of Education*, vol. 12, no. 2, pp. 127–41.

Slattery, Patrick (1995) 'A Postmodern Vision of Time and Learning: a Response to the National Education Commission Report Prisoners of Time', *Harvard Educational Review*, vol. 65, no. 4, pp. 612–33.

Sleegers, Peter and Wesselingh, Anton (1993) 'Decentralisation in Education: a Dutch Study', *International Studies in Sociology of Education*, vol. 3, no. 1, pp. 49–67.

Smith, Neil and Katz, Cindy (1993) 'Grounding Metaphor: Towards a Spatialised Politics', in Michael Keith and Steve Pile (eds), *Place and the Politics of Identity* (London: Routledge).

Soja, Edward (1985) 'The Spatiality of Social Life: Towards a Transformative Theorisation', in D. Gregory and J. Urry (eds), *Social Relations and Spatial Structures* (London: Macmillan).

Soja, Edward and Hooper, Barbara (1993) 'The Spaces that Difference Makes: Some Notes on the Geographical Margins of the New Cultural Politics', in Michael Keith and Steve Pile (eds), *Place and the Politics of Identity* (London: Routledge).

Stacey, Judith (1988) 'Can There Be a Feminist Ethnography?' *Women's Studies International Forum*, vol. 1, no. 1, pp. 21–7.

Stacey, Judith (1990) *Brave New Families: Domestic Upheaval in Late Twentieth Century America* (New York: Basic Books).

Sunnari, Vappu (1997) *Gendered Structures and Processes in Primary Teacher Education – Challenge for Gender-sensitive Pedagogy*, Northern Gender Studies 4, Universities of Oulu and Lapland, Femina Borealis 5, Oulun yliopistopaino 4, Oulu.

Thomson, Rachel (1995) 'Unholy Alliances: the Recent Politics of Sex Education' in Liz Dawtrey, Janet Holland and Merril Hammer (with Sue Sheldon) (eds), *Equality and Inequality in Education Policy* (Clevedon: Multilingual Matters in association with the Open University).

Thomson, Rachel and Scott, Sue (1992) *Learning About Sex: Young Women and the Social Construction of Sexual Identity* (London: Tufnell Press).

Thorne, Barrie (1993) *Gender Play: Girls and Boys in Schools* (Buckingham: Open University Press).

Tolonen, Tarja (1998a) 'Everyone at School Thinks I am a Nerd' – Schoolboys' Fights and Ambivalence about Masculinities', *Young*, vol. 6, no. 2, pp. 4–18.

Tolonen, Tarja (1998b) 'Ideal Girls and Ideal Boys: Youth Cultural Descriptions on Embodiment', a paper presented at BSA Conference, University of Edinburgh.

Tomkins, J. (1986) 'Indians: Textualism, Morality and the Problem of History', in H. L. Gates (ed.), *Race, Writing and Difference* (Chicago: Chicago University Press).

Troman, Geoff (1996) 'No Entry Signs: Educational Change and Some Problems Encountered in Negotiating Entry to Education Settings', *British Educational Research Journal*, vol. 22, no. 1, pp. 71–88.

Troyna, Barry (1992) 'Can you See the Join? An Historical Analysis of Multicultural and Antiracist Education Policies', in Dawn Gill, Barbara Mayor and Maud Blair (eds), *Racism and Education: Structures and Strategies* (London: Sage/Open University).

Turner, Bryan S. (ed) (1993) *Citizenship and Social Theory* (London: Sage).

Walkerdine, Valerie (1984) 'Some Day my Prince will Come', in Angela McRobbie and Mica Nava (eds), *Gender and Generation* (London: Macmillan).

Walkerdine, Valerie (1992) 'Progressive Pedagogy and Political Struggle', in Carmen Luke and Jennifer Gore (eds), *Feminisms and Critical Pedagogy* (New York: Routledge).

Walkerdine, Valerie (1997) 'Successful Girls and Failing Boys? Thoughts Towards a New Millennium', plenary paper given at 'Transitions in Gender and Education' Conference, Warwick University.

Walkerdine, Valerie (1998) *Counting Girls Out? Girls and Mathematics* (London: Falmer Press).

Walkerdine, Valerie and Lucey, Helen (1989) *Democracy in the Kitchen: Regulating Mothers and Socialising Daughters* (London: Virago).

Weeks, Jeffrey (1996) *Invented Moralities: Sexual Values in an Age of Uncertainty* (Cambridge: Polity Press).

Weiler, H. N. (1990) 'Comparative Perspectives on Educational Decentralization: an Exercise in Contradiction?', *Educational Evaluation and Policy Analysis*, vol. 12, pp. 433–48.

Wexler, Philip with the assistance of Warren Crichlow, June Kern and Rebecca Martusewicz (1992) *Becoming Somebody: Toward a Social Psychology of School* (London: Falmer Press).

Whitty, Geoff (1989) 'The New Right and the National Curriculum State Control or Market Forces?', *Education Policy*, vol. 4, no. 4, pp. 329–41.

Whitty, Geoff, Rowe, Gabrielle and Aggleton, Peter (1993) 'Subjects and Themes in the Secondary-School Curriculum', *Research Papers in Education*, vol. 9, no. 2, pp. 159–81.

Williams, Raymond (1961) *The Long Revolution* (Harmondsworth: Penguin).

Witte, John F. (1990) 'Choice and Control: an Analytical Overview', in William H. Clune and John F. Witte (eds), *Choice and Control in American Education*, vol. 1: *The Theory of Choice and Control in American Education* (London: Falmer Press).

Woods, Peter (1990) *The Happiest Days? How Pupils Cope with School* (London: Falmer Press).

Yuval-Davis, Nira (1997) *Gender and Nation* (London: Sage).

Index

Aapola, Sinikka, 17, 98, 113, 166
Abercrombie, Nicholas, 12, 13
abstract citizen, 5, 7
abstract pupil, 5, 7, 55, 142
    and difference in schools, 36–7, 98
abstract school, 7
access to schools, 58
Acker, Sandra, 92
activity in schools, 184–5
age, and friendship groups, 113
Aittola, Tapio, 124
Alapuro, Risto, 20
anxieties of students, 124–6
Anyon, Jean, 108, 156
Apple, Michael W., 23, 27, 31, 33
Arnesen, Anne-Lise, 34
Arnot, Madeleine, 22, 26, 27, 30, 36, 40
Aronowitz, Stanley, 23
Atkinson, Paul, 54, 99
Australia, and markets in schooling, 23

Baker, David P, 46
ballroom metaphor, 2, 6, 164
Bartky, Sandra L., 172
Bhabha, Homi K., 19
Billig, Michael, 5, 36
binary opposites
    culture/nature, 10–11
    female/male, 3
    and neutral 'pupils', 21
Blum, Lawrence A. Q., 47
bodies
    in authority, 188–90
    changes in the teenage years, 165–6
    'curriculum of the body', 2, 137
    and dress styles, 167–72, 173–5
    pedagogy of the body, 137
    in the physical school, 165–91
    and sport, 185–8
Bowles, Samuel, 91

boys
    in the classroom, 117, 118
    in crowds, 119–24
    and cussing, 131
    disruptive behaviour, 74–5
    and dress styles 168, 169–70, 174
    emotions expressed by, 125–6
    and gender balancing acts, 114, 115
    gender-blenders, 174
    hairstyles, 171
    having and using voice, 180, 181, 184
    heterosexuality of, 123–4
    and individuality, 16
    and male teachers, 107
    and movement in space, 159, 160, 177, 195
    name-calling, 132–4
    and pleasure, 127
    quiet, 122–3, 156, 163
    self-evaluation, 84, 85
    and spatial praxis, 156
    and sport, 186–8
    teasing, 132
    and time–space paths, 153
    underachievement in schools, 36–7, 196–7
Bracey, P., 44
Brenner, Johanna, 25
Britain, 4–5
    citizenship in, 28
    curriculum development, 200–1
    education for citizenship, 38–9, 45–6, 50
    equal opportunities policies, 26, 27, 37
    and ethnic minorities, 37, 113–14
    and gender differentiation in sport, 185
    gender relations, 25, 194–5
    gender segregation in schools, 21
    London schools: buildings,

Britain – *continued*
139–40, 141, 142–3; cussing
in, 131; dress styles and school
uniforms, 167–70, 173, 174–5,
190–1; expressions of heterosexual desire, 127–8;
extra-curricular activities,
108–9, 110; friendship groups,
114, 196; gender balancing
acts, 114–15; gender distribution of teachers, 106; and
gender issues, 195–6; hairstyles, 171; nationalism/
internationalism in, 95–7; Oak
Grove, 58, 139, 140, 201;
students' spatial metaphors,
158; teacher/student relations,
108; teachers, 68–9, 70–1,
80–1, 188–90; Woburn Hill,
58, 96, 140, 141, 201
and nation building through
education, 20
National Curriculum, 38–9, 42–4,
46, 48–9
New Right politics and policies, 24,
25; in education, 26, 27, 28,
29, 32, 33, 34, 35, 194
school-based curricula, 49, 50
and social democratic policies in
education, 26, 28
teachers, and physical contact with
pupils, 188–90
British nationality, concept of,
95–6
Brophy, Jere E., 37
buildings (school), 137–43
Finland, 138–9
lockers, 140
modern, 138
rebuilding work, 138
students' views on, 142–6
and time–space paths, 149–50
toilets, 140
Victorian, 137–8
see also classrooms
bullying, 127, 129–31, 132, 135
Burr, Vivian, 3
Butler, Judith, 13, 97

Californian schools
buildings, 142
classrooms, 141
and individual citizens, 198, 199
individuals and differences in the
curriculum, 46–7, 98–9
power relations, 155–6
professional pupils, 75–6
and race, 195, 198
caretakers (school), 103, 104, 105
Carrigan, T., 108, 172
child-care provision, Britain, United
States and Finland, 25, 194–5
choice, and the marketisation of
education, 30–3
Christian-Smith, Linda, 128
citizens
from pupils to, 99–100
making gendered, 92–4
making individual, 82–7
making knowing, 76–81
making sexual, 97–8
national, 19–21
in space, 17–19
students as 'citizens-to-be', 44–6
citizenship 4
in Britain, 28
and difference, in the national
curricula, 38–47
education for, 38–9, 44–6, 99
in Finland, 28, 44–5
and individuality, 4, 198–200; and
difference, 9–12
and New Right politics and
policies, 31
and social justice, 21–2, 31
classrooms, 138, 141
locked doors, 149
seating plans, 145–6
students' views of, 143, 144–5
Clifford, Janet, 56
Cohen, David, 33
Cohen, R., 25, 31
Connell, R. W., 97, 121, 172–3
control
in the official school, 88–92
in the physical school, 143, 166–7,
190–1; and time–space paths,
153–4

teachers and physical contact,
    188–90
Corrigan, Paul, 126, 141
Crawford, June, 55
crosscultural approach, 2, 6–7, 55,
    193
cultural citizenship in Finland, 44
cultural individualism, 12–13
curricula
    national, 38–47
    in schools, 47–50
'curriculum of the body', 2, 137
cussing in schools, 131, 197

Dale, Roger, 26, 29, 30
dance metaphor, 2, 5, 6, 53–4, 192–3
    and anxiety and boredom, 124
    and the official school, 54, 65, 66,
        99–100, 101, 128
    and the physical school, 54, 165,
        190
    and space, 164
Darmanin, Mary, 25
David, Miriam, 29, 30
Davies, Bronwyn, 2, 12, 16, 76, 82,
    88, 90, 92, 150, 156
Davies, Paul, 30
decentralisation in educational
    policy, 4, 33–4
Delamont, Sara, 54, 99, 172
Denzin, Norman, 56
Dewey, John, 148
difference, 3
    and citizenship in the national
        curricula, 38–47
    individuality and citizenship, 4,
        9–12
    in the official school, 92–9
    in schools, and the 'abstract pupil',
        36–7, 98
    and spatial relations, 160–1
Donald, James, 2, 11, 29
dress codes, 167–72, 173–5
    school uniforms, 167–70
    for sport, 185

education for citizenship, 38–9
educational systems, establishment
    of national, 19–20

embodiment, 6
    and citizenship, 11
    and classroom observers, 59
    and the physical school, 136, 166
    of teachers, 166
emotions, in the informal school,
    124–8, 135
England/Wales *see* Britain
English teaching, in the British
    National Curriculum, 43
Epstein, Debbie, 24, 97, 123–4, 134,
    172
equality of opportunity, 51
    in Britain, 26, 27, 37, 202; school
        policies on, 94, 98
    and choice, 30, 32–3
    in Finland, 26, 27, 37, 200, 202;
        curriculum, 49
    and standards, 34–5
ethnicity
    in Britain, 37, 42, 50, 113, 197
    in Finland, 37, 41–2, 45, 49, 50,
        113, 197–8
    and friendship groups, 113–14
    and hairstyle, 171
    racial segregation in California, 47
    teasing, cussing and name-calling,
        131, 197
ethnographic research, 3, 4, 5
    ethics and anonymity, 62–3
    and lesson notes, 63–4
    methods, 59–64, 204–8
    planning, 53–9
Evans, John, 185

families, and New Right politics and
    policies, 30
Feintuck, Mike, 29, 34
female teachers
    and girls, 107, 117
    and physical contact, 189
    of sports, 186
    and staffroom culture, 106
    and the teacher/student relations,
        107, 108
femininity, and students' dress
    styles, 173, 174–5, 190
feminism
    and citizenship, 21, 22

feminism – *continued*
  and ethnography, 54–5, 56–7
  and poststructuralism, 3–4
File, Nigel, 43–4
Fine, Michelle, 98
Finland, 4–5
  boys' underachievement debate,
    196
  cultural homogeneity and dress,
    173–4
  education for citizenship, 38,
    44–5
  education system, 26–7, 28–9, 30,
    34, 35, 36, 194, 200, 201, 202
  equality and quality in, 34–5, 200
  gender relations, 25, 194, 195
  Helsinki schools: buildings, 138–9;
    City Park, 57–8, 138, 139, 140,
    141, 201; dress styles, 167,
    170–1, 173–4; extra-curricular
    activities, 108, 109; gender
    balancing acts, 114–15; gender
    categorization by teachers,
    93–4; gender distribution of
    teachers, 106; and gender
    issues, 195; gender separation
    in sports, 186; Green Park, 57,
    58, 138–9, 140, 141, 201; hair-
    styles, 171; having and using
    voice, 179–82; lessons in
    manners, 73–4; nationalism/
    internationalism in, 94–5;
    pupil professionalism, 73; and
    sex education, 98; sports
    lessons, 186, 188; students'
    space in, 145; and students'
    spatial metaphors, 158;
    teachers, 69–70, 76–80, 108
  and multiculturalism, 37, 40–2
  and nation building through
    education, 20–1
  and neo-liberalism, 28
  school-based curricula, 47–8, 49–50
  social-democratic welfare state, 23,
    25, 194
Fish, Stanley E., 56
Fitzclarence, Lindsay, 123, 124
Flintoff, Ann, 185
Foster, Victoria, 162

Foucault, Michel, 55, 140
friendships, 110–14, 116, 118–19,
    135, 196
Fuhrman, Susan H., 25, 27
Fullinwider, Robert, 41–2

Garside, Ros, 43
gaze
  and ethnographic research, 55–6,
    59–61
  and girls' embodiment, 172
  in the physical school, 166
gender, 3
  and the 'abstract pupil', 36
  and adolescence, 166
  balancing acts, 114–15
  Britain, United States and Finland,
    25, 194–7
  and classroom seating
    arrangements, 146
  and dress styles, 168–72, 173–5
  and ethnography, 54–5
  and friendship groups, 111–12
  and individuality, 200
  making gendered citizens, 92–4
  and marginality, 203
  neutrality in educational
    documents, 39–40
  at official celebrations, 109
  segregation: in national education
    systems, 20–1; in sport, 185–6
  and single-sex groups, 115
  and spatial demarcations, 161
  and spatial positioning, 162–3
  and spatial praxis, 156
  and sport, 185–8
  and students as individual citizens,
    84–7
  and the teacher/student relations,
    107
  see also boys; female teachers; girls;
    male teachers
gender-blenders, 174
Gewitz, Sharon, 28
Giddens, Anthony, 53, 57, 143, 148,
    163
Gillborn, David, 37
Gintis, Herbert, 91
Gipps, Caroline, 37

girls
anxiety experienced by, 125
collaboration among, 116–19
and cussing, 131
and dress styles, 168–9, 171, 172, 173–4
and female teachers, 107, 117
and gender balancing acts, 114–15
hairstyles, 171
having and using voice, 180–4, 195–6
heterogeneity of, 126
and individuality, 13–15, 16–17
and mental flight, 159
and movement in space, 177–8, 190
name-calling, 132–3, 134
and pleasure, 126–7
quiet, 127, 154, 163, 182, 183
self-evaluation, 84–7
and spatial praxis, 156
and sport, 186–7
teasing, 132, 153
and time–space paths, 153
Giroux, Henry, 23
'good pupils', 99
Good, Thomas L., 37
Goodson, Ivor, 43, 76
Gordon, Tuula, 3, 5, 12, 13, 22, 26, 27, 36, 61, 72, 73, 87, 90, 102, 109, 111, 116, 123, 148, 149, 152, 157, 159, 160, 165, 172, 184, 204
Graham, D., 48
Green, Andy, 2, 20, 81

Halpin, David, 72
Harré, Rom, 12
Harvey, David, 18
Haywood, Chris, 98
heterosexuality in schools, 123–4
Hey, Valerie, 33, 35, 60, 61, 87, 104, 114, 116, 117, 118–19, 132, 162
Hill, Dave, 35
Hillcole Group, 26
Hirvi, Vilho, 35
history teaching, in the British National Curriculum, 43–4
Holland, Janet, 98, 171, 172

homophobia in schools, 123
name-calling, 133–4
hooks, bell, 182
Hooper, Barbara, 18
humour, students' sense of, 127
Hunt, Robyn, 16, 76, 82, 92
Husu, Liisa, 25
Hynninen, Pirkko, 108, 122

individual students, 12–17
individualism
and citizenship, 4, 9–12, 198–200; making individual citizens, 82–7
and dress styles, 174
in national education systems, 21
and New Right politics and policies, 31
and women in Britain, 194–5
informal school, 53, 101–35, 193
anxiety and pleasure, 124–8
and the dance metaphor, 53–4, 101, 128
extra-curricular activities, 108–10
friendships, 110–14, 116, 118–19, 135
gender issues, 114–24
and individual citizens, 199
marginalisation processes, 128–34, 201–2
and power relations, 134–5
support staff, 102–5
see also teachers
internationalism issues, in the official school, 94–7

Jackson, Philip, 75
Jakku-Sihvonen, Ritva, 40
Johnson, Richard, 20, 97, 172
Jones, Carol, 10, 22
Jones, Kathleen, 4

Kaarninen, Mervi, 20
Karakasidou, Anastasia N., 19
Katz, Cindy, 18, 148
Kehily, Mary, 98, 108, 120, 121, 123, 126
Keith, Michael, 19, 142
Kenway, Jane, 4, 24, 35, 119, 123, 124, 126

Knight, John, 24, 25, 33, 34
Kozol, Jonathan, 99

Lahelma, Elina, 3, 39, 61, 73, 90,
    108, 109, 148, 149, 157, 159,
    165
Lees, Sue, 133, 172
Lefebvre, Henri, 18, 157
Lehtonen, Jukka, 124, 134
Lesko, Nancy, 2
Lincoln, Yvonne, 56
Lindström, Aslak, 40
Lucey, Helen, 163
Lukes, Stephen, 12

Mac an Ghaill, Máirtín, 98, 107,
    120-1, 134, 186
McKiernan, D., 42-3
McLean Taylor, Jill, 183
McRobbie, Angela, 4, 57
male teachers
    of sports, 186
    and staffroom culture, 106
    and teacher/student relations, 107,
        108
Marcus, George E., 56
marginalisation in schools, 17,
    128-34, 201-2
marketisation of education, 29-33,
    37, 51
    and school uniforms, 168
    teachers' views on, 70-1
Markkola, Pirjo, 20
Marshall, T. H., 10
Marx, Karl, 21
masculinity
    and boys in crowds, 120
    construction of hegemonic, 108,
        172-3; and sport, 186
    crisis of, 27, 123
    and dress styles, 174
    and male teachers, 107
    and quiet boys, 123
Massey, Doreen, 19, 56, 148
materialist feminism, 4
memory work, 55
Metso, Tuija, 114
Meyer, John W., 46
Middleton, Sue, 34, 51

Mills, Martin, 66
Mirza, Heidi S., 153
Molloy, Maureen, 53-4
Morley, David, 56
multiculturalism
    in Britain, 42-4, 50, 197
    in Finland, 37, 40-2, 49, 197-8
Murphy, Patricia, 66
music teaching in Finland, 94-5

name-calling in schools, 127, 132-4,
    197
nation states
    and nature/culture, 10-11
    and space, 18-19
national citizens, 19-21
national curricula, citizenship and
    difference in, 38-47
nationality
    and the 'abstract pupil', 36
    in Finland, 40-2
nationalism/internationalism
    issues in schools, 94-7, 198
Nayak, Anoop, 108, 120, 121, 123,
    126
NBE, *Finnish Framework Curriculum*,
    38, 39, 40-1, 76
neo-conservatism in education, 28-9,
    31
neo-liberalism in education, 28-9, 31
new ethnography, 4
New Right politics and policies, 2, 4,
    23-4
    in education systems, 9, 22, 24-35,
        194, 201, 202
    and sex education, 97-8
New Zealand, and markets in school-
    ing, 23
Ní Chartheígh, Dearbhal, 34
Niemelä, Pirkko, 25
Norris, Nigel, 29, 78
Nummelin, Raija, 98
nurses, support role of school nurses,
    103

official school, 53, 65-100, 193
    between control and agency, 88-92
    and the dance metaphor, 53-4, 65,
        66, 99-100, 128

informalising, 102–10
making gendered citizens, 92–4
making individual citizens, 82–7, 199
making knowing citizens, 76–81
making sexual citizens, 97–8
and professional pupils, 6, 71–6, 99–100
see also teachers
Ozga, Jenny, 26, 29

Palmu, Tarja, 109
Parkinson, Kay, 52
Pateman, Carole, 4, 10
pedagogy, 65–6
physical school, 53, 136–64, 193
and bodies, 165–91
buildings, 137–43
and the dance metaphor, 53–4, 136, 164
and embodiment, 136
and individual citizens, 199
see also space; teachers
Pile, Steve, 19, 142
pleasure, 124–8
Popkewitz, Thomas S., 20
poststructuralism, 3–4
power
and resistance: in the official school, 91–2; and spatial praxis, 154–6, 163, 164
and societal patterns, 202
power relations, and the informal school, 134–5
Probyn, Elspeth, 56
professional pupils, 6, 71–6, 99–100
space and place, 143
pupils
abstract pupil, 5, 7, 36–7, 55, 98, 142
'good pupils', 99
as national citizens, 21
professional, 6, 71–6, 99–100, 143
and students, 71

Ramazanoglu, Caroline, 172
Redman, Peter, 121, 186
resistance
and power: in the official school, 91–2; and spatial praxis, 154–6, 163, 164
Riddel, Sheila I., 40
rights, citizenship, 11, 12
Roche, Maurice, 24, 31
Roman, Leslie, 57, 62
Ruddock, Jean, 92
Runnymede Trust 42

school buildings *see* buildings (school)
school uniforms, 167–70, 190–1
Scott, Sue, 98
Scraton, Sheila, 185
sex education, 97–8, 104, 172
sexual harassment, 108, 112
and dress styles, 170
sexuality
and the control function of schools, 172–5
and the informalisation of teacher/student relations, 108
and name-calling, 133, 196
and the official school, 97–8
students and heterosexual relationships, 112, 127–8
Shaw, Jenny, 60, 111, 124
Shilling, Chris, 142, 146
Singh, M., 34
single-sex groups, 115
Skeggs, Beverley, 108
Slattery, Patrick, 148
Sleegers, Peter, 33, 34
Smith, Neil, 18, 148
social class
and the 'abstract pupil', 36, 37
and friendship groups, 114
and London schools, 201
social constructionism, 3, 166
'social contract', 9
social democratic policies in education, 26, 28, 29–30
social justice
and citizenship, 21–2, 31
and New Right politics and policies, 31, 35
and social democratic policies in education, 26
Soja, Edward, 18, 19, 138

space
  citizens in, 17–19
  defining, 136–7
  demarcations and limits, 161–2
  and embodiment, 2
  movement in, 158–60, 175–9
  physical and social, 163
  and place: of students, 143–6; of
      teachers, 146–7
  in school buildings, 141–3
  and social relations as spatial,
      160–3
  spatial metaphors, 136–7, 156–8,
      160–1
  spatial praxis, 137, 154–6, 163, 164
  time–space paths, 53, 148–54, 158,
      160, 163, 175
sport, 185–8
Stacey, Judith, 56–7
staffrooms, 66, 67, 105–6, 143, 147,
      149
standards, versus equality, 34–5
students
  anxieties of, 124–6
  and boredom, 124
  as 'citizens-to-be', 44–6
  dress styles, 167–72, 173–5
  friendships, 110–14, 116, 118–19
  gender balancing acts, 114–15
  hairstyles, 171
  having and using voice, 179–85,
      195–6
  and heterosexual relationships,
      112, 127–8
  individual, 12–17
  informalisation of teacher/student
      relations, 106–8
  loners, 111
  and mental flight, 158–9
  and movement in space, 158–60,
      175–9
  and name-calling, 127, 132–4
  self-descriptions of, 82–7
  single-sex groups, 115
  space and place, 143–6, 147
  and spatial metaphors, 156–8
  spatial praxis and resistance, 154–6
  and time–space paths, 53, 148–54,
      158, 163, 175

  see also boys; girls; pupils
Sunnari, Vappu, 84
supermarket metaphor, 32
support staff in schools, 102–5
surveillance
  and ethnographic research, 55–6
  in the physical school, 166

teachers
  and the informal school, 105–8;
      informalisation of
      teacher/student relations,
      106–8; staffroom culture,
      105–6; and support staff,
      102–3, 104; and teasing, 135
  and movement in space, 178–9
  and the official school, 66–71,
      73–4; control and agency,
      88–92; and issues of national-
      ism/internationalism, 94–7;
      making gendered citizens,
      92–4; and students' self-evalu-
      ations, 85, 86; teaching
      methods, 76–81
  and the physical school: and
      control, 167; embodiment of,
      166; physical contact with
      pupils, 188–90; and school
      buildings, 138; space and
      place, 146–7, 163
  staffrooms, 66, 67, 105–6, 143, 147
  and time–space paths, 150–1, 160
  see also female teachers; male
      teachers
teasing, 127, 129, 131–2, 135, 153
Thomson, Rachel, 97, 98, 172
Thorne, Barrie, 113
time–space paths, 53, 148–54, 158,
      160, 163, 175
Tolonen, Tarja, 121, 123, 127, 170,
      173
Tomkins, J., 56
Troman, Geoff, 58
Troyna, Barry, 37
Turner, Bryan, 20–1

uniforms (school), 167–70
United States, 3, 4
  gender relations, 25, 195

gender segregation in schools, 21
and nation building through
  education, 20
New Right politics and policies, 23,
  24, 25, 35
in education, 27, 29, 31, 32, 33, 35
see also Californian schools

voice, having and using, 179–85,
  195–6

Walkerdine, Valerie, 19, 84, 87, 163,
  182
Weeks, Jeffrey, 11, 15
Weiler, H. N., 33–4
welfare states, and New Right politics
  and policies, 30

Wessenligh, Anton, 33, 34
Wexler, Philip, 2, 66, 99, 152, 156
Whitty, Geoff, 25, 39
Williams, Raymond, 10
within-gender differences, 3
Witte, John F., 33
women's employment patterns,
  Britain compared with Finland,
  25, 194–5
Woods, Peter, 2, 127, 130
working-class girls, and individuality,
  16–17
working-class students, and
  time–space paths, 152

Yuval-Davis, Nira, 10, 19, 21